Out-frames
How NLP Coaching Works

Dr Richard Bolstad
and Julia Kurusheva

Transformations International Consulting & Training
PO Box 35111, Browns Bay, Auckland 0753, New Zealand
www.transformations.net.nz
ISBN 978-0-473-23519-2

Dedication
To all our students and clients, from whom we learned this

Out-frames
Table of Contents

Coaching, NLP and Multiple Frames

What Coaching Is

Primarily, this is a book for those who have trained in NLP or Neuro-Linguistic Programming. More generally though, this is a book for all those who want to help others achieve more success and satisfaction in their lives. We could have said that this is a book on the use of NLP in therapy or counselling, but those words contain some unfortunate limitations. They link what is being done to a nineteenth and twentieth century model which helped people to heal psychological wounds from the past. Coaching is a somewhat more future oriented term.

The metaphor of coaching emerged in university sports and academic study, and was first used to describe an activity at Oxford University in 1831 (before this, a "coach" was a physical means of getting from one's present situation to one's desired destination). A sportsperson or a sports team now hires a coach to help them enhance and maximize their potential during training and reach their goals in sports events. A student may be given a coach to help them study with maximum effectiveness and pass their exams. This metaphor contains many important presuppositions which have been taken into the new fields of life coaching and business coaching in the last 3 decades: presuppositions such as the focus on action and goals, the ongoing nature of the coaching contract, and the client directed process.

Janet Harvey, president of the International Coaching Federation (ICF), one of the world's largest life coaching organizations, says that life coaching emerged in the 1980s from the Human Potential movement. The following eleven core coaching competencies were developed by the ICF to support greater understanding about the skills and approaches used within today's coaching profession as defined by the ICF.

A. Setting the Foundation
   1. Meeting Ethical Guidelines and Professional Standards
   2. Establishing the Coaching Agreement
B. Co-creating the Relationship
   3. Establishing Trust and Intimacy with the Client
   4. Coaching Presence
C. Communicating Effectively
   5. Active Listening
   6. Powerful Questioning
   7. Direct Communication

D. Facilitating Learning and Results
    8.   Creating Awareness
    9.   Designing Actions
    10. Planning and Goal Setting
    11. Managing Progress and Accountability

Coaching is not quite the same as training, counselling or mentoring. Coaching in business is based on the understanding that businesspeople, like sportspeople, want more than mere training in some system of achievement, more than counselling to help with their achievement problems or blockages, and more than mere mentoring to follow a path that someone else has already walked. They have a unique potential which can be released fully by guiding them to clarify their strengths, their values and their purpose, set and plan action towards goals, and regularly review their own path. Like a sports coach, a coach in the business setting meets with their clients regularly and guides them to constantly improve what they do.

What Coaching Is Not

I recommend that people get clear about the nature and intention of coaching before committing themselves to coaching sessions. It helps firstly to clarify the difference between coaching and mentoring. Mentoring is a relationship where someone with experience in the client's field shares that experience and advises about career decisions towards a future similar to the path taken by the mentor, while coaching is a relationship where a coach helps the client utilise their own experience to set their own goals and work towards those. It also helps to clarify the difference between coaching and therapy or counselling. Therapy tends to be past-oriented, problem-focused and progress measured while coaching is future-oriented, solution-focused and performance measured. Clients who do not know the difference would think that either they need to have a problem to benefit from coaching, or they can only benefit from a coach who understands their particular job.

Training and consulting are also subtly different to coaching, although effective coaching may utilize both. Training tends to be based on a learning agenda set by the trainer and aimed at transferring skills and understandings from trainer to trainee, while coaching is based on the coachee's agenda and utilises their skills and understandings. Consulting tends to be based on skills and expertise delivered by the consultant to an organization or person, while coaching is based on developing the skills and expertise of an individual coachee. Training is useful when a group of people or a team identify shared educational needs and want to be "on the same page" with a subject. For example, training may ensure a consistent response to corporate clients with a particular common need. Coaching is an ongoing commitment to maximising performance. Also, once a person is expert at their job, research shows that training delivers less and less benefit to them in that context. University of California researchers Stuart Dreyfus and Hubert Dreyfus (1980) studied experts from a number of different fields and found that learning by reviewing their own cases was a far more effective mechanism for improving performance rather than giving them an ever increasing list of guidelines and techniques, in the way that training tends to do. Beginners benefit from being taught rule and guidelines, but experts learn most from studying their own unique real life applications of those guidelines.

Even in a business context, coaching is driven by the client's goals rather than the organisation's goals. This creates a context where extraordinary personal changes can happen, which then benefit the organisation itself. In his research Hewlett Packard and Nokia management coach Dr Trygve Roos found that many business clients chose to work on what would be seen as personal issues, which none-the-less had a profound effect on their business achievement. He gives examples (Roos, 2002, p 4) of a client with a phobia of flying which had altered all his career choices, and a client with a phobia of pigeons who had structured all his business meetings to avoid the need to walk past public parks. These are not issues that a client might choose to alert her/his manager to, but they significantly affect productivity and corporate outcomes. As an example of the efficiency of his work with specific issues, Roos worked with 25 clients who wanted to give up smoking cigarettes (Roos, 2002, p 91). 19 ceased smoking after a single 45 minute session, and another one after two sessions. At follow-up 24 months later, only 5 of the original 25 had started smoking again, a success rate of 75%, over twice the usual best results of longer aversion and other therapies for smoking.

This means that when coaching supports clients to enjoy their life more, to be happier, it supports their business success. Amazingly, both white and blue collar workers are more likely to report feeling "happy" when they are on the job than when they are in their leisure time (Csikszentmihalyi, 1990, p 158). Signalled by a beeper at random times and asked to rate their level of happiness, those studied by Mihaly Csikszentmihalyi were happy 54% of the time while at their work, but only 18% of the time while engaged in leisure activities. Work has the fundamental ingredients which Csikszentmihalyi's research shows leads to happiness – work offers challenges and provides an opportunity to use skills to overcome these challenges. When employees are not happy in their work, they either experience the challenges as too high for their skill level (stressful), or too low (boring). In the business setting, coaching helps each employee identify the goals that bring them back into the area where their skills are extended and yet they feel capable. For the individual employee, coaching enables the creation of a satisfying life and a satisfying career.

I recommend that people check four main things when they select a coach. Firstly, what training does this person have as a coach? A coach is not a mentor; it is not enough for them to know the field where their client works. A background in traditional counselling gives great listening skills but may focus the coach unduly on problems rather than on positive life goals and career achievements. A training in coaching itself or in a coaching field such as NLP (Neuro Linguistic Programming) is, I believe, the most effective preparation. Secondly, does this person belong to an organisation of coaches that gives them ethical and professional back-up? Coaching is based on the same ethical principles as any other effective consulting or organisational development process, and I recommend you check that your coach is clear about issues such as confidentiality and that they focus on your outcomes rather than the outcomes of the coach or some other stakeholder. Thirdly, does your coach have some form of peer support, coaching supervision or coaching themselves? It just makes sense that they themselves use the same performance enhancing process they are selling you. Fourth and most important, do you get a sense of rapport with them, a sense that they understand your internal experience and are committed to you? This last piece is something you can only make a decision about once you have interacted with the person themselves.

From a coaching perspective, as I have said, there are risks with the traditional role of a "counsellor" or "psychotherapist". In their search for a term not tainted by the expectations of "counsellor" and "psychotherapist", Carkhuff and Berenson (1977) used the term "helper". Their concern was based on some important research. For example, in 1951, E. Powers and H. Witmer published one of the most extensive and well designed studies of the results of counselling and therapy, "An Experiment in the Prevention of Delinquency". In this study 650 high risk boys aged 6-10 were chosen and grouped into pairs based on various demographic variables. One of each pair was then assigned to counselling (either client-centred or psychoanalytic), and linked up to support services such as the YMCA. After an average five years of counselling, the boys were followed up. Counsellors rated 2/3 of the boys in their care as having "benefited substantially" from the counselling, and the boys agreed, saying it gave them more insight and kept them out of trouble.

Such is success, isn't it? Well, except for one detail. The treated boys were more likely to have committed more than one serious crime, had higher rates of alcoholism, mental illness, stress related illness, and lower job satisfaction than those left untreated. This remained true at 30 year follow-up, and the researchers lamely suggest that there "must be" some positive benefits, but they were unable to find them. Just because counsellors believe that counselling "feels good" doesn't mean it helps. This 1951 study demonstrates the risks of dependency-producing models of "coaching" in general. The boys and their counsellors valued "their relationship", but it did not empower the boys to change; it disabled them (Zilbergeld 1983, p132-134)

The Emergence of a Coaching-Based Business Culture

Research in 2011 by Qa Research, an independent marketing research agency in the United Kingdom, found that 80% of business organisations surveyed had used or were now using coaching (Franze ed., 2011, p 1). They said "There is broad consensus on the purpose of coaching – four out of the five leading reasons given were connected with providing benefits for individuals. Organisations are more likely to engage in coaching for personal development (53%) than improving specific areas of performance (26%). Good coaching should be a facilitative process, with an emphasis on unlocking capabilities through guiding and questioning, rather than on teaching or instructing. As such, it is as much to do with personal skills as it is business and workplace skills. The research, however, suggests that the focus at present is skewed towards the latter – more organisations (95%) use coaching to focus on business and workplace skills than on personal skills (70%). The scope of the coaching provided appears to be linked to selection of coaches. When line managers are used to coach people who report to them, they tend to focus the coaching on business and workplace skills. But when organisations use internal coaches who are not line managers, they are more likely to say that coaching focuses equally on business and workplace skills and personal skills (76% vs. 59% of those that use line managers)."

Coaching has proven itself in the global economy. It has stayed where other management and self-development tools have come and gone as fads. The reason is firstly because it helps build strengths within the person and within the organisation, rather than impose models from outside. Secondly, the coaching interaction concretely embodies the changes managers often want to see in their organisational culture. It empowers employees from the first day it is used. It is a bridge between talking about change and actually creating change from the grass roots of the organisation to the leaders. A manager not using coaching is a manager wasting vast potential; potential which they already pay for in salaries.

Coaching training with ICF has been sometimes limited to the core competencies, rather than being built around them. The International Association of Coaching Institutes (ICI), which we are trainers with, provides an NLP (Neuro-Linguistic Programming) based model of coaching competency. This has three additional requirements for coaching training, aside from the core Coaching Process competencies, including:

- Development of an Individualised Conception of what Coaching is
- Basic knowledge in Conflict Management
- Integration of NLP-models with other useful coaching systems and methods

This last requirement affirms the goal of this book: to provide multiple models or "frames" through which to understand and enrich coaching. To understand why NLP based coaching is committed to having multiple frames, let's now introduce you to NLP itself.

What is NLP?

My aim in this chapter is not so much to review the vast field of NLP as used in coaching, but to give an introduction which will enable those new to NLP to make sense of the rest of this book, which is primarily written for NLP Practitioners. The term Neuro Linguistic Programming (NLP) was first coined in 1976, although it is expanded from the term "neuro-linguistics" used by Alfred Korzybski in 1930 in his research on the way language shapes our brain's experience of the world. Richard Bandler was a fourth year student in Dr John Grinder's linguistics class at the University of California in Santa Cruz, when the two of them began the development of NLP in 1972. The richness of NLP owes much to the network of people that this association focused. Their network of professional contacts, whose ideas contributed to the development of NLP, included:

- Virginia Satir (the family therapist in whose work Richard Bandler initially observed the language patterns that became known in NLP as the metamodel),
- Gregory Bateson (systems theorist and psychotherapist, whose partner Margaret Mead had studied trancework with Dr Milton Erickson),
- Dr Milton Erickson (medical doctor and innovative hypnotherapist)
- George Miller (the neuroscientist who proposed the "TOTE" model for understanding how our cognitive strategies achieve results),
- Noam Chomsky (developer in the study of language: linguistics),
- Robert Spitzer (head of Science and Behaviour Books, who edited Fritz Perls' work for publication).
- Fritz Perls, developer of Gestalt psychotherapy.

"The Structure of Magic Volume I" was the first book jointly published by Bandler and Grinder, in 1975. It presents NLP as a meta-discipline (above and beyond other disciplines such as education, health care or business), based on "modelling" (creating models to explain how experts in any discipline achieve their results). By studying experts in a field such as psychotherapy (where the first such experts studied were Dr Milton Erickson, Virginia Satir and Fritz Perls) the NLP developers claimed that it is possible to identify cognitive patterns which can then be taught to others in that field, or even in other fields, to enhance performance. This modelling process then generates not only a list of cognitive patterns which are useful in various circumstances, but also a list of "training" or "installing" techniques for transferring the cognitive skills to another person. These lists of patterns and techniques are usually thought of as the content of "NLP", but they are actually merely a sampling of the results of the core NLP process – modelling.

For example, Donald Moine at the University of Oregon studied 45 minute long audiocassette recordings of insurance salespeople. His sample included top producers from their companies, as well as "average" producers of sales. The highly successful salespeople used far more of a precise set of "language patterns", already documented by NLP in the work of Virginia Satir and Dr Milton Erickson, and explained later in this book. The patterns included embedded suggestions, complex equivalents, mind reading, metaphors, pacing, and modal operators of possibility. This artfully vague and suggestive language was part of the most successful salespeople's skill in enabling others to change (Moine, 1981). Having identified which patterns successful salespeople use (largely unconsciously, for the original users) Moines was then able to teach those patterns to other salespeople wanting to communicate more successfully in the sales situation.

Given that the first "models" studied by the developers of NLP were psychotherapists, it is understandable that many of the first patterns of excellence identified using NLP have immediate application in the related fields of psychotherapy and coaching. NLP, to restate, is not just "a kind of psychotherapy". It does have uses in psychotherapy, coaching and 100 other fields.

A study of NLP use in Psychotherapy was organised by Martina Genser-Medlitsch and Peter Schütz in Vienna, Austria in 1996. The test sample of 55 therapy clients and the control group of 60 clients on a waiting list were matched by pattern of symptoms, age, family circumstances, education level, therapy experience etc. The test group were seen by members of a group of 37 NLP Master Practitioners (22 men and 15 women) who used a full range of NLP techniques (for those who know the names of NLP techniques, they used reframing, setting outcomes, parts work, metamodel, metaphor, trance, time line work, anchoring, belief changes, submodality shifts, strategies, and the trauma-phobia process). Clients were assessed with a number of questionnaires before therapy, after therapy, and at 6 month follow-up. The assessments checked occurrence of individual discomforts, clinical psychological symptoms, coping strategies used for stress management, locus of control (whether the people felt in control of their lives), and subjective evaluation of the therapy by the client and the therapist. Diagnoses (ICD9) ranged from schizo-affective and other psychotic disorders, through alcohol dependence, endogenous depressions, psychosomatic disorders, and other issues to post traumatic stress disorders. These disorders were more severe initially in the test group than in the control group on all scales, and their use of psychiatric drugs was higher. On average, treatments lasted 12 sessions (1-48) over a period averaging 20 weeks.

After treatment 1.9% of clients who had NLP therapy felt no different, 38.9% felt better and 59.3% felt considerably better. None of those treated felt worse. In the control group meanwhile, 47.5% felt no different, 29.5% felt better and 6.6% felt considerably better. 9.8% of the controls felt worse and 4.9% felt considerably worse. At 6 month follow-up, 52% of clients who had had therapy felt considerably better, 28% felt better, 12% felt there was no change, and 8% felt worse. Meanwhile, the therapists rated 49% of their treatments as having met objectives well, 47% as having somewhat met objectives, and 4% as of little or no success.

After therapy, the clients who received NLP scored higher in their perception of themselves as in control of their lives (with a difference at 10% significance level), reduced their use of drugs, used more successful coping methods to respond to stressful situations, and reduced symptoms such as anxiety, aggression, paranoid thinking, social insecurity, compulsive behaviours, and depression. The research showed that a small number of positive changes also occurred in the control group and could not be accounted for by the therapy, including some of the reduction in psychosomatic symptoms, social isolation and some paranoid thinking. Altogether, positive changes in 25 of 33 symptom areas (76%) occurred as a result of the therapy, positive changes in 3 areas occurred in both groups, and no significant changes occurred in 5 areas.

Peter Schütz followed up this research in 2010. A controlled study of NLP in Psychotherapy, conducted then by Peter Schütz, Melita Stipančić and others, studied clinical symptoms and personality disorders in clients who were followed up for 5 months, demonstrating significant positive changes comparable to those usually found in longer Cognitive Behavioural Therapy regimens (Stipančić et alia 2010, Wake, L. et alia, ed.s 2013).

While remembering my cautions about the problem-focused model of "psychotherapy", and remembering that the patterns and techniques used by these NLP psychotherapists are not the core of NLP itself, this research also indicates the potential success of using an NLP model in coaching practice.

While modelling is the most central agreed characteristic of NLP, it is not the only such core organizing principle. NLP is often described as being based on a set of unique assumptions or presuppositions, of which two are central. These are a) The map is not the territory and b) Life is systemic.

Alfred Korzybski used a metaphor to describe the first of these presuppositions. He suggested that our internal experience of the world is like a map, and that this map is never the same as the real world or "territory". He took the example (1994, p 750) of a map including the cities of Paris, Dresden and Warsaw. He noted that in a useful map,

Dresden is given as between Paris and Warsaw, which parallels the relationship that occurs when you drive from one place to the other across the actual territory. At best, a map can contain *similar relationships* to the real territory, but obviously the map will always have some differences from that territory. For example, the map will never have all the detailed side roads that you find in the real territory. This means that no map, including the collage of maps that have come to be called NLP, is "real". Some maps are more useful than others for specific results (just as a subway map may be more useful than a road map for getting across a large city, even though it is no more real than the street map).

The second core presupposition of NLP comes from the work of Gregory Bateson. Bateson used the analogy of a man cutting down a tree with an axe (Bateson, 1991, p 164) to explain the system-based nature of reality. He points out that in order to swing the axe, the man needs to pay attention to where the last cut was. The cut, it could be said, causes him to swing in a certain place. And each cut could also be said to result from the specific properties of the axe; how heavy it feels, and how well balanced. So the axe, it might be claimed, controls the cut, which controls the man. Actually, of course, Bateson is claiming that the tree-cutting is a system (an interconnected process where each part responds to the actions of the other parts and in turn influences them). Simple cause and effect descriptions of such a system (e.g. claiming that the man causes the tree to be cut down) may be useful for communication, but have little use scientifically. Even the arbitrary divisions between man, axe and tree merely simplify reality in ways which suit our communication style.

The situation has more complexity than this though, because Bateson goes on to point out that all system descriptions only have meaning in contexts. The man's action with the axe and the tree cannot be understood without knowing, for example, how the man came to cut the tree. If his job involves cutting trees, perhaps he gets told to cut a certain kind of tree, or told to cut at a certain speed. Those things also influence the actions in that man-axe-tree system (which we now need to consider a corporation-supervisor-man-axe-tree system). We could go on forever. In the "mental world" of ordinary human communication, we put a frame around the area we are considering. That frame includes the time we think about (for example, does the man-axe-tree situation begin with the man's lifting the axe, with the tree growing to a certain shape, or with the cut shaping the trunk) and the spacial area (do we consider the forest, the area of the tree, the area of the cut, or the ecosystem). To link this idea with the first presupposition of NLP (the map is not the territory), new frames allow new maps of reality, and thus new choices about our actions. This "reframing" of experience, to use Bateson's term, is central to NLP, and to the book you are reading.

NLP and the Brain: Sensory System Use

How does NLP suggest that we can identify the patterns by which successful people achieve their results, if that is what NLP does? It suggests that we pay attention to the details of how people use their brains. Everything we experience of the world comes to us through the neurological (brain) channels of our sensory systems. The greatest spiritual transcendence and the most tender interpersonal moments are "experienced" (transformed into internal experiences) as images (visual), sounds (auditory), body sensations (kinesthetic), tastes (gustatory), smells (olfactory) and learned symbols such as these words (digital), all inside our brains. Those experiences, furthermore, can be re-membered (put together again) by use of the same sensory information. Let's take a simple example.

Think of a fresh lemon. Imagine one in front of you now, and feel what it feels like as you pick it up. Take a knife and cut a slice off the lemon, and hear the slight sound as the juice squirts out. Smell the lemon as you lift the slice to your mouth and take a bite of the slice. Taste the sharp taste of the fruit.

If you actually imagined doing that, you mouth is now salivating. Why? Because your brain followed your instructions and thought about, saw, heard, felt, smelled and tasted the lemon. By recalling sensory information, you recreated the entire experience of the lemon, so that your body responded to the lemon you created. Your brain treated the imaginary lemon as if it was real, and prepared saliva to digest it. Seeing, hearing, feeling, smelling and tasting are the natural "languages" of your brain. Each of them has a specialised area of the brain which processes that sense. Another NLP term for these senses is "Modalities". When you use these modalities, you access the same neurological (brain) circuits that you use to experience a real lemon. As a result, your brain treats what you're thinking about as "real".

Understanding this process immediately illuminates a number of our coaching clients' challenges. The person with Post Traumatic Stress Disorder (PTSD) panics when they are reminded of disturbing past events - they use the same "think-of-a-fresh-lemon" process to recreate vivid and terrifying flashbacks to these traumatic events. And knowing how these brain circuits allow them to do that also shows us a number of ways to solve the problem, as we'll see.

Our perception of the world is a complex process by which we interact with the information delivered from our sense modalities. Biochemist Graham Cairns Smith points out that there are areas of the neural cortex (outer brain) which specialise in information from each of the senses (he lists the modalities as olfactory, gustatory, somatosensory, auditory and visual). However there is no direct connection between the sense organ (the retina of the eyes, for example) and the specialised brain area which handles that sense. The cortex is the outer area of the brain, and each sense has an area of cortex specialised for it. The visual cortex, for example, is at the back of the brain. A great deal of redesigning has to happen at other places, before the raw sensory data gets to areas of the cortex where we can "perceive" it.

Consider the case of vision, for example. Impulses from the retina of the eye go first to the lateral geniculate body (see diagram below), where they interact with data from a number of other brain systems. The results are then sent on to the visual cortex, where "seeing" is organised. Only 20% of the flow of information into the lateral geniculate body comes from the eyes. Most of the data that will be organised as seeing comes from areas such as the hypothalamus, a mid-brain centre which has a key role in the creation of emotion (Maturana and Varela, 1992, p 162). What we "see" is as much a result of the emotional state we are in as of what is in front of our eyes. A hungry person notices food, a frightened person notices danger. In NLP terminology, this understanding is encapsulated in the statement "The map is not the territory". The map your brain makes of the world is never the same as the real world.

Your brain has a very specific way of incorporating the information about your emotions into the actual picture you are seeing. The emotional information is "coded" visually (and in the other senses) as a result of some specific detailed distinctions made within the cortex. Inside the visual cortex, there are several areas which process "qualities" such as colour, brightness and distance. When you are hungry, food often looks bigger and brighter (television advertisers know this – they makes the food on their adverts bigger and brighter too). In NLP these qualities are known as visual "submodalities" (because they are produced in small sub-sections of the visual modality). The first fourteen visual submodalities listed by Richard Bandler (1985, p 24) were colour, distance, depth, duration, clarity, contrast, scope, movement, speed, hue, transparency, aspect ratio, orientation, and foreground/background.

To give a sense of how these submodalities "code" emotional information, consider the following study. In research by Emily Balcetis, an assistant professor in NYU's Department of Psychology, and David Dunning, a Cornell professor of psychology, volunteers tossed a beanbag towards a gift card (worth either $25 or $0) on the floor. They were told that if the beanbag landed on the card, they would be given the card. Interestingly, the volunteers threw the beanbag much farther if the gift card was worth $0 than if it was worth $25 — that is, they underthrew the beanbag when attempting to win a $25 gift card, because they viewed that gift card as being closer to them. These findings indicate that when we want something, we actually view it as being physically close to us. Moving an object, in our imagination, closer to us makes us see it as more significant. This is then the basis for several NLP processes such as the "visual swish", in which an image of a desired future self is moved quickly closer and becomes brighter.

One of the most important submodalities is the difference in visual awareness created by stepping out of a remembered or imagined experience to be what NLP calls "dissociated", versus stepping in to be what NLP calls "associated". Training the brain to dissociate from disturbing events is a key submodality shift, as demonstrated in research by Brad Bushman and Dominik Mischkowski (2013). They subjected research students to a situation designed to evoke anger and anxiety. They then asked the students to review the events. Some students were told to adopt a self-immersed perspective ("see the situation unfold through your eyes as if it were happening to you all over again") and then analyze their feelings surrounding the event. Others were told to use the self-distancing perspective ("move away from the situation to a point where you can now watch the event unfold from a distance…watch the situation unfold as if it were happening to the distant you all over again") and then analyze their feelings. The third control group was not told how to view the scene or analyze their feelings. Each group was told the replay the scene in their minds for 45 seconds. The researchers then tested the participants for aggressive thoughts and angry feelings. The difference was dramatic; those students who had dissociated themselves were substantially less distressed and less angry. This distancing is the basis of the famous NLP phobia-trauma process.

In his book "The Trauma Trap", Dr David Muss MD documents his extensive use of this NLP Trauma Process with victims of PTSD: A policeman involved in the Hillsborough soccer disaster describes how his flashbacks (sudden horrific memories of the trauma), insomnia and alcohol abuse disappeared after two sessions. A patient (Barbara Drake) tells how one session with Dr Muss completely resolved flashbacks and other symptoms resulting from a sexual abuse experience. These and the other stories documented by Muss parallel our own experiences as trainers and Master Practitioners of NLP. Muss says "I know that it has worked for every patient I have dealt with so far, without exception." (Muss, "The Trauma Trap", 1991, p 10). Muss did a pilot study with 70 members of the West Midlands Police Force, who had witnessed major disasters such as the Lockerbie air crash. Of these, 19 qualified as having PTSD. The time between trauma and treatment varied from six weeks to ten years. All participants reported that after an average of three sessions they were completely free of intrusive memories and other PTSD symptoms. Follow-up ranged from 3 months to 2 years, and all gains were sustained over that time.

By the time NLP emerged in the 1960s, researchers already understood that each sensory system had a specialised brain area, and that people had preferences for using particular sensory systems. In their original 1980 presentation of NLP, Dilts, Grinder, Bandler and DeLozier (1980, p 17) point out that all human experience can be coded as a combination of internal and external vision, audition, kinesthesis and olfaction/gustation. The developers of NLP noticed that we also process information in words and that words too have a specific brain system specialised to process them, as if they were a sensory system. They described this verbal type of information as "auditory digital", distinguishing it from the auditory input we get, for example, in listening to music or to the sound of the wind.

The standard NLP diagram of "eye accessing cues" (below) shows that visual thinking draws the eyes up, auditory to the sides and kinesthetic down. Note that auditory digital is placed down on the left side (suggesting that all the accessing cues on that side may correspond to the dominant hemisphere, where verbal abilities are known to be processed). In left handed subjects, this eye pattern is reversed about 50% of the time.

Eye movements are clues as to the area in their brain from which a person is getting (accessing) information. A second aspect of thinking is which sensory modality they then "process" or re-present" that information in. Accessing and representing are not always done in the same sensory system. A person may look at a beautiful painting (Visual accessing) and think about how it feels to them (kinesthetic representation). The person's representing of their experience in a particular language can be identified by the words (predicates) they use to describe their subject. For example, someone might say "I see what you mean." visually, "I've tuned in to you." auditorally, or "Now I grasp that." kinesthetically. The person who looks at the beautiful painting and represents it to themselves kinesthetically might well say "That painting feels so warm. The colours just flow across it." They experience the painting, in this case, as temperature and movement.

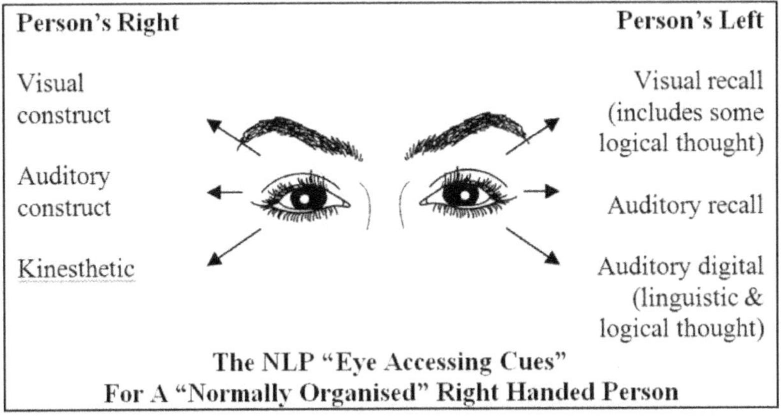

Everything in the brain and nervous system works both ways. If place "A" affects place "B", then place "B" affects place "A". We saw previously that if changing submodalities affects whether you feel excited looking at a picture, then changing the feeling of excitement will also change the submodalities of your image.

In the same way, if thinking visually causes your eyes to be drawn up more, then placing the eyes up more will help you to visualise. Specifically, looking up to the left (for most people) will help them recall images they have seen before. Dr F. Loiselle at the University of Moncton in New Brunswick, Canada (1985) tested this. He selected 44 average spellers, as determined by their pretest on memorising nonsense words. Instructions in the experiment, where the 44 were required to memorise another set of nonsense words, were given on a computer screen. The 44 were divided into four subgroups for the experiment.

Group One were told to visualise each word in the test, while looking up to the left.

Group Two were told to visualise each word while looking down to the right.

Group Three were told to visualise each word (no reference to eye position).

Group Four were simply told to study the word in order to learn it.

The results on testing immediately after were that Group One (who did actually look up left more than the others, but took the same amount of time) increased their success in spelling by 25%, Group Two worsened their spelling by 15%, Group Three increased their success by 10%, and Group Four scored the same as previously. This strongly suggests that looking up left (Visual Recall in NLP terms) enhances the recall of words for spelling, and is twice as effective as simply teaching students to picture the words. Furthermore, looking down right (Kinesthetic in NLP terms) damages the ability to visualise the words. Interestingly, in a final test some time later (testing retention), the scores of Group One remained constant, while the scores of the control group, Group Four, plummeted a further 15%, a drop which was consistent with standard learning studies. The resultant difference in memory of the words for these two groups was 61% .

NLP and the Brain: Strategies

To achieve any result, such as relaxation, each of us has a preferred sequence of sensory "representations" which we go through. For some people, imagining a beautiful scene is part of their most effective relaxation strategy. For others, the strategy that works best is to listen to soothing music, and for others simply to pay attention to their breathing slowing down as the feeling of comfort increases.

The concept of Strategies was defined in the book Neuro-Linguistic Programming Volume 1 (Dilts et alia, 1980, p 17). Here the developers of NLP say "The basic elements from which the patterns of human behaviour are formed are the perceptual systems through which the members of the species operate on their environment: *vision* (sight), *audition* (hearing), *kinesthesis* (body sensations) and *olfaction/gustation* (smell/taste).... We postulate that all of our ongoing experience can usefully be coded as consisting of some combination of these sensory classes." Thus, human experience is described in NLP as an ongoing sequence of internal representations in the sensory systems.

These senses were written in NLP notation as V (visual), A (auditory), K (kinesthetic), O (olfactory) and G (gustatory). To be more precise, the visual sense included visual recall, where I remember an image as I have seen it before through my eyes (V^r); visual construct, where I make up an image I've never seen before (V^c); and visual external, where I look out at something in the real world (V^e). So if I look up and see a blue sky, and then remember being at the beach, and then feel good, the notation would go: $V^e \rightarrow V^r \rightarrow K$. Notice that, at each step, I did have all my senses functioning (I could still feel my body while I looked up), but my *attention* shifted from sense to sense in a sequence. The digital senses (thinking in symbols such as words) have also been incorporated into this NLP strategy notation, so that we can describe one of the common strategies people use to create a state of depression as $K^i \rightarrow A_d \rightarrow K^i \rightarrow A_d$ …. (Feel some uncomfortable body sensations; tell themselves they should feel better; check how they feel now, having told themselves off; tell themselves off for feeling that way, and repeat ad nauseum!)

The developers of NLP used the T.O.T.E. model to further explain how we sequence sensory representations. The "TOTE" was developed by neurology researchers George Miller, Eugene Galanter and Karl Pribram (1960), as a model to explain how complex behaviour occurred. Ivan Pavlov's original studies had shown that simple behaviours can be produced by the stimulus-response cycle. When Pavlov's dogs heard the tuning fork ring (a stimulus; or in NLP terms an "anchor"), they salivated (response). But there is more to dog behaviour than stimulus-response.

For example, if a dog sees an intruder at the gate of its section (stimulus/anchor), it may bark (response). However, it doesn't go on barking forever. It actually checks to see if the intruder has run away. If the intruder has run away, the dog stops performing the barking operation and goes back to its kennel. If the intruder is still there, the dog may continue with that strategy, or move on to another response, such as biting the intruder. Miller, Gallanter and Pribram felt that this type of sequencing was inadequately explained in Pavlov's simple stimulus-response model. In Miller and Pribram's model, the first stimulus, (seeing the intruder) is the Trigger (the first T in the "TOTE"; Pavlov called this the "stimulus", and in NLP we also call this an "anchor") for the dog's "scaring-intruders-away" strategy. Obviously, the submodality intensity of the trigger is what actually activates the strategy (in this case the closeness of the intruder). The barking itself is the Operation (O). Checking to see if the intruder is gone yet (checking that the submodalities are reduced) is the Test (second T). Going back to the kennel is the Exit from the strategy (E). This might be written as $V^e \rightarrow K^e \rightarrow V^e/V^c \rightarrow K^e$. Notice that the checking stage (Test) is done by comparing the result of the operation (what the dog can see after barking) with the result that was desired (what the dog imagines seeing – a person running away). In the notation, comparison is written using the slash key "/".

Let's take another example. When I hear some music on the radio that I really like (trigger or anchor), I reach over and turn up the radio (operation). Once it sounds as loud as I enjoy it sounding (test), I sit back and listen. The strategy, including the end piece where I listen (another whole strategy really) is $A^e \rightarrow K^e \rightarrow A^e/A^r \rightarrow K^e \rightarrow A^e$.

To revisit the strategy for depression mentioned above, we can now diagram it as $K^i \rightarrow A_d \rightarrow K^i /K^c \rightarrow A_d$. The first K^I is the *trigger, stimulus* or *anchor* which starts the strategy. The person feels a slightly uncomfortable feeling in their body. The next step, the A_d, is where they talk to themselves and tell themselves off for feeling that way. Next, they compare the feeling they get internally now (after telling themselves off) with the feeling they got before. (K^i /K^c). Noticing that it feels worse, they tell themselves off some more (the final exit A_d). The feeling of depression can be thought of as the result of repeatedly running this strategy, called "ruminating" by researchers into the problem (Seligman, 1997, p 82-83).

Once we understand that every result a person achieves is a result of a strategy which begins with some trigger and leads them to act and test that action, then we have a number of new choices for changing the way they run their strategy and the results they get.

Emotional states are best considered as "meta" to the representational systems. They are vast, brain-wide commentaries on the entire set of representations and physiological responses present. Our states meta-comment on *and* alter the representations (from the primary senses as well as from the digital senses) "below them". For example, when a person is angry, they may actually be physically unable to hear their partner or spouse telling them how much they love them. The interference from the emotional state reduces the volume of the auditory external input. This often results in a completely different strategy being run! Put another way, the "state" determines which strategies we find easy to run and which we are unable to run well.

Strategies are learned behaviours, triggered by some specific sensory representation (a stimulus). What does "learned" mean? The human brain itself is made up of about one hundred billion nerve cells or neurons. These cells organise themselves into networks to manage specific tasks. When any experience occurs in our life, new neural networks are laid down to record that event and its meaning. To create these networks, the neurons grow an array of new dendrites (connections to other neurons). Each neuron has up to 20,000 dendrites, connecting it simultaneously into perhaps hundreds of different neural networks.

Steven Rose (1992) gives an example from his research with new-hatched chicks. After eating silver beads with a bitter coating, the chicks learn to avoid such beads. One peck is enough to cause the learning. Rose demonstrated that the chicks' brain cells change instantly, growing 60% more dendrites in the next 15 minutes. These new connections occur in very specific areas —what we might call the "bitter bead neural networks". These neural networks now store an important new strategy. The strategy is triggered each time the chick sees an object the right shape and size to peck at. This is a visual strategy of course. The trigger (seeing a small round object) is Visual external (V^e) and the operation (checking the colour) is also Visual external (V^e). The chick then compares the colour of the object it has found with the colour of the horrible bitter beads from its visual recall (V^e/V^r) and based on that test either pecks the object or moves away from it (K^e). We would diagram this strategy: $V^e \rightarrow V^e \rightarrow V^e/V^r \rightarrow K^e$.

Obviously, the more strategies we learn, the more neural networks will be set up in the brain. California researcher Dr Marion Diamond (1988) and her Illinois colleague Dr William Greenough (1992) have demonstrated that rats in "enriched" environments grow 25% more dendrite connections than usual, as they lay down hundreds of new strategies. Autopsy studies on humans confirm the process. Graduate students have 40% more dendrite connections than high school dropouts, and those students who challenged themselves more had even higher scores (Jacobs et alia, 1993).

How do messages get from one neuron to another in the brain? The transmission of impulses between neurons and dendrites occurs via hundreds of precise chemicals called "information substances"; substances such as dopamine, noradrenalin (norepinephrine), and acetylcholine. These chemical float from one cell to another, transmitting messages across the "synapse" or gap between them. Without these chemicals, the strategy stored in the neural network cannot run.

The particular mixture of chemicals present when a neural network is laid down must be recreated for the neural network to be fully re-activated and for the strategy it holds to run as it originally did. If someone is angry, for example, when a particular new event happens, they have higher noradrenalin levels. Future events which result in higher noradrenalin levels will re-activate this neural network and the strategy they used then. As a result, the new event will be connected by dendrites to the previous one, and there will even be a tendency to confuse the new event with the previous one. If my childhood caregiver yelled at me and told me that I was stupid, I may have entered a state of fear, and stored that memory in a very important neural network. When someone else yells at me as an adult, if I access the same state of fear, I may feel as if I am re-experiencing the original event, and may even hear a voice telling me I'm stupid.

This is called "state dependent memory and learning" or SDML. Our memories and learnings, our strategies, are *dependent* on the state they are created in. Since this is a system, what we see, hear, smell, taste or touch may also "trigger" or "anchor" a state of mind by activating a neural network that occurred when that sensory stimulus was present previously, as Pavlov discovered. In a controlled research study published in Germany (Reckert, 1994), Horst Reckert describes how in one session he was able to remove students' test anxiety using the simple technique of anchoring, based on this principle. He had the students recall a powerfully relaxed time, while pressing on a specific point on their hand to "anchor" the event, and then had them use that same pressure on their hand as they thought about the challenging situation. This connected the feeling of relaxation to the experience of sitting in the test room. This is the same principle you experience when you hear a song on the radio that reminds you of the feeling you had years ago when that song first came out.

To summarise what we have learned about the brain in this chapter so far, one could say that all human success, and most human challenges, can be described in terms of the strategies that people use in their brain. These strategies can be described as learned sequences of visual, auditory, kinaesthetic, olfactory-gustatory and auditory digital responses. They can be modified by simply rehearsing a new strategy, by anchoring or triggering a strategy from a more functional situation, or by altering the submodalities of the experience so that different strategies are activated.

NLP and the Brain: Unconscious Strategies

Researchers have known for some time that decision-making is often improved if the person has a break from the task they are attempting. In 2013, brain imaging research from Carnegie Mellon University, published in the journal "Social Cognitive and Affective Neuroscience," showed that the brain regions responsible for making decisions continue to be active even when the conscious brain is distracted with a different task. The research provided some of the first evidence showing how the brain unconsciously processes decision information in ways that lead to improved decision-making. "This research begins to chip away at the mystery of our unconscious brains and decision-making," said J. David Creswell, assistant professor of psychology in CMU's Dietrich College of Humanities and Social Sciences and director of the Health and Human Performance Laboratory. "It shows that brain regions important for decision-making remain active even while our brains may be simultaneously engaged in unrelated tasks, such as thinking about a math problem. What's most intriguing about this finding is that participants did not have any awareness that their brains were still working on the decision problem while they were engaged in an unrelated task." (Cresswell et alia, 2013).

This kind of unconscious processing is utilized in several NLP processes based on hypnotherapy, such as Core Transformation, Time Line Therapy™ and Ericksonian hypnotherapy. A large body of research verifies the healing power of communication with the "unconscious mind" in the distracted state of hypnosis or trance. Studies show that suggestions made in hypnosis can over-ride what would have been considered "incurable congenital conditions". For example, the British Medical Journal in 1952 published a study of a 16 year old boy with congenital ichthyosis erythroderma, whose skin was covered in a horny layer which wept fluid at the joints. In a week following hypnosis, small areas of the body were clear of this problem, and the results spread to the rest of the body over the second week. (Crasilneck and Hall, 1985, p376).

Ernest Rossi developed a model of hypnosis based on state dependent neural networks. He says "All methods of mind-body healing and therapeutic hypnosis operate by accessing and reframing the state-dependent memory and learning systems that encode symptoms and problems." (Rossi and Cheek, 1988, p 111). Thus, the areas of the mind previously known as the "subconscious" or "unconscious" are now recognised by Rossi as being simply neural (brain) networks which are dissociated from usual awareness due to the very different emotional state in which they were encoded. Communication with such neural networks can be done by re-establishing the state in which they are encoded (i.e. by creating an altered or "trance" state). Rossi points out that such neural networks are often poorly connected to the cortex and to the auditory digital (verbal) areas of the brain. He suggests that it is easier to communicate with them by having them signal using finger movements or some similar body movement. These are called "ideomotor" signals in the literature, because the ideas of the neural network are transferred directly into motor responses without "conscious thought".

Ernest Rossi's co-writer David Cheek has done a great deal of research on the ideomotor phenomenon. He showed, for example, that he was able to evoke hand movements for "yes" and "no" in response to his questions to 1000 hospital patients under full general anaesthetic (Cheek, 1981). Milton Erickson first learned to create "ideomotor signals" from Leslie Le Cron in the 1920s. He used a number of different methods such as hand movements, finger jerks, head nods, and the movement of a pendulum suspended from the fingers (Erickson, 1981, p 111-180). Erickson's method of inviting ideomotor signals, like his method of trance induction, was unique to each specific client he worked with. He described his conversation with them as a "utilisation" process. The specific language patterns used by him, to facilitate trance, were analysed by Bandler and Grinder (1975) and called the "Milton Model". Much of his language was based on presuppositions. For example, Erickson might say to a client "Are you in a deeper trance now than the trance you are in as you fall asleep, or is this a lighter trance for now?" In answering the question, either "yes" or "no", the client must presuppose that she or he is already in a trance.

The brain remembers the sequence of life events in an area called the hippocampus , using what NLP has termed a "time line". A time line is a spacial metaphor in which events are thought of as occurring along a line which stretches out in one direction to the past, and in another direction to the future. Examples of this way of mentally organising events are referred to in everyday speech; for example when we say "I'm going to put that whole experience *behind* me now." Or "I'm looking *forward* to seeing you again." This set of submodality distinctions for time was first described by Connirae and Steve Andreas (1987, p 1-24). Since then, a number of other NLP Practitioners have developed ways to work with the brain's coding of memory. These include "Re-imprinting" and "Change Personal History" (Dilts, Hallbom and Smith, 1990) and "Time Line Therapy™" (James and Woodsmall, 1988). Like Parts Integration, these techniques seem to have a significant effect on physical health conditions. They tend to involve viewing the original traumatic events from a new time perspective, and while connecting to emotional resources from other areas of the person's life.

A one year research study (May 1993-May 1994) into the treatment of asthmatics, using Time Line Therapy™, was done in Denmark. Results were presented at a number of European conferences, including the Danish Society of Allergology Conference (August 1994), and the European Respiratory Society Conference (Nice, France, October 1994). The study was run by General Medical Practitioner Jorgen Lund and NLP Master Practitioner Hanne Lund, from Herning, Denmark. Patients were selected from 8 general practices. 30 were included in the NLP Intervention group, and 16 in the control group. All received basic medical care including being supplied with medication. Most had never heard of NLP before, and many were completely unbelieving in it, or terrified of it. Their motivation to do NLP was generally low. The intervention group had an initial day introduction to NLP and Time Line Therapy™, and then 3-36 hours (average 13) of NLP intervention. The NLP focus was not mainly on the asthma; it was on how the people lived their daily lives. The results affected both the peoples general lives, and their asthma. Patients tended to describe their change subjectively as enabling them to be "more open", get "colossal strength and self confidence" "a new life" etc.

The lung capacity of adult asthmatics tends to decrease by 50ml a year average. This occurred in the control group. Meanwhile the NLP group increased their lung capacity by an average of 200ml (like reversing four years of damage in a year!). Daily variations in peak flow (an indicator of unstable lung function) began at 30%-40%. In the control group they reduced to 25% but in the NLP group they fell to below 10% . Sleep disorders in the control group began at 70% and dropped to 30%. In the NLP group they began at 50% and dropped to ZERO. Use of asthma inhalers and acute medication in the NLP group fell to near ZERO.

Hanne Lund points out that the implications of this project reach far beyond asthma management. The patients who used NLP did not consciously do something different in order to cure their asthma. They had the unconscious areas of the brain respond differently to solve their problems. Lund says "We consider the principles of this integrated work valuable in treatment of patients with any disease, and the next step will be to train medical staff in this model." (Lund, 1995).

An unconscious problem-solving strategy can be "installed" far more casually, of course, by rehearsing the person through it conversationally in a metaphor (a story). Joseph O'Connor gives a fascinating example (O'Connor and Seymour, 1994, p 184). " I went to the newsagent's the other day and found a very traumatised elderly lady telling the shopkeeper how she had just been mugged. The story went on and got worse. Awaiting my moment, I interrupted and recounted the tale of my friend who was beaten up in her home and could not seem to get the incident out of her head. Then, a few weeks later, when she realised what she was doing, she said, 'Being beaten up is bad enough, but I'll be damned if I'll give them the satisfaction of ruining my life' and she decided to push the whole incident so far away that it was as though she had forgotten all about it....' Can I have a Guardian please?' The old lady paused, her eyes focused off into the distance, and then her state changed and she calmly walked out of the shop. The unexpected thing was that as I left with my paper, the person behind me smiled and said two words: 'Nice work.'."

NLP and the Brain: Rapport

NLP has also studied how experts use their brain when they are communicating with others: how they create feelings of cooperation and trust for example. In 1995 a remarkable type of neuron was discovered by researchers working at the University of Palma in Italy (Rizzolatti et alia, 1996; Rizzolatti and Arbib, 1998). The cells, now called "mirror neurons", are found in the pre-motor cortex of monkeys and apes as well as humans. In humans they form part of the specific area called Broca's area, which is also involved in the creation of speech. Although the cells are related to motor activity (i.e. they are part of the system by which we make kinaesthetic responses such as moving an arm), they seem to be activated by visual input. When a monkey observes another monkey (or even a human) making a body movement, the mirror neurons light up. As they do, the monkey appears to involuntarily copy the same movement it has observed visually. Often this involuntary movement is inhibited by the brain (otherwise the poor monkey would be constantly copying every other monkey), but the resulting mimickery is clearly the source of the saying "monkey see, monkey do".

In human subjects, when this area of the brain is exposed to the magnetic field of transcranial magnetic stimulation (TMS), thus reducing conscious control, then merely showing a movie of a person picking up an object will cause the subject to involuntarily copy the exact action with their hand (Fadiga et alia, 1995). This ability to copy a fellow creature's actions as they do them has obviously been very important in the development of primate social intelligence. It enables us to identify with the person we are observing. When this area of the brain is damaged in a stroke, copying another's actions becomes almost impossible. The development of speech has clearly been a result of this copying skill. Furthermore, there is increasing evidence that autism and Aspergers syndrome are related to unusual activity of the mirror neurons. This unusual activity results in a difficulty the autistic person has understanding the inner world of others, as well as a tendency to echo speech parrot-fashion and to randomly copy others' movements (Williams et alia, 2001).

Mirror neurons respond to the facial expressions associated with emotions as well, so that they enable the person to directly experience the emotions of those they observe. As you watch someone else, your mirror neurons copy the things you see and hear (they imagine you doing that) and by synchronising with that person you start to feel what they are feeling. The more you copy their behaviours, the more your brain understands what it is like for them, and the more they will feel understood. Obviously this usually works best when it happens so subtly that neither person is conscious of the copying.

William Condon has meticulously studied videotapes of conversations, confirming these patterns. He found that in a successful conversation, movements such as a smile or a head nod are involuntarily matched by the other person within 1/15 of a second. Within minutes of beginning the conversation, the volume, pitch and speech rate (number of sounds per minute) of the peoples voices match each other. This is correlated with a synchronising of the type and rate of breathing. Even general body posture is adjusted over the conversation so that the people appear to match or mirror each other (Condon 1982, p 53-76). As a person adjusts their facial expression and other nonverbal behaviour to match others' they actually use the same pattern of brain activation that the other person is using. When their mirror neurons respond and they copy the person's actions, they thus feel what that person is feeling. This results in what researchers call "emotional contagion" – what NLP calls rapport (Hatfield et alia, 1994).

There is now extensive evidence that human beings synchronise their behaviour with each other continuously and unconsciously. The more the two people feel bonded to each other, the more this occurs. Mothers synchronise their movements with their own baby much more than with other babies, for example (Bernieri et alia, 1988). One of the advantages, interestingly, is that when someone synchronises their movements with yours, you perceive them more fully. For example, you are more able to recognise their face in a series of similar faces afterwards (Macrae et alia, 2008). However the most dramatic changes are changes in your responsiveness to their suggestions.

In one of the first experiments demonstrating this, the experimenter (pretending to be just another subject in a group experiment) adopted the real subjects' postures slowly and smoothly, just a few seconds after the subject. The subject then identified that experimenter as being more likeable (Chartrand and Bargh, 1999). Lawrence Rosenblum notes that "Numerous other studies have revealed similar social benefits. Being subtly imitated by a "negotiator" would make you more likely to agree with his or her opinion (Maddux et alia, 2008). Being imitated by a pretend cola salesman would make you more likely to rate the soda favourably and drink more of it during your interaction. You'd give a higher tip to a waitress who imitates your order verbatim rather than paraphrasing (van Baaren et alia, 2004). And you'd even rate a computer animated "interviewer" as more persuasive and positive if it subtly imitated your own head nodding (Bailenson and Yee, 2005). Finally, when GPS driving directions are conveyed by a voice that matches your own vocal emotion, you're less distracted than if provided directions by a voice not matching your emotion (Jonsson et alia, 2008)." In Lawrence Rosenblum's book "See What I'm Saying" (Rosenblum, 2010, p 211) he lists several other examples of this research. People who sing in time with each other (as opposed to singing the same song but not in unison) or walk in step with each other for a few minutes (as opposed to simply walking beside each other) are then much more cooperative with each other. They also report "a feeling of connectedness and trust with their partner subjects" after doing this (Wiltermuth and Heath, 2009). In NLP this feeling of synchronising and connectedness is called "rapport".

Seattle's Washington University researchers and marital therapists John and Julie Gottman have been in the forefront of a revolution in couples work. Their in depth research on more than a thousand couples over the last thirty years has demonstrated that the "rapport" created by this synchronising is the core ingredient in marital success. Gottman's researchers have shown that they can accurately predict whether a couple will divorce just by listening to and watching a five minute conversation between the couple, by identifying the specific language patterns used and seeing the specific non-verbal responses they make to each other (Gottman and Silver, 1999, p 3). They can predict divorce with 96% accuracy and pinpoint the exact year it will happen with 80% accuracy. Gottman's research demonstrates the power of what NLP calls matching and mirroring, and the rapport it creates. Couples who can understand each other actually adjust their bodies to experience what the other person is experiencing. They breathe in time with each other, sit in similar positions, use similar voice tonality, and even their heart rates match. Their brain patterns synchronise. Even when they argue, synchronisation, such as nodding in time with the other person, continues (Gottman, 1999, p 27).

NLP and the Brain: Language Patterns

As its name suggests, Neuro Linguistic Programming began with the linguistic analysis of the communications used by psychotherapists such as Virginia Satir, Milton Erickson and Gregory Bateson. John Grinder and Richard Bandler categorised the patterns in these therapists work, using recognised linguistic labels. The result has been three main collections of patterns that successful communicators use while talking. My intention is not to teach these patterns here, but to give readers some sense of what I'm referring to by "language patterns". In actual coaching, as we'll discuss later, these patterns need to be used with considerable care, skill and appropriate timing, to be anything more than "moralistic intrusions".

1) The Metamodel. This model, based on Virginia Satir's work, generates a series of questions for eliciting clearer, more reality-based descriptions of a client's experience (Grinder and Bandler, 1975). The appropriate question is identified based on the category of statement (the "metamodel pattern") made by the client. The NLP Practitioner restates the person's experience (called "pacing" it) and then asks the question; for example:

Presupposition. If the client says "I wonder why I made such a mess of my marriage." I might challenge the presupposition that the person has accepted before asking this question - the presupposition that they did "make a mess" of their marriage. I might say "You say you wonder why that happened. Can I check: how do you know that you made a mess of your marriage?"

Mind Read. If the client says "I can tell my wife hates me." I might ask "You say you can tell. I'm curious: What do you see or hear that tells you that?"

Lost Performative (where a judgement is performed and the judger is not identified). If the client says "It's wrong to talk back to your boss." I might ask " You suggest that it's wrong to talk back. Can I check: According to whom is it wrong?"

Complex Equivalent (where two things are said to be equivalent to each other). If the client says "I failed the exam so I guess I'm a hopeless case." I might ask " You seem to be saying that failing the exam is almost the same as being a hopeless case. I'm puzzled: How does not passing the exam mean that you as a person are a hopeless case?"

Universal Quantifier. If the client says "*Nothing* I do *ever* works" I might ask "You say Nothing and Ever. I wonder, has there *ever* been a single time when you did something and it worked?"

Modal Operator of Impossibility. If the client says "I *can't* relax and trust myself when I'm at work." I might ask " You say you can't do that. Can I check: What would happen if you did?" or "What stops you?"

Unspecified Verb. If the client says "My father really *hurts* me." I might ask "When you say he really hurt you, I'm not sure: How, specifically, does he hurt you?"

Unspecified Noun. If the client says "People have been telling me I need to listen more." I might ask "When you say people have told you that, I'm unclear: Which people? Who, specifically told you that?"

Simple Deletion. If the client says "I'm really unhappy." I might ask "I get that you are really unhappy, and I'm not sure: About what?"

Dr Thomas Macroy at Utah State University did a detailed study of 31 families, members of which were asked to rate their level of satisfaction with the family. Next, a family session was held for each family and recorded on audiotape. The audiotapes were analysed for the occurrence of 150 specific metamodel patterns. In those families where people were less satisfied, substantially more metamodel patterns were being used, especially deletions and unspecified nouns. This study supports the notion that challenging metamodel patterns is an important way to enhance the ability to achieve satisfaction socially (Macroy, 1978).

2) The Milton model. This model also begins with the metamodel language categories listed above. Instead of challenging them with a question, though, it utilises them purposefully. Interestingly, Milton Erickson used these categories to create indirect suggestions for successful hypnotherapeutic change. He also used many other identified categories of language such as Pacing (acknowledging what the client is already experiencing) and Metaphor (Bandler and Grinder, 1975). Following is an example of this "constructive" use of such patterns to suggest change in an "artfully vague" way. The words in bold would be said with a slightly different voice tonality, to create "Embedded Suggestions" (another Milton model pattern) in the paragraph, but you probably already realise how easily **you can use this**.

"Your reading this now (pacing), and you might **be very interested** (mind read) to hear a story about the way that Milton Erickson talked (use of metaphor beginning). And the fact that you've chosen to **enjoy this right now** (presupposition) is a good thing (lost performative), because just reading this kind of example means that **you're learning much** about the way that Milton would talk to people (complex equivalent), and every time (universal quantifier) you re-read this, you *can* find that you (modal operator of possibility) **learn more** (unspecified verb) of the kind of things that Milton said (unspecified noun) and no doubt you realise that this is how Milton Erickson assisted people to **make changes** (simple deletion).

While the Milton model is the opposite of the kind of clear

communication which makes ongoing co-operation possible, it has a different kind of use. It is the language of influence. Erickson used this language to suggest changes. Donald Moine at the University of Oregon studied 45 minute long audiocassette recordings of insurance salespeople. His sample included top producers from their companies, as well as "average" producers of sales. The highly successful salespeople used far more embedded suggestions, complex equivalents, mind reading, metaphors, pacing, and modal operators of possibility. This artfully vague and suggestive language was part of their skill in enabling others to change (Moines, 1981). They might say, for instance "I notice you've been looking at those products for a few minutes now (pacing) and so I can see that you're interested in buying one (mind reading) and that means (complex equivalent) you probably want know which one will work best for you, so you can (modal operator of possibility) choose the right one quickly (embedded suggestion)".

3) The Sleight of Mouth patterns (also called criteria utilisation patterns). These are a series of ways to "Reframe" (using Gregory Bateson's term) a person's experience. They were first codified by Robert Dilts (Dilts, 1999). The Sleight of Mouth patterns include the use of the metamodel and Milton model as well as a number of other patterns which intentionally alter the person's sense of what a specific event "means" (i.e. what the psychological "complex equivalent" of the event is for them). For example, a client may say "My mother was always depressed, so I guess I'll always be depressed." This is a complex equivalent statement, telling us that, currently, the meaning of this person's mother having been depressed is that they will always be depressed. i.e. "My mother was always depressed = I will always be depressed." There are a great many things I can do to break this equivalence (i.e. to "deframe" the statement) or to create a new more useful equivalence (i.e. to "reframe" it). The original Sleight of Mouth framework lists twenty or so patterns. For example:

1) Use the metamodel questions to de-frame: I could ask "Was she always depressed? Was there ever a single moment when she wasn't depressed?", or "How, specifically, do you plan to "always be depressed"?", or "How does her being depressed mean that you have to be?"

2) Use the Milton model to reframe: I could tell a story (metaphor) about Ted Turner, whose father committed suicide after a lifetime of depression; Ted loved life and went on to turn his father's failing advertising business into multimedia giant CNN Time Warner, and to give the largest single donation to charity ever given by one person. As I

tell this story, I could include embedded suggestions and a new complex equivalent, having Ted say to himself, "Ted, you saw how your father got himself depressed, and so you know more than anyone how to **enjoy life fully**."

3) Apply the person's way of thinking (and even their wording) to itself. This might involve saying "That's always a depressing kind of guess to be nurturing, isn't it."

4) Identify an issue that's more important. I might say "Rather than thinking about what happened to you or your mother in the past, isn't it more important to think about how you could become a positive role model for your own children?"

5) Identify the intention behind the person's statement and discuss that instead. I could point out "I guess your intention is to protect yourself from being disappointed by trying and failing. I wonder if you've noticed that the only way to really protect yourself from a sense of failure is to know you did your very best to live the kind of life you really want to live."

Is a simple language pattern like a Sleight of Mouth reframe enough to change a severe emotional problem? Sometimes it is. Dr Lewis Baxter (1994) showed that clients with obsessive compulsive disorder had raised activity in neural networks inside the caudate nucleus of the brain (demonstrated on PET scans of the brain). Drugs such as Prozac raise serotonin levels and the caudate nucleus activity is thus reduced. Baxter found that when clients repeated a simple reframe to themselves, the PET scan showed the same raising of serotonin levels and the same lowering of activity in the caudate nucleus. Precisely chosen words affect state-dependent neural networks.

An Example of a One Session NLP Coaching Intervention

As mentioned, my aim here is not to teach NLP, but simply to give those new to it a sense of how NLP based coaching works. I urge you to get training in NLP to what is called "Master Practitioner" level before attempting to use the methodology as a coach. One place to find out about this is our internet site (www.transformations.net.nz).

What would an actual NLP session look like then? In an article introducing NLP, NLP co-developers Steve and Connirae Andreas present a transcript of their work with a 26 year old office worker named Kate, who suffered anxiety after seeing a car accident on her way to work (Andreas and Andreas, 1992, p 24-28). In the actual accident, she saw two people killed, and believed that only her own quickly "slamming on the brakes" had saved her from the same fate. Kate had worked successfully in the office at the Andreas' training business for two years and now was unable to focus on her job because of obsessing about the accident. Kate said that the image of the dead man's face kept "zooming in to her mind" whenever she was in a car, especially when someone else was driving, or when she went past the place where the accident happened. The strategy for her problem, then, was triggered by her seeing the driver or the place. After zooming in on the memory of one of the dead men's faces from the accident, she would then check what she needed to do, and feel frozen and unable to control events (a kind of recreated version of slamming on the brakes). Kate said this also reminded her of the feeling she had when she was a child and her mother physically abused her. Because Kate's life experience functions as a system, it is not possible to understand fully the meaning (the map) she creates from one experience (the particular territory) without realizing that it connects to all the other experiences she has had.

Both Steve and Connirae spent some time just listening to Kate's story and acknowledging her distress (pacing it to build rapport), and non-verbally matching her gestures and speech. The feeling of rapport and trust that they built in this time made Kate feel safe enough to risk changing her response. The visual submodality pattern of zooming in on a remembered image would provide the structure for Connirae's NLP intervention. In a sense, Connirae has modelled how Kate uses her brain to create a fast emotional shift, and she can use that model to teach Kate to run her brain to get the results she wants. Rather than imposing some abstract NLP 'technique" on Kate, she builds rapport with and "utilizes" Kate's own skill. Firstly, she assisted Kate to design a picture of a "Kate who could deal with that kind of situation really well…. She has the resources to deal with it effectively…. You can know that by the expression on her face, the way she moves, breathes and gestures, the sound of her voice, etc." At this time, Connirae's language use was particularly careful, as she presupposed the possibility of change and "reframed" Kate's beliefs. When Kate said that she thought maybe the resourceful image needed medical training to feel safer, Connirae pointed out that "What this Kate knows is not medicine, it's how to use whatever information and skills she has to act in the best way possible. She may also make mistakes once in a while – all of us do – but she also has the resources to learn from them, and use these learnings next time." This is an important clarification of the outcome they are going for, which is not some perfect safety (requiring a change in what Korzybski would call "the territory"), but a realistic trust in her own inner resources (a change in what Korzybski would call her "map" of what happens).

Steve and Connirae explain: "Connirae knew what made Kate panic: the memory of zooming in on the man's face. She had also helped Kate create an image of her capable self…. The next step is to connect these two images in her mind, so that every time Kate thinks of the man's face, it will automatically transform into the image of seeing herself with the resources to deal with this kind of situation…. NLP teaches many ways to connect images in our minds and each of us is unique in what works best for us. Connirae already knew that "zooming in" had an impact on Kate, so she decided to use that to connect the two images. She first tested her guess, to find out if Kate felt more attracted to the capable Kate of the future if she brought the image closer and zoomed in on it. When she tried this she smiled and said "Yes." Then she asked her to clear her visual screen in preparation for linking the two images. "Now see the unconscious man up close and zoomed in. As soon as you can see that, also see a very small image of the capable Kate, way out on the horizon…. Now let the image of the capable Kate zoom in close very rapidly at the same time as the image of the man in the accident quickly "unzooms" and moves off so far away you can't see it anymore." "

Kate expressed doubt that she was "really seeing" these images, and Connirae reassured her that she only needed to "pretend" to see them. She continued "Now blank your internal screen and do the same thing five more times." After running this process, called a "Swish", Connirae tested to check how Kate felt. The Swish "installed" a new strategy which was automatically (unconsciously) triggered each time something reminded Kate of the dead man's face. The entire process of planning and running the Swish took about an hour of coaching time. She immediately felt much better thinking about the accident, and was able to drive home past the scene of the accident without the usual panic that she had been suffering. At a follow-up seven years later, Kate reported that she had never again had the problem, even when she had come across and assisted at other car accidents. The Swish process changes the submodalities on the original event, in this case by shifting the remembered images far away. It also uses the same submodality pattern in reverse to bring in a metaphorical "resourceful" self-image.

Why are the Particular Frames in "Out-frames" so Important?

In the brief introduction to NLP, given above, you can already get a sense of the initial complexity of some of the tools we are using, and the value of some organizing models to explain when it will be useful to do what. NLP trainer Steve Andreas says (1999) "I think that someone who uses the NLP methods exceptionally well has several ways of gathering all the different skills and techniques under a single overarching framework of understanding." Here, however, our aim is to give you more than just "a single overarching frame". We want to give you a range of such models to combine and choose from.

Way back in 1977, two leading trainers in the new field of counselling, Robert Carkhuff and Bernard Berenson, presented an extraordinary "meta-model" of helping skills called "Beyond Counselling and Therapy" (Carkhuff and Berenson, 1977). Shifting away from the problem focused frame of traditional "counselling", they viewed the helping process through the different "frames" of crisis theory, educational theory, and five specific psychotherapeutic models (the Existential, Psychoanalytic, Behaviourist and Client Centered models). Their aim was to show how each of these "frames" sheds light on the process of helping and yet, used by itself, unnecessarily limits the process. They emphasized that helping can be "for better or for worse" and that helpers who are limited by using only one model of helping can actually prevent their clients from coping effectively with life. The exquisitely flexible therapist Milton Erickson is said to have stated this in the extreme: "I create a different model of psychotherapy for every client I see."

Like Carkhuff and Berenson, we urge you to expand and multiply your frames for thinking about the process of coaching in order to enhance your success. Our interest is practical, and these frames emerged out of our own work with coaching clients, and our guidance of new coaches struggling to understand how to be more successful in their sessions. Each of the following chapters presents an out-framing of the coaching session which relates it to a wider context.

NLP training provides a vast plethora of techniques, categorisations and language pattern tabulations. Like most new NLP Practitioners, I originally found this overwhelming, and when I asked "How do I know when to do what?" I was told "Trust your unconscious mind". This answer contradicts the entire basis of NLP, which is modelling the "unconscious skill" of experts and making it explicit. The answer left me unsatisfied, and I resolved to apply "modelling" to my own work. The RESOLVE model (Chapter 2) was the first meta-frame I developed, and gives an overview of NLP work. In this section I introduce the choosing of NLP processes based on the depth of the person's challenge (Neurological Levels), the level of motivation (Motivational Interviewing) and the personality of the client (Personal Skills).

As I worked with clients in the NLP world, it quickly became obvious that much of the time my entire session would be spent eliciting what NLP called a "well-formed" goal or outcome. Explaining what is and is not a goal then became a frame in itself, as discussed in the section When is a Goal Not a Goal? (Chapter 3). It also became clear to me that some clients had unhelpful patterns of response to their challenges, and that these general patterns of response were more important to deal with than their actual "problems". These "Patterns of Chronicity" explain change more effectively than the specific "Ecology issues" related to the particular goal the person was working on, as I explain in When Ecology is Unecological (Chapter 4).

As Julia Kurusheva and I began travelling round the world training, we were increasingly asked to deliver "one session" NLP work. While this type of work is not mainstream coaching, it is frequently what clients ask for, and it is what NLP training implies will be possible. Such brief work also prevents the formation of client dependency on counselling/coaching, and avoids an interminable "working on" problems. It was for this situation that Julia developed her Sprint model summarising the key steps for efficient one session work. Discussed in Changing Someone's Life in a Single Session (Chapter 5), the Sprint model has been shown to accurately predict the success of longer term client work as well, so it reveals itself as a model for efficiency, rather than just an emergency first-aid model.

The models that we develop when we are first working in a field, to explain what we are doing, are not necessarily the most useful models for explaining the real complexities of that field. The Wheel of Change (Chapter 6) was a model that I developed only after two decades of NLP work, by rethinking everything that I had experienced. It is a model of the change process that is based on client uniqueness rather than Practitioner steps. More than any of the other models, it explains why different types of intervention and different models of coaching may work better with different clients and even different practitioners.

Coaching usually presupposes that client problems and goals are individual matters that can be best solved by the person individually, without the presence of others, and even without reference to others. Our clients' lives, however, are largely lived in the presence of others and with constant reference to them. The assumption of individuality is a cultural and gender bias that emerged from the origins of NLP. Cultural, Gender and Relationships in NLP Coaching (Chapter 7) expands the frame of NLP coaching to think in terms of culture, of gender, and of sustaining these relationships and creating successful interpersonal results.

The illusion that we are separate from the world itself is an even more pervasive error of perception, and is assisted by our languages themselves, as they divide and categorise the undivided flow of experience and convert it mentally into "things". Undoing Life to Living (Chapter 8) reverses this trend and invites us to convert these "things" back into the lived and ever changing events that they emerged from. In the process, "problems" themselves merge back into the flow of life.

In the final section, I update NLP based on the research about memory reconsolidation which emerged in the years 2013-2015. Since all our internal experiences are recorded as "memory" it is possible to reinterpret what we do with NLP as a vast project of helping the brain to re-consolidate memories, as it naturally does continuously anyway.

Bibliography:

Andreas, S. and Andreas, C. "Neuro-Linguistic Programming" p 14-35 in Budman, S.H., Hoyt, M.F. and Friedman, S. The First Session In Brief Therapy Guildford Press, New York, 1992

Andreas, S. "What Makes A Good NLPer?" p 3-6 in Anchor Point, Vol 13, No. 10, October 1999

Arbib, M.A. "From monkey-like action recognition to human language: an evolutionary framework for neurolinguistics." Behavioural and Brain Sciences, 28, 105-167, 2005

Aziz-Zadeh, L., Iacoboni, I., Zaidel, E ., Wilson, S., & Mazziotta, J. "Left hemisphere motor facilitation in response to manual action sounds." European Journal of Neuroscience, 19, 2609-26 1 2, 2004

Bailenson, J. N. & Yee, N. "Digital chameleons: Automatic assimilation of nonverbal gestures in immersive virtual environments." Psychological Science, 16, 814-819, 2005

Balcetis, E. and Dunning, D. "Wishful Seeing: How Preferences Shape Visual Perception" Current Directions in Psychological Science February 1, 2013 22: 33-37

Bandler, R. and Grinder, J. Patterns of the Hypnotic Techniques of Milton H. Erickson, M.D. Volume 1, Meta, Cupertino, California, 1975

Bandler, R. and Grinder, J. The Structure of Magic I, Science and Behavior Books, Palo Alto, California, 1975

Bandler, R. Using Your Brain For A Change Real People Press, Moab, Utah, 1985

Bateson, G. A Sacred Unity, HarperCollins, New York, 1991

Baxter L. R. "Positron emission tomography studies of cerebral glucose metabolism in obsessive compulsive disorder." Journal of Clinical Psychiatry, 1994, 55 Supplement: p 54-9.

Bayliss, ,A.P., Paul, M.A., Cannon, P. R., & Tipper, S. P. "Gaze cueing and affective judgments of objects: I like what you look at." Psychonomic Bulletin & Review, 13, 1061-1066, 2006

Bayliss, A.P. and Tipper, S.P. "Predictive gaze cues and personality judgments: Should eye trust you?" Psychological Science, 17, 514-520, 2006

Bernieri, F. J., Reznick, S., & Rosenthal, R. "Synchrony, pseudosynchrony, and dissynchrony: Measuring the entrainment process in mother-infant interactions", Journal of Personality and Social Psychology, 54, 243-253, 1988

Bolstad, R. <u>RESOLVE: A New Model Of Therapy</u> Crown House, Bancyfelin, Wales, 2002

Brynie, F.H. Brain Sense American Management Association, New York, 2009

Bushman, G. Kross, E. and Mischkowski, D. Journal of Experimental Social Psychology, 2013

Carkhuff, R.R. and Berenson, B.G. Beyond Counselling and Therapy, Holt, Rinehart and Winston, New York, 1977

Carkhuff, R.R. The Art Of Helping Human Resource Development, Amherst, Massachusetts, 1973

Casile, A., & Giese, M. A. "Nonvisual motor training influences biological motion perception", Current Biology 16, 69-74, 2006

Charney, E. J. "Postural configurations in psychotherapy", Psychosomatic Medicine, 28, 305-315, 1966

Chartrand, T. L., & Bargh, J. A. "The chameleon effect: The perception-behavior link and social interaction", Journal of Personality and Social Psychology 76, 893-910, 1999

Cheek, D., "Awareness of Meaningful Sounds Under General Anaesthesia." in Theoretical and Clinical aspects of Hypnosis, Symposium Specialists, 1981

Chen, X., Striano, T., &. Rakoczy, R. "Auditory-oral matching behavior in newborns." Developmental Science, 7, 42-47, 2004

Condon, W. S. "Cultural Microrhythms" p 53-76 in Davis, M. (ed) <u>Interactional Rhythms: Periodicity in Communicative Behaviour</u> Human Sciences Press, New York, 1982

Creswell, J. D., Bursley, D.K., and Satpute, A. B.. Neural Reactivation Links Unconscious Thought to Decision Making Performance. Social Cognitive and Affective Neuroscience, 2013

Csikszentmihalyi, M. Flow Harper Collins, New York, 1990

de Guzman, G. C., Tognoli, E.,Lagarde, J., Jantzen, K. J., & Kelso, J.A.S. "Effects of biological relevance of the stimulus in mediating spontaneous visual social coordination." Societal for Neuroscience: Abstract Viewer/Itinerary Planner, Program No. 867.21, 2005

Diamond, M. <u>Enriching Heredity: The Impact of the Environment on the Brain</u> Free Press, New York, 1988

Dilts, R. <u>Sleight Of Mouth</u> Meta Publications, Capitola, California, 1999

Dilts, R., Grinder, J., Bandler, R. and DeLozier, J. <u>Neuro-Linguistic Programming: Volume 1 The Study of the Structure of Subjective Experience</u>, Meta Publications, Cupertino, California, 1980

Dilts, R., Hallbom, T. and Smith, S. Beliefs: Pathways To Health And Wellbeing Metamorphous, Portland, Oregon, 1990

Dreyfus, Stuart "Formal Models vs. Human Situational Understanding: Inherent Limitations on the Modeling of Business Expertise". 1981, University of California, Berkeley.

Dreyfus, Stuart and Dreyfus, Hubert. "A five Stage Model of the Mental Activities Involved in Directed Skill Acquisition". 1980.

Erickson, M.H. and Rossi, E.L. <u>The February Man</u> Brunner/Mazel, New York, 1989

Erickson, M.H. Experiencing Hypnosis Irvington, New York, 1981

Fadiga, L., Craighero, L., Buccinor G., & Rizzolatti, G. "Speech listening specifically modulates the excitability of tongue muscles: A TMS study." European Journal of Neuroscience, 1 5, 399-402, 2002

Fadiga, L., Fogassi, G., Pavesi, G. and Rizzolatti, G. "Motor Facilitation during action observation: a magnetic stimulation study" p 2608-2611 in Journal of Neurophysiology, No. 73, 1995

Franze, L. ed. "Creating a Coaching Culture" Institute of Leadership and Management, London, 2011

Gazzola, V., Aziz-Zadeh, L. and Keysers, C. "Empathy and the somatotropic auditory mirror neuron system in humans." Current Biology, 16, 1824-1829, 2006

Genser-Medlitsch, M. and Schütz, P., "Does Neuro-Linguistic psychotherapy have effect? New Results shown in the extramural section." Martina Genser-Medlitsch and Peter Schütz, ÖTZ-NLP, Vienna, 1997

Gottman, J.M. and Silver, N. <u>The Seven Principles For Making Marriage Work</u> Three Rivers Press, New York, 1999

Gottman, J.M. <u>The Marriage Clinic</u> W.W. Norton and Co., New York, 1999

Greenough, W.T., Withers, G. and Anderson, B. "Experience-Dependent Synaptogenesis as a Plausible Memory Mechanism" p 209-229 in Gormezano, I. And Wasserman, E. ed <u>Learning and Memory: The Behavioural and Biological Substrates</u> Erlbaum & Associates, Hillsdale, New Jersey, 1992

Hadjikhani, N., Joseph, R. M., Snyder, J., & Tager-Flusberg, H.

"Anatomical differences in the mirror neuron system and social cognition network in autism." Cerebral Cortex, 16, 1276-1282, 2006

Hamilton, A., Wolpert, D., & Frithz U. "Your own action influences how you perceive another person's action." Current Biology 14, 493-498, 2004

Jacobs, B., Schall, M. and Scheibel, A.B. "A Qualitative Dendritic Analysis of Wernicke's Area in Humans: Gender, Hemispheric and Environmental Factors" in Journal of Comparative Neurology, 327.1, p 97-111, 1993

James, T. and Woodsmall, W. Time Line Therapy And The Basis Of Personality, Meta Publications, Cupertino, California, 1988

Korzybski, A. Science and Sanity, Institute of General semantics, Englewood, New Jersey, 1994

Lund, H. "Asthma Management" p 4-6 in The Time Line Therapy Association Journal, Vol 5, Summer 1995

Macroy, T.D. "Linguistic surface structures in family interaction" in Dissertation Abstracts International, 40 (2) 926-B, Utah State University, 133 pp, Order = 7917967, 1978

Maturana, H.R. and Varela, F.J. <u>The Tree Of Knowledge</u> Shambhala, Boston, 1992

Miller, G., Galanter, E. and Pribram, K. <u>Plans And The Structure Of Behaviour</u>, Henry Holt & Co., 1960

Moine, D. "A psycholinguistic study of the patterns of persuasion used by successful salespeople" in Dissertation Abstracts International, 42 (5), 2135-B, University of Oregon, 271pp, Order = 8123499, 1981

Muss, D. "A New Technique For Treating Post-Traumatic Stress Disorder" in British Journal of Clinical Psychology, 30, p 91-92, 1991

Muss, Dr D. The Trauma Trap. Doubleday, London, 1991

O'Connor, J. and Seymour, J. <u>Introducing Neuro-Linguistic Programming</u>, Harper Collins, London, 1990

Roos, T. Mental Coaching, Trafford Publishing, Victoria, Canada, 2002

Stipančić, M., Renner, W., Schütz, P. and Dond, R. "Effects of Neurolinguistic Psychotherapy on psychological difficulties and perceived quality of life" in Counselling and Psychotherapy Research, 10 (1) pages 39-49, 2010

Wake, L., Gray, R.M. and Bourke, F.S. eds <u>The Clinical Effectiveness of Neurolinguistic Programming</u> Routledge, London, 2013

Zilbergeld, B. The Shrinking of America, Little Brown & Co, Boston, 1983

RESOLVE

A Model of NLP Changework

RESOLVE is an acronym for a series of steps used in NLP based change work. Steve Andreas says (1999) "I think that someone who uses the NLP methods exceptionally well has several ways of gathering all the different skills and techniques under a single overarching framework of understanding." In meeting this aim, the RESOLVE model has a similar function to Carkhuff and Egan's "Developmental Models of Helping" (Carkhuff, 1973; Egan, 1975). Most models of psychotherapy propose some structuring of the session, or of the process of psychotherapy. In NLP terms, there are several key elements of this process which enable NLP "tools", such as the Trauma process, to work effectively.

The co-developers of NLP (especially Richard Bandler and Dr John Grinder) did not initially teach a framework for understanding the vast array of new patterns they revealed and developed. Dr Tad James was one of the first NLP trainers to do so. His General Model of Therapy (James, 1995) evolved out of his own modelling of Richard Bandler's client work. My colleague Bryan Royds grouped all the NLP interventions we had studied, based on this model. Margot Hamblett and I expanded this grouping and formalised it into the RESOLVE model, which is now taught in a number of NLP training programs round the world. The book RESOLVE (Bolstad, 2002) expands on this model and the research behind it. Videotapes are also available from the course in which I teach the use of the model and from client sessions which demonstrate its use.

Consulting: A Resourceful State For The Helper

The depressed, confused or anxious person is hiring me as a consultant (like a consultant in the business setting) to give them advice and support to put into action a plan that will change their life. If it is to work, this will be a collaborative relationship, in which they will need not only to "help", but also to experimentally follow the advice the consultant gives. I have no magic way of solving their problems for them. But if they do the things I suggest, I believe that they will experience change. I often say "NLP doesn't work. *You* work…. NLP just explains how you work, perfectly.". The other side of this is that if I am not hired as a consultant, I accept that. I do not carry on trying to "sell my services".

A consultant in a business context is hired to suggest strategies to enable their client to meet the client's goals. There are several implications to this arrangement, which I consider appropriate to the NLP setting:

- The consultant has some expertise in the area where they recommend changes, as well as some expertise in co-operating with clients. In the 1960s and 1970s, counselling developers Robert Carkhuff and Bernard Berenson published a number of research studies showing that helping interactions tend to influence clients either for better *or* for worse. They identified several measures of successful human functioning, and showed that helpers who function well on these dimensions are able to assist others to function well on these dimensions too. Helpers who function poorly on these dimensions actually influence clients to deteriorate in their functioning! (Carkhuff and Berenson, 1977, p 5, p 35). Carkhuff and Berenson likened most psychotherapists to professional lifeguards with extensive training in rowing a boat, throwing a ring buoy, and giving artificial respiration, but without the ability to swim. "They cannot save another because, given the same circumstances, they could not save themselves." What this emphasizes is that effective change agents are models of the skills they want to convey to their clients. What you do matters far more than what you tell your clients to do.

- The consultant elicits, clarifies and works towards the *client's* goals, not towards the consultant's own goals. The client is in charge of their own business. The consultant needs to be "hired" either formally or informally. That is, they offer their expertise in response to a request. They are not just a person who enjoys interfering in others lives. The client can choose to action the consultants suggestions, or not. Without this action, the consultant's work is recognised to be of little significance. The consultant is in charge of the process of consulting; the client is in charge of the content of their business.

- Consultants operate with certain explicit professional guidelines, such as confidentiality, and avoidance of double relationships (e.g. combining a consulting relationship with a sexual relationship) with clients. In return they expect their clients to operate with some guidelines such as turning up to arranged meetings on time.

Adopting this consultant role is itself a therapeutic step. As I spell out for my clients what kind of relationship I want, I am modelling healthy relating for them. I am also treating them as if they are "at cause" in their life, rather than a helpless victim. The NLP attitude and the consulting role are conveyed very simply at the beginning of any encounter. In doing this, I convey my own sense of resourcefulness; the ability to swim without being caught up in the currents of dependency and despair which many clients are dealing with. Creating this consulting contract is the first step of the RESOLVE model. Part of the practitioner's resourceful attitude is knowing that, just as in the sports situation where the "coaching" metaphor comes from, change is the client's job and not the coach's. This requires a skill in dissociating rather than in getting caught up in the client's horror of what happened to them.

Establishing Rapport

Once I am clear on my role as a consultant, there are several steps still remaining before we can "change" the client's life. The first is known in NLP as building rapport. The developers of NLP noted that the chances of a helper being able to lead someone to change their strategy were increased by the helper elegantly joining the person's reality first. "When you join someone else's reality by pacing them, that gives you rapport and trust, and puts you in a position to utilise their reality in ways that change it." (Bandler and Grinder, 1979, p 81). For example, one of the set of strategies that often help create anxiety is to make scary internal visual images. If I talk with the visually anxious person about what they can *see* as they sit beside me, there is an increased chance that when I gradually shift my comments to talk more about kinesthetic relaxation, the person will follow this lead into the new strategy of relaxation (Yapko, 1981). Examination of films and videotapes of therapy sessions and other conversations by communication researchers (Ivey et alia, 1996, p 60; Condon 1982, p 53-76; Hatfield et alia 1994) now confirms the significance of what researchers call "interactional synchrony" or "movement complementarity". This same process is variously referred to in the NLP literature (e.g. Bolstad and Hamblett, 1998, p 68-72) as "non-verbal matching", "pacing" or "rapport skills".

What are these non-verbal rapport skills? NLP developers propose that when conversation flows smoothly, people breathe in time with each other, and co-ordinate their body movements as well as their voice tonality and speed. The more this matching of behaviour happens, the more the other person gets a sense of shared understanding and at-one-ness or "rapport". Also, the more this matching happens, the more the other person will be open to useful suggestions, and adopt the emotional responses of the helper or therapist. All learning and change depends on this willingness of the client to be open to new responses.

William Condon has meticulously studied videotapes of conversations, confirming these patterns. He found that in a successful conversation, movements such as a smile or a head nod are matched by the other person within 1/15 of a second. Within minutes of beginning the conversation, the volume, pitch and speech rate (number of sounds per minute) of the peoples voices match each other. This is correlated with a synchronising of the type and rate of breathing. Even general body posture is adjusted over the conversation so that the people appear to match or mirror each other. Elaine Hatfield, John Cacioppo and Richard Rapson, in their book *Emotional Contagion*, show that matching another person's behaviour in these detailed ways results in the transfer of emotional states from one person to another. If I feel happy, and you match my breathing, voice, gestures and smiles, you will begin to feel the same emotional state. This is the source of empathy, and also of much therapeutic change.

In 1995 a remarkable area of neurons (nerve cells) was discovered by brain researchers working at the University of Palma in Italy (Rizzolatti et alia, 1996; Rizzolatti and Arbib, 1998). The cells, now called "mirror neurons", are found in the pre-motor cortex of the brains of monkeys and apes as well as humans. In humans they form part of the specific area called Broca's area, which is also involved in the creation of speech. Although the cells are related to motor activity (i.e. they are part of the system by which we make kinesthetic responses such as moving an arm), they seem to be activated by visual input. When a monkey observes another monkey (or even a human) making a facial expression or body movement, or vocalising, the mirror neurons light up. As they do, the monkey appears to involuntarily copy the same movement it has observed visually. This ability to copy a fellow creatures actions as they do them has obviously been very important in the development of primate social intelligence. It enables us to identify with the person we are observing and to experience the emotions of fellow humans empathically. When this area of the brain is damaged in a stroke, copying another's actions becomes almost impossible. The development of speech has clearly been a result of this copying skill.

In his study of intimate relationships, John Gottman has shown that by identifying such synchronization during a five-minute video, he can predict whether or not a couple will stay together for the next decade (predicting divorce with 95% accuracy and the precise year of divorce with 80% accuracy).

By revealing the nonverbal basis of rapport, NLP has been able to add considerably to the skills which a helper uses to convey empathy. Research identifying the effectiveness of *verbal* pacing (reflective listening; restating what the person said) first emerged in 1950, and a summary of the 50 years of continuing evidence for this core helping skill is presented by Allen Bergin and Sol Garfield (1994) in their Handbook of Psychotherapy. Building rapport in NLP terms also includes pacing the person's core metaprograms and values as these are revealed. Clients have been shown, for example, to prefer a counsellor whose word use matches their own representational system (visual, auditory, kinesthetic or auditory digital) by a ratio of three to one! (Brockman, 1980).

Specifying Outcomes

Once rapport is established, chunking down to detailed plans becomes very significant. While using vague language helps to build a feeling of rapport, the ongoing use of vague language is part of the system by which many clients maintain their problem. For example, Thomas Macroy (1998) found that when family communication was analysed in terms of the NLP metamodel, those families who were most dissatisfied were also using the most deletions, distortions and generalisations in their language (especially deletions). Research on the Solution Focused Therapy model (a model closely allied with NLP) confirms that clients improve after questions from their helper which focus on what outcome the client has. Also, the amount of discussion of solutions and outcomes in the first session is strongly correlated to the chances that the client will continue with the change process (Miller et alia, 1996, p 259). William Miller has done an overview of the research into successful psychotherapy, in which he identifies that enabling the client to set their own goal for therapy significantly increases their commitment to therapy and enhances the results (Miller, 1985). Solution focused therapists focus their entire intervention on eliciting the client's own outcomes and solutions. As de Shazer reports, this results in 75% success over four to six sessions (Chevalier, 1995). That is to say, setting an outcome is itself a change process.

Richard Wiseman did a very large study showing the same result. He tracked 5,000 people who had some significant goal they wanted to achieve (everything from starting a new relationship to beginning a new career, from stopping smoking to gaining a qualification). Dramatic and consistent differences in goalsetting made the mere 10% who were successful stand out from the other 90%. Most of all, successful goalsetters described their goal in positive terms, and considered carefully what challenges they would face actually doing the work to achieve it ("ecology" in NLP).

Guiding the person to do this involves using meta-model questions to help the person shift from general nominalizations ("I want happiness") and unspecified verbs ("I want to nurture myself more") to sensory specific descriptions ("I will take ten minutes each day to focus on what I have done well and write three examples of actions I'm pleased with in my diary").

Opening Up The Client's Model Of The World

Once we have a wellformed outcome, are we ready to make the changes? The answer is maybe. More of the "art" of NLP happens at the next stage in consulting than at any other. Here I need to open up the client's model of the world, so that they allow for the possibility of change. The one core factor in the client's "personality" that reliably predicts how well they will respond to the change process itself is whether they experience themselves as having an internal locus of control. Clients who believe that they are in charge of their own responses ("At cause", to use the NLP jargon) do far better in numerous research studies with a variety of different models of therapy (Miller et alia, 1996, p 319, 325). Furthermore, research shows that this sense of being in control is not a stable "quality" that some clients have and others do not; it varies over the course of their interaction with the helper. Successful therapy has been shown to result first in a shift in the "locus of control", and then in the desired success (Miller et alia, 1996, p 326). In their study of NLP Psychotherapy, Martina Genser-Medlitsch and Peter Schütz in Vienna (1997) found that NLP clients scored higher than controls in their perception of themselves as in control of their lives (with a difference at 10% significance level).

Dealing first with this meta-level change, dramatically increases your chances of enabling someone to change. There are three steps to putting someone "at cause" with their situation. These are 1) demonstrating the general possibility of change, 2) demonstrating the specific possibility of changing the client's current problem, and 3) demonstrating the possibility of using a selected, specific change technique to change that problem. Completing these tasks means that reframing is *always* part of my work as an NLP Practitioner. For me, this step of the RESOLVE model, more than any other, is the key to transformative change. It is done with a series of metaphors, reframes, sleight of mouth patterns, and presuppositional questions.
level).

Dealing first with this meta-level change, dramatically increases your chances of enabling someone to change. There are three steps to putting someone "at cause" with their situation. These are 1) demonstrating the general possibility of change, 2) demonstrating the specific possibility of changing the client's current problem, and 3) demonstrating the possibility of using a selected, specific change technique to change that problem. The first step is to give a concrete physical demonstration of change happening easily, and quickly as a result of changing internal representations.

For example, I have every client do a visualisation exercise near the start of their session. They turn around and point behind them with their arm, and then come back to the front. Next they imagine themselves going further, and notice what they would see, feel and say to themselves if their body was more flexible and they could turn around further. Then, keeping their feet in the same place, they turn around again and notice how much further they can go, instantly and without any extra effort (Bolstad and Hamblett, 1998, p 81). Another example of a simple demonstration of change is the lemon visualisation from near the start of the book. In this I say "Think of a fresh lemon. Imagine one in front of you now, and feel what it feels like as you pick it up. Take a knife and cut a slice off the lemon, and hear the slight sound as the juice squirts out. Smell the lemon as you lift the slice to your mouth and take a bite of the slice. Taste the sharp taste of the fruit. If you actually imagined doing that, you mouth is now salivating. Why? Because your brain followed your instructions and thought about, saw, heard, felt, smelled and tasted the lemon. By recalling sensory information, you recreated the entire experience of the lemon, so that your body responded to the lemon you created."

To demonstrate the possibility of changing this client's specific problem, I want to show them that their problem has a strategy (a sequence of internal representations that creates the result they have been getting). I will access, elicit and experimentally alter the person's problem strategy:

1) Pre-test the strategy. Tad James (1995, p 28) emphasised that the process of helping someone change (like all strategies) involves a test before the change intervention and a related test after the intervention. I ask, "When you think about it now, can you get back enough of a sense of that problem so you'd know if that changed?" Until they can, it would be risky to go on. After all, how will they know whether they've succeeded? Of course, some people say they only get the problem in a certain situation. I tend to say, with an air of conviction "Okay, let's go there now!". Once we have a pre-tested response from this comment, I can easier check what's different later on, in our post-test to verify the change.

2) Elicit the strategy. I say "Wow! That's impressive. How do you do that? How do you know it's time to start?..." These questions presuppose that the client "does" something. By answering them, the client has established that if a change process didn't work, it's because they are still "doing" the old behaviour well enough to get the problem. The whole stage of opening up the person's model of the world is a process of reframing, of meta-level change preparing for the simple shifting of the strategies which happens next.

3) Have the person dissociate from and experimentally alter the strategy. I ask "What if I changed that strategy in this small way. Would it still work?" Answering this question requires the person to rehearse a different strategy, and experimentally change their old way of behaving.

The third step of this stage is to pre-frame the specific change techniques identified as useful by the consultant. This includes answering the question "How does this technique relate to my problem and my outcome?" (i.e. "Why are we doing this?"), and the question "Does this technique work?". Stories of other clients who have benefited from the change technique are an elegant way to answer both questions, as well as rehearsing the client through the process.

Each type of change technique is based on certain assumptions, which are discussed from the Practitioner's point of view in Chapter three. It is easy to assume that our clients share these assumptions, which we may easily take for granted after using the techniques so many times. For example, the following pre-frames are useful before making an intervention in each of the ten categories (from Chapter three). These may be introduced by demonstrations such as the pointing exercise, by metaphorical stories, by giving examples of clients' use of the process, by presupposing them, or by directly teaching them.

For example, when I use Hypnotherapy, I use certain specific techniques for communicating with a client's unconscious mind. A client will occasionally ask me "What do you mean by the term "unconscious mind"? Unconscious means out to it, like in a coma. Either my mind is working, in which case I'm conscious, or it isn't, in which case I'm unconscious. I don't see how you can communicate with what is unconscious." When I hear this question, I'm aware that something of the backup for using hypnotherapy, the operating system, is missing. This backup includes certain beliefs about what is possible, and the opportunity to notice certain internal events. Amongst hundreds of choices, I might say "Until I mention it now, you weren't conscious of the speed you were breathing, and the depth you were breathing to. But you can be conscious of that now, right? In fact, now that you're conscious of it, you can change the speed and breathe slower, or faster, shallower or deeper. Check it out now. You can run your breathing with your conscious mind. Of course, if you do, then it's hard to get much else done. So being conscious of breathing may be useful for an athlete, but not necessary at some other times.... So how were you deciding which speed to breathe at when you weren't conscious of it? That action of your brain that decided that is what I'm calling your unconscious mind. Now, when I play some classical music here, your breathing rate will tend to slow down, without you thinking about it consciously. That's what I mean by communicating with your unconscious mind. The music communicates with the part of your brain which is deciding how fast you'll breathe. So, in the same way, would it be useful to you to be able to communicate with the part of your mind which chooses what to memorise, or chooses how quickly you heal?"

Choosing A Change Process

Leading is the step in the RESOLVE model where the official "NLP change process" is done. In selecting which process to use, I assess three factors in particular:

1. The "Neurological Level" of the challenge
2. The Client's Personal Strengths in terms of association-dissociation and "chunking up – chunking down"
3. Motivational Interviewing Stages of Change

Neurological Levels

Firstly, let me explain the Neurological levels model. When a client says "I can't seem to create the right state of mind to manage the pressure in my job." NLP trainer Robert Dilts points out that you could respond to this at a number of different "neurological levels" depending on which word or phrase in the sentence you attend to.

1) The final phrase "...in my job." refers to the **Environment** where the problem happens. One way to create change is to change the environment (e.g. by finding a different job). Often this is the first level of change that clients themselves have tried.
2) The phrase "...manage the pressure..." refers to the specific **Behaviours** which the client is unable to do. Change can be created at this level (e.g. by showing the client specific behaviours which will reduce the sense of pressure; by setting a resource anchor). Often this is the first level of change that consultants want to try.

3) The phrase "...create the right state of mind..." refers to the **Capabilities** which the client would need in order to solve the problem. More profound change can be achieved at this level (e.g. by showing the client new strategies for creating useful states of mind in any circumstances).

4) The phrase "...can't seem to..." refers to the level of **Beliefs and Values**. It would be the same if the client said "I don't want have to create the right state of mind to manage the pressure in my job." "...don't want to..." is a Beliefs and Values level issue. Fundamental changes can occur for clients when they resolve issues at this level (e.g. by changing their beliefs about what is possible using Time Line processes).

5) The deepest level in the statement is the level of the word "I...", the level of **Identity**. At this level, change can occur by giving the client a new experience of who they are as a person (e.g. by using parts integration to integrate the part of them that gets anxious with the part of them that knows they are capable of doing their job). Many of our attempts to get clients to change do not work because change needs to occur at this much more profound level.

6) There is a level before the person says anything, though. This level is the level Dilts calls **Spirit**, and involves the person's connection with greater systems of which they are a part (communities, the universe etc). Inspirational leaders often achieve change at this level by use of metaphor and profound reframing.

The important thing about using the neurological levels in changework is that, as a generalisation, a problem at one level needs to be dealt with by a solution at a level at least one "higher" than the problem. For example, a person who is gets panicky whenever they are in an elevator tends to think they have an "elevator" problem. This environment level issue needs to be solved by a behaviour level change (such as the NLP trauma cure). A person who cannot learn a new strategy for resolving conflicts in their relationships may think they have a problem of capability, but this capability level issue needs to be solved by a beliefs and values level change (such as reframing their beliefs about what conflict means and dealing with the disturbing event on the time line). Change at a "higher" level affects all the levels below it, virtually instantly. When a client changes their belief about anxiety, they find they can learn new ways to manage it, and they behave in different ways to previously.

Some clients specifically ask for change at a certain level. Coaches often have their own preferences about which level they want to work at. It is useful to be able to accept, for example, that not every client comes in wanting spiritual transformation, or fundamental changes in their self-image. Sometimes a person just wants to get rid of their panic in the elevator. And, after all, once they have changed that, they may decide to learn a strategy that enables them to relax in any situation, and that may change their beliefs about what is possible.

- When a person states that they want something external to change (environment level), we at least help them change their behaviour or anchored responses.
- When they state that they want to behave differently, we at least help them install new skills and strategies (capability level).
- When they say they want new capabilities, we at least help them change their beliefs about the situation and the possible responses.
- When they say they want to change their priorities (values) or let go of old beliefs, we at least help them to change their sense of who they are and what their overall purpose is.
- When someone wants to change at that deeper (identity) level, we help them connect with a sense of what is greater than them that can give their life meaning (spirituality).

Personal Strengths Model

Milton Erickson, the hypnotherapist who was modelled by the developers of NLP, continuously urged the identification and utilisation of clients "problem" strategies in therapy. He says "This author has repeatedly stressed the importance of utilising patients' symptoms and general patterns of behaviour in psychotherapy. Such utilisation renders unnecessary any effort to alter or transform symptomatology as a preliminary measure to the re-education of patients in relation to the crucial problems confronting them in their illness." (Erickson, 1980, Vol IV, p 348). In the following section I provide a simple, easy to use, format for NLP Practitioners to quickly identify a client's "pattern of behaviour" and utilise it by providing NLP processes which pace it. I will show you how every client who enters your office is revealing their *strengths* by the very way they claim to have a "problem". My model is based on an earlier model developed by Carl Jung.

In developing the metaprograms model of personality, NLP began with Jung's categories of Thinker, Feeler, Sensor and Intuitor. In Jung's model, the terms Thinker, Feeler, Sensor and Intuitor refer both to personality types and also to skills for living, which people develop to various extents. He explains (Jung, 1964, p49) "These four functional types correspond to the obvious means by which consciousness obtains its orientation to experience. *Sensation* (i.e. sense perception tells you that something exists; *thinking* tells you what it is; *feeling* tells you whether it is agreeable or not; and *intuition* tells you whence it comes and where it is going."

In NLP terms, four important analogues of Jung's skills are the ability to:

1) Dissociate (distance oneself from experiences, seeing them from outside; corresponding to Thinker)
2) Associate (step into experiences, feeling them from inside; corresponding to Feeler) ,
3) Chunk up (Be aware of the global "big picture"; corresponding to Intuitor)
4) Chunk down (Be aware of the specific details; corresponding to Sensor)

These four skills or metaprograms (amongst others!) are essential for living an enjoyable life. They are also necessary prerequisites for all other internal processing, including the processing we call NLP techniques. To experience anchoring, for instance, you need to be able to associate into experiences. To run the phobia cure you need to be able to dissociate. To set a well formed outcome you need to be able to chunk down, and to do the parts integration process you need to be able to chunk up.

When a client comes seeking change, they bring their own personal skills; ones they've developed over a lifetime. Certain upbringings support the development of skills for dissociating; encouraging the person to step out of their experience. Certain upbringings support the development of skills for associating into and fully "living" experiences. Some upbringings nurture both abilities. It's the same for chunking skills.

Anchoring processes require associating into a specific situation (stepping into an experience and feeling it from the inside). A client who is excellent at associating will generally be good at anchoring. They've been doing it already (possibly using it to create phobias, but the skill is intact). They may or may not have acquired the skill to dissociate that is presupposed in the phobia/trauma cure. If we use collapsing anchors before the phobia cure, or create a resource anchor first, we are utilising their strength (pacing) before leading them to new skills.

Submodality change processes require being able to dissociate somewhat from the experience you are eliciting submodalities for. Some submodality processes (such as the phobia/trauma cure) specifically require making dissociated, constructed images. Time Line Therapy™ (in which the person imagines floating up above the Time Line of their life) requires dissociating from the experiences on the Time Line. A client who is excellent at dissociating will generally be good at Time Line Therapy™ (see James and Woodsmall, 1988). They may find checking an experience in the time line less convincing, but will experience the change from being way up above and before the problem event. Someone who "feels" cut off from their experience may appreciate healing their limiting decision (to be cut off) from above the time line before coming back and anchoring themselves to a powerful resource state.

It's the same with chunking. Using the detailed NLP questioning style called the Metamodel or using solution focused questions to clarify your thoughts and set specific goals requires chunking down. The person skilled at chunking down to the thousand details of their day and getting anxious may appreciate setting a sensory specific goal before you do trancework and chunk up to some generalised "change". On the other hand, using the "artfully vague" language patterns developed by Milton Erickson to induce trance presupposes the ability to chunk up, as do techniques which ask for the purpose or "higher intention" of your behaviour. A client who gets depressed because "everything" is hopeless may find it easier to use parts integration before setting specific goals.

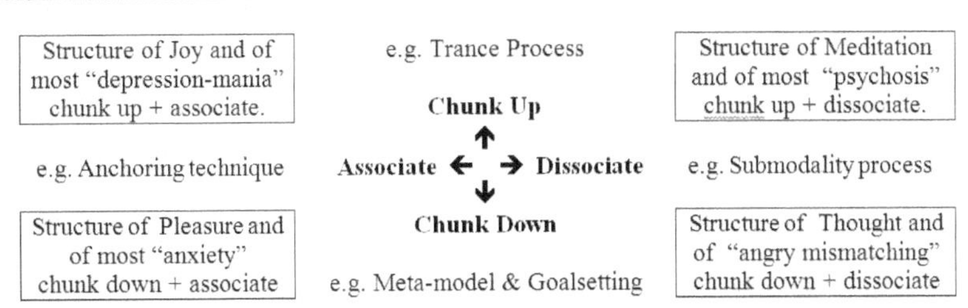

As an NLP Practitioner, you'll discover that some techniques work better with certain clients. It's not random. Clients have strengths. This four-skill model is one method for "diagnosing" those strengths. Some clients can do everything you suggest easily; that's great -they have all four skills.

In a sense, every time you use an NLP technique with a client, you help them to develop the skills presupposed by it. In that way, it's not only the specific issue that changes. Your client develops the skills required by the technique; which are simultaneously the skills to live an enjoyable life. NLP techniques are training skills for life.

As Jung noted in his model, people generally utilise a pair of the basic skills most of all. In our model, for example, a person may use skills to associate into a chunked up experience (*"Everything feels* like this.") which could be used to create euphoria or "depression". This person may benefit from developing their ability to chunk down and dissociate, using submodality processes and dissociated goal setting.

Someone who uses skills to dissociate in a chunked up way (*"Everything I'm conscious of* is like this") could have used these skills to create a state of meditation or "psychosis". They could benefit from taking aboard techniques to chunk down and associate, such as strategy installation and associated goalsetting.

If your client uses skills to associate into chunked down experiences (*"These specific details feel* like this"), which can be used to generate pleasure or "anxiety disorders", they might benefit from learning how to chunk up and dissociate, with such trance techniques as Time Line Therapy™.

Lastly, the person who uses skills to dissociate in a chunked down way (*"These specific details I'm conscious of* in this way") which support planning successful action or extreme mismatching (what in psychiatry might be called a borderline personality disorder) could benefit from developing the skills of chunking up and associating into life with parts integration, anchoring and trance work.

What all this means is that when a client steps into your office and tells you they have a "problem", they are describing a skill they have. As you listen to how they describe their difficulty, they will either say it affects everything, or it affects specific things. They will say either that they feel intensely or that they have difficulty identifying their feelings. In any case, they are telling you which strengths they are using, and thus telling you which NLP processes they are already running inside. Within five minutes, you can identify which NLP processes are most likely to work for them as you help them change. This enables you to select from the ten types of intervention, discussed in section three of this book, the most effective type to pace the person's current skills.

As I was developing this model, a client came to see me asking for NLP processes to help her create a sense of spiritual awakening. This, she said, was something she had never really had access to. I initially assumed that she wanted to experience processes such as Core Transformation (A process involving chunking up to a profound "core state"; see Andreas, 1992), but as I attempted to lead her through this and other similar techniques, she continuously interrupted and disagreed with the instructions. In describing her goal, she had actually described in intricate detail what needed to change for her to achieve "spiritual awakening", but complained that while she could "think about it" the description had no feeling with it. As soon as I recognised her style as chunking down and dissociating, I offered to change to another technique. She was delighted to be introduced to the far more detailed and dissociated submodality belief change, which she reported gave her the real experience of spiritual opening.

This example emphasises that diagnostic terms such as "depression", "phobia" and "psychosis" only roughly correspond to the metaprograms that we are sorting for here. I am interested in which strengths people actually demonstrate in relation to this particular challenge at this particular time, rather than which label someone has given them.

	Chunk Up / Associate e.g. depression, joy	Chunk Up / Dissociate e.g. psychosis, awareness
Spirit	Core Transformation	Dis-identification
Identity	Parts Integration	Time Line Therapy
Values-Beliefs	Meta-Stating	SMD Belief Change
Capabilities	Chain Anchors	Swish
Behaviour	Resource Anchor	Trauma Cure
Environment	Community Involvmt.	Move to Retreat Centre
	Chunk Down / Associate e.g. anxiety, fun	Chunk Down / Dissociate e.g. borderline PD, goals
Spirit	Drop Through	Mind Backtracking
Identity	Re-imprinting	Core Questions
Values-Beliefs	Mind To Muscle	Values Elicitation
Capabilities	Strategy Installation	Ideomotor Signals
Behaviour	Collapse Anchors	Plan Towards Outcome
Environment	Tidy Up Environment	Move > New City

Finally, Jung's original model also contained another distinction which can be added to the Personal Strengths model. This is Extraversion-Introversion (Whitmont, 1991, p 139-140). Some clients will describe their problem in an introverted way ("This is what happens inside me") and some will describe their problem in an extraverted way ("This is what happens between others and me."). This is a third axis on the model, making it a three dimensional chart. This distinction has been less significant in NLP consulting because most NLP processes are done internally. None-the-less, some variation along this continuum does occur. Time Line Therapy™ is clearly a more introverted way of using Time Line than Robert Dilt's Re-imprinting on the Time Line, where the person actually walks along the floor. Dealing with relationships and setting tasks are two examples of more extraverted techniques used in the NLP context.

The above table does not seek to categorise NLP Processes, but merely to give examples of where they could be used in terms of this model.

Motivational Interviewing Stages of Change

The final consideration by which I choose what to do is to assess which stage of deciding to change the client is at. This tells me their current level of motivation to take action.. To explain, let me summarise the Motivational Interviewing model. Brief Motivational Interviewing is another multi-staged model for helping people make life changes. Unlike the models we have considered so far, though, it did not emerge out of studies of psychotherapy. It emerged out of studies of peoples own individual response to the need to change (Finney and Moos, 1998, p 157). James Prochaska, John Norcross and Carlo Diclemente interviewed 200 people who quit smoking on their own, to find out what happened (Prochaska et alia, 1994). How did these people change a behaviour that psychotherapists have found so hard to alter? The researchers followed up with studies of people who had given up a number of other self defeating behaviours, finding the same patterns.

Prochaska and DiClemente (Prochaska et alia, 1994; Miller and Rollnick, 1991, p 14-18) found that successful self-changers cycle through a series of six stages. Helping a person in one stage, they say, requires an entirely different approach to helping someone at another. Part of what makes therapy less successful is that everyone is being treated as if they were at the same "stage". The methodology of Motivational Interviewing does not focus on the content of the problem (e.g. by educating an alcoholic about the dangers of drinking) but on the process of becoming motivated to quit. The authors describe "resistance" as a result of applying a change strategy designed for the wrong stage of change (e.g. treating a person in the contemplation stage as if they should be ready for action). The stages can be diagrammed in a cycle as below.

Summarising, the stages and the effective responses to each stage are:

Pre-contemplation. The person doesn't consider the problem an issue at this stage. Helpers can refuse to collude with the problem, and simply seek permission to give information.

Contemplation. The person seesaws between wanting to change and keeping their old pattern. Helpers can assist the person to explore and clarify their values (what's important to them) and to use decision-making processes.

Commitment. The person says they really want to change. Helpers can assist the person to set goals, and can provide preparatory tasks for the person, to check out their intention to act.

Action. Once the person is ready to act, a helper can elicit and alter their old strategy for creating the problem, and integrate the conflicting neural networks to resolve the problem.

Maintenance. At this stage the person needs to build a new lifestyle by integrating change at the level of their life mission, values, and time line. Helpers can also teach interpersonal skills, state changing skills, and other useful new strategies to back up their change.

Recycling. Finally, it is important to have the person think through how they would respond to possible future "lapses" into the old patterns and have them check that they can continue supporting their new choices.

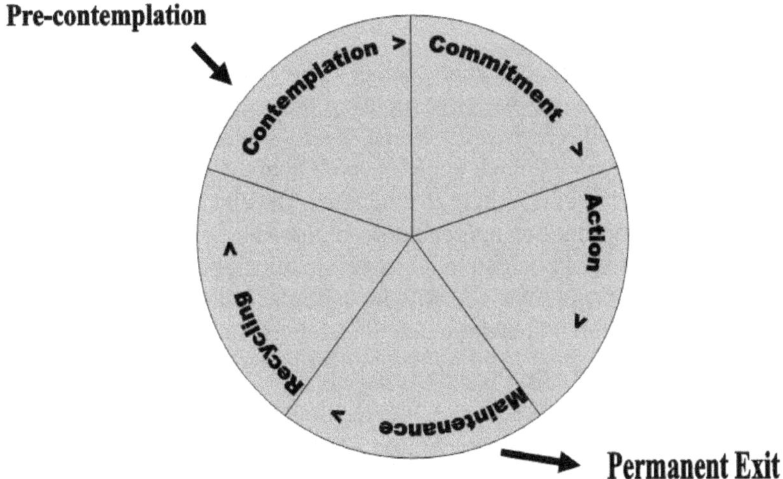

Verifying The Change

Once I have a client who is "at cause" and knows their outcome, I am indeed ready to run standard NLP change processes. I do not merely run the process and send the person home of course. Solution focused therapists have studied the difference in the way they ask about the results of change processes afterwards (for example when the client returns to the next session). In studies replicated several times, they have found that if they ask questions which imply the possibility of failure (e.g. "Did the change process work?") they get a different result than if they ask questions which presuppose success (e.g. "How did that change things?"). When asked a question that presupposes change, 60% of clients will report success. If the question presupposes failure, 67% will report that their situation is the same as it was before (Miller et alia, 1996, p 255-256).

Many times I have seen a client tell me that "nothing has changed" one minute, and then report that they have actually achieved every goal they set for our time together. What causes the shift? My willingness not to assume that their memory of events *is* reality, but instead to ask persistently, firstly..."So what has changed in your life (or in your experience of the situation that was a problem)? No matter how small the changes seem at first, what is different?", and then secondly, to genuinely congratulate them - "Wow, that's great. How did you do that?" and then thirdly, to keep asking "And what *else* has changed?" These three questions come from the Ericksonian school of Solution Focused Therapy (Chevalier, 1995). In asking them, I'm coaching the client to sort for solutions.

Milton Erickson explained that change is an unconscious process, and that the conscious mind needs re-assuring that change has occurred. He says (Erickson and Rossi, 1979, p 10) "Many patients readily recognise and admit changes they have experienced. Others with less introspective ability need the therapist's help in evaluating the changes that have taken place. A recognition and appreciation of the trance work is necessary, lest the patient's old negative attitudes disrupt and destroy the new therapeutic responses that are still in a fragile state of development". Here Erickson refers to pacing a client's strategy for being convinced.

Ecological Exit

Verifying the changes for the client leaves us one key task still to do. A number of studies have led helpers to recognise the importance of futurepacing the changes their clients initiate (having the client imagine themselves back in their actual life using their new skills). This process functions both to check out the appropriateness of their plans, the "ecology" in NLP terms, and also to install the expectation of success in the person's future (Mann et alia, 1989; Marlatt and Gordon, 1985). Allen Ivey and others have their clients write a "future diary" of their success a year into the future. Alan Marlatt has clients step into the future and fully consider what might make them change their mind about their changes, and then has them plan to prevent that. Both approaches have been shown to deliver far more robust change than parallel programs which skip this futurepacing stage. Of course, if any undesirable consequences of the change are detected at this stage, the process shifts back to clarifying outcomes.

It is also important to have the client plan for situations which may challenge what we have done or even temporarily evoke the old response. Prochaska and Diclemente, who describe this as part of the Recycling step in their stage model, remember, say, "Just as one swallow doesn't make a spring, one slip doesn't make a fall."

The Stages Set Out

In summary, there are seven stages that successful consulting takes the NLP Practitioner and client through:

Resourceful consultant approach
Establish rapport
Specify person's outcome
Open up person's model of the world
Lead the person to their outcome
Verify change
Exit process

1. Resourceful State: To explore the RESOLVE model, I want to give an example from the work of NLP co-developer Richard Bandler. In this example session, Bandler works with Susan, who suffers panic attacks where she imagines that people in her family may have died in a car accident (Bandler, 1984, p 1-31). Bandler begins the session by asking Susan to tell him what she wants him to do, and explaining that he is not a magician (p 5).

Richard: Okay Susan. Now why don't you tell me what it is that you would like? I don't know. We just got brought here and wired up, so you have to give me a hint.

As Susan replies, she is accepting the roles Bandler has defined. She has begun contributing her share to the process of change. This simple statement by Bandler communicates much of the attitude of the NLP consultant, as described above.

2. Establish Rapport: Next, Bandler uses pacing statements to build rapport. For example (Bandler, 1984, p 7).

Susan: It's a fear of losing friendships or close relationships. Even when I anticipate a loss that isn't even real I get a panic attack.
Richard: The situation that you are worried about being in is the one of anticipating and thinking about the loss?

These simple checks assure Susan that Bandler understands her concern. This makes it safer for him to playfully challenge her later in the process of change.

3. Specify Client's Outcome: In his work with Susan's anticipatory anxiety, Richard Bandler checks carefully that she has a sensory specific and ecological outcome. When she first tells him that fear is her problem, he asks her, "Is the fear appropriate?" checking the ecology of making this change (Bandler, 1984, p 7). She tells him it's not, and says she wants some distance from her problem. He checks her outcome more fully to elicit a clear description of what it would be like for her to be changed (p 16):

Richard: If you were to have distance how would you know you had it?
Susan: Well I believe I wouldn't feel those feelings. I'd have confidence, some self confidence and I think I could say to myself, well, just because they're not here now doesn't mean that you've lost them and it really doesn't matter. Maybe something happened. And also you can go on. So what if they don't show up. You can go on.

4. Open Up The Person's Model Of The World: Bandler does a number of things to open up Susan's model of the world and "pre-frame" the possibility of change. He asks her to explain to him the strategy she uses to get anxious (1984, p.9)

Richard: But how do you do it? How do you know, how do you get the panic?
Susan: Do you mean what feelings do I get?
Richard: Let's say I had to fill in for you for a day. So one of the parts of my job would be if somebody was late I'd have to have the panic for you. What do I do inside my head in order to have the panic?
Susan: You start telling yourself sentences like ..."
Richard: I've got to talk to myself.
Susan: So and so is late, look they're not here. That means that they may never come.
Richard: Do I say this in a casual tone of voice?
Susan: No

He continues asking her in similar detail about the visual aspects of her strategy for producing panic. He checks that, by bringing the pictures up close, she can bring on a feeling of panic, and then he compliments her on her success (p 16-17).

Richard: You've obviously mastered this. By the way, do you know that this is an accomplishment?
Susan: You mean to master the panic?
Richard: I bet you a lot of people here couldn't panic.
Susan: Probably not. Not like I do I'm sure.

Far from being the "dysfunctional" person in the interaction, Susan is now described as very skilled. From this point on, Bandler is operating as a consultant to help her reach her own goal. In a sense, she is no longer "owning the problem". She is now actively involved in changing herself. She happily accepts Bandler's direct instructions to change her way of thinking; instructions which would have come across as insulting and intrusive if given at the very start.

Leading: Bandler guides Susan through the NLP Swish technique (Bandler, 1984, p 21). This process begins with her using her ability to scare herself by seeing the picture of a car accident as if she were involved in it. The "swish" gets her to alter this picture rapidly, shifting to what NLP calls a dissociated viewpoint (giving her the distance she has been asking for). Repeating this several times "installs" the new perspective in her brain.

Richard: Go ahead and make the picture bright and focus on it. Close your eyes again, move right in and as you approach very closely to it you begin to feel the panic. What I want you to do is to see in the small, lower left hand corner a little tiny dark square that has a picture of you the way you would be if you had made this change. It's real darkened in the corner but suddenly the big picture begins to get darker and the other one begins to expand and become brighter until it fills the whole screen. But you can do it faster than that. There you go. Hurry up. Until you can see yourself the way you would be. Now I want you to do the exact same thing. I want you to do it five times real fast.

Verify Change: Richard ensures that Susan is fully convinced that she has changed. He tells her (Bandler, 1984, p 24-25):

Richard: You go ahead this time and go back and look at that panic. See if you can hold it. I want you to try as much as you can in vain.
Susan: It's hard. I just keep getting white.
Richard: What do you mean?

Susan: I'm having trouble doing it.
Richard: I thought you'd mastered that.
Susan: I am a master at panic. Right now all I'm getting is white….
Richard: Try it once more. Just to be sure.
Susan: I really just can't do it.

Ecological Exit: Once he has this clear, unequivocal statement verifying the change, Bandler moves on to "futurepacing" (planning for the future effects of the change). He reminds Susan that she believed this would change her future. He says (Bandler, 1984, p 25-26):

Richard: You've got to keep your promise. You said it would change your whole life.
Susan: Yeah.
Richard: Now you have to keep your end of the bargain.
Susan: Well I think if I don't have this problem that it is going to change. Because it's going to affect everything.
Richard: You're not going to be able to do it.
Susan: That would be wonderful.
Richard: Try it
Susan: I've tried it.
Richard: Try it now.
Susan: I just can't get it. I just can't get it.
Richard: Well if it was so easy before and it's so hard now, that's an indication. You can go try it in the real world. I tell you what. Why don't you go outside by the coffee machine and I'll meet you there in ten minutes?

Eight months later, Susan was interviewed by Michael Saggese about her experience. She told him (p28-30):

Susan: When I left the studio that day I knew I felt really good but I was still a little sceptical of what had happened because my panics are so bad and so painful to me. I went home that evening and the same situation occurred. Someone was supposed to come and they didn't show up for several hours. And I didn't get upset at all. I was able to lie down and take a nap. It didn't upset me at all. I was just truly amazed….

Summary: The RESOLVE Model of Consulting

Resourceful state for the consultant
Establish rapport
Specify person's outcome
Open up person's model of the world

Lead the person to their outcome
Verify change
Exit process

The RESOLVE model begins with understanding that all change requires the guide themselves to begin in a resourceful state. During the first three steps, the consultant alternately uses two key verbal skills. The first is verbal pacing, which is the linguistic expression of the rapport skills by which they align with the person and create a sense of shared understanding or empathy. The second is open questioning, by which the consultant guides the person to identify and specify their outcome. A key shift then occurs at the stage of Opening up the Client's Model of the World. At this stage it becomes clear to the client that they have the resources to change, and are in charge of creating the outcomes they have chosen. The purpose of helping is thus for the consultant to be a support person who assists the client to identify their own goals and design their own solutions. The consultant is clear that they do have some specialised knowledge which will assist the client to do that. Having run whatever NLP change processes they select, the consultant then helps their client verify that change has happened, and then install

Bibliography

Andreas, S. "What Makes A Good NLPer?" p 3-6 in Anchor Point, Vol 13, No. 10, October 1999

Bandler, R. and Grinder, J. Frogs Into Princes, Real People Press, Moab, Utah, 1979

Bandler, R. Magic In Action, Meta Publications, Cupertino, 1984.

Bergin, A. and Garfield, S. Handbook of Psychotherapy and Behaviour Change, Wiley & Sons, New York, 1994

Bolstad, R. and Hamblett, M. Transforming Communication Addison-Wesley-Longman, Auckland, 1998

Bolstad, R. RESOLVE: A New Model Of Therapy Crown House, Bancyfelin, Wales, 2002

Brockman, W.P. "Empathy revisited: the effects of representational system matching on certain counselling process and outcome variables", Dissertation Abstracts International 41(8), 3421A, College of William and Mary, 167pp., 1980

Carkhuff, R.R. and Berenson, B.G. Beyond Counselling and Therapy, Holt, Rinehart and Winston, New York, 1977

Carkhuff, R.R. The Art Of Helping Human Resource Development, Amherst, Massachusetts, 1973

Chevalier, A.J., On The Client's Path, New Harbinger, Oakland, California, 1995

Condon, W. S. "Cultural Microrhythms" p 53-76 in Davis, M. (ed) <u>Interactional Rhythms: Periodicity in Communicative Behaviour</u> Human Sciences Press, New York, 1982

Egan, G. <u>The Skilled Helper</u> Brooks/Cole, Monterey, California, 1975

Erickson, M.H. and Rossi, E.L. <u>Hypnotherapy: An Exploratory Casebook,</u> Irvington, New York, 1979

Fiedler, F.E. "Factor analysis of psychoanalytic, non-directive and Adlerian therapeutic relationships" p 32-38 in Journal of Consulting Psychology, No. 15, 1951

Finney, J.W. and Moos, R.H. "Psychosocial Treatments for Alcohol Use Disorders" p 156-166, in Nathan, P.E. and Gorman, J.M. <u>A Guide To Treatments That Work</u>, Oxford University Press, New York, 1998

Genser-Medlitsch, M. and Schütz, P., <u>"Does Neuro-Linguistic psychotherapy have effect? New Results shown in the extramural section."</u> Martina Genser-Medlitsch and Peter Schütz, ÖTZ-NLP, Vienna, 1997

Gordon, D. and Meyers-Anderson, M. <u>Phoenix: Therapeutic Patterns of Milton H. Erickson</u> Meta publications, Capitola, California, 1981

Hatfield, E., Cacioppo, J. and Rapson, R. <u>Emotional Contagion</u> Cambridge University Press, Cambridge, 1994

Hischke, D. " A definitional and structural investigation of matching perceptual predicates, mismatching perceptual predicates, and Milton-model matching." In Dissertation Abstracts International 49(9) p 4005

Jablensky, A., Sartorius, N., Ernberg, G., Anker, M., Korten, A., Cooper, J.E., Day, R., and Bertelsen, A., "Schizophrenia: manifestations, incidence and course in different cultures. A World Health Organisation ten country study." In <u>Psychological Medicine,</u> Supplement 20, p 1-97, 1992

James, T. "General Model For Behavioural Intervention" in <u>Time Line Therapy® Practitioner Training</u> (manual. Version 3.1), Time Line Therapy™ Association, Honolulu, 1995

James, T. and Woodsmall, W. Time Line Therapy And The Basis Of Personality, Meta Publications, Cupertino, California, 1988

Kopelowicz, A. and Liberman, R.P. "Psychosocial Treatments for Schizophrenia", p 190-211 in Nathan, P.E. and Gorman, J.M. <u>A Guide to Treatments That Work</u>, Oxford University Press, New York, 1998

Lambert, M. and Bergin, A. "The Effectiveness of Psychotherapy" in Bergin, A. and Garfield, S. <u>Handbook of Psychotherapy and Behaviour Change</u> Wiley, New York, 1994

Macroy, T.D. "Linguistic surface structures in family interaction" in Dissertation Abstracts International, 40 (2) 926-B, Utah State

University, 133 pp, Order = 7917967, 1978

Mann, L., Beswick, G., Allouache, P. and Ivey, M. "Decision workshops for the improvement of decisionmaking: Skills and confidence" in Journal of Counselling and Development, 67, p 478-481, 1989

Marlatt,G. and Gordon, J. Relapse Prevention: Maintenance Strategies in the Treatment of Addictive Behaviours Guilford, New York, 1985

Miller, S. D., Hubble, M.A. and Duncan, B.L. Handbook of Solution Focused Brief Therapy, Jossey-Bass, San Francisco, 1996

Miller, W. "Motivation for treatment: a review with special emphasis on alcoholism." In Psychological Bulletin, Vol 98 (1), p 84-107, 1985

Miller, W.R. and Rollnick, S. Motivational Interviewing, The Guilford Press, New York, 1991

Peele, S. Diseasing of America, Houghton Mifflin, 1989, Boston

Prochaska, J.O., Norcross, J.C. and Diclemente, C.C. Changing For Good, William Morrow & Co., New York, 1994

Ragge, K. The Real AA: Behind the Myth of 12 Step Recovery, See Sharp Press, Tucson, 1998

Rizzolatti, G., Fadiga, L., Gallese, V. and Fogassi, L. "Premotor cortex and the recognition of motor actions" p 131-141 in Cognitive Brain Research, No. 3, 1996

Rizzolatti,G. and Arbib, M.A. "Language within our grasp" p 188-194 in Trends in Neuroscience, No. 21, 1998

Schachter, S. "Recidivism and self-cure of smoking and obesity" in American Psychologist 37: P 436-444, 1982

Schachter, S. and Singer, J.E. "Cognitive, social and physiological determinants of emotional state" in Psychological Review, 69 (12) p 379-399, 1962

Trimpey, J. Rational Recovery, Simon & Schuster, New York, 1996

Whitmont, E.C. The Symbolic Quest: Basic Concepts of Analytical Psychology Princeton University, Princeton, New Jersey, 1991

Jung, C. ed. Man And His Symbols Dell, New York, 1976

Yapko, M.D. Hypnosis and the Treatment of Depressions, Brunner/Mazel, New York, 1992

Yapko. M., "The Effects of Matching Primary Representational System Predicates on Hypnotic Relaxation." in the American Journal of Clinical Hypnosis, 23, p169-175, 1981

Zilbergeld, B. The Shrinking of America, Little Brown & Co, Boston, 1983

Richard Bolstad and Julia Kurusheva

When Is A Goal Not A Goal?

The Failure Of Most Goal-setting

Goals are theoretically central to all coaching. When I teach NLP, I find that most people *believe* that they know how to set and achieve goals. However when we actually check people's real life results, we find that most people, most of the time, do not set and achieve goals at all.

Richard Wiseman (2009, p 88-93) did a very large study of goalsetting. He tracked 5000 people who had some significant goal they wanted to achieve (everything from starting a new relationship to beginning a new career, from stopping smoking to gaining a qualification). He followed people up over the next year, and found firstly that only 10% ever achieved their goal. It wasn't just bad luck. Dramatic and consistent differences in the psychological techniques they used made those 10% stand out from the rest.

Those who failed tended either to think about all the bad things that would happen or continue to happen if they did not reach their goal (what NLP calls away from motivation, and what other research calls counterfactual thought) or to fantasise about achieving their goal and how great life would be if they somehow magically got what they wanted. They also tried to achieve their goal by willpower and by attempts to suppress "unhelpful thoughts". Finally, they spent time thinking about role models who had achieved their goal, often putting pictures of the role model on their fridge or other prominent places, to remind them to fantasise and wish they were like those people. Although the unsuccessful 90% were convinced that these strategies would help them, none of these techniques worked, and furthermore, the successful 10% did not waste their time doing these things.

The key to the problem 90% of us have lies in a series of complete misunderstandings about what a goal actually is. I am going to suggest that, mostly, the 90% failed because they did not actually have goals. In this chapter I want to distinguish goals from five completely separate cognitive structures: values, directions, problems, affirmations and competitive targets. All of these five structures may be useful, and using several of them at once is perfectly workable, but these last five are not goals. Starting "goal-setting" with one of the other structures in mind means not actually achieving the results that goal-setting promises.

Problems

The first thing that Wiseman found unsuccessful people did was to think a lot about how bad things have been for them, and how they are not where they want to be. Wiseman says "For example, when asked to list the benefits of getting a new job, successful participants might reflect on finding more fulfilling and well-paid employment, whereas their unsuccessful counterparts might focus on a failure leaving them trapped and unhappy." (Wiseman, 2009, p 92) Focusing on problems and what we don't want is paying attention to the past. It feels very different to focusing on the goal, outcome or solution to those problems, and it has very different, and less useful, results.

In 2000, Dr Denise Beike and Deirdre Slavik at the University of Arkansas conducted an interesting study of what they called "counterfactual" thoughts. These are thoughts about what has gone "wrong", along with what they could have done differently. Dr. Beike enlisted two groups of University of Arkansas students to record their thoughts each day in a diary in order to "look at counterfactual thoughts as they occur in people's day-to-day lives." In the first group, graduate students recorded their counterfactual thoughts, their mood, and their motivation to change their behaviour as a result of their thoughts. After recording two thoughts per day for 14 days, the students reported that negative thoughts depressed their mood but increased their motivation to change their behaviour. They believed that the negative thoughts were painful but would help them in the long term.

To test out this hope, the researchers then enlisted a group of students to keep similar diaries for 21 days, to determine if any actual change in behaviour would result from counterfactual thinking. Three weeks after completing their diaries the undergraduate students were asked to review their diary data and indicate whether their counterfactual thinking actually caused any change in behavior. "No self-perceived change in behaviour was noted," Dr. Beike told Reuters Health. Counterfactual thoughts about negative events in everyday life cause us to feel that we "should have done better or more," Dr. Beike said. "These thoughts make us feel bad, which motivates us to sit around and to feel sorry for ourselves." So what does work? The study found that "credit-taking thoughts", in which individuals reflect on success and congratulate themselves, serve to reinforce appropriate behavior and help people "feel more in control of themselves and their circumstances." (Slavik, 2003).

It is quite common, when working with a new client, for them to explain to me that their goal is "Not to be anxious". This contains no different information that the statement "My problem is being anxious". It does not tell me what they want instead. NLP Trainer Steve Andreas has a great metaphor for this. Imagine, he says, that you get into a taxi and tell the driver "I don't want to be here." And when the driver, in a puzzled way, says "Yes, but where do you wasn't to be instead of here?" you reply "Well, somewhere else." There is no point in the driver moving her or his car until you learn to state a goal.

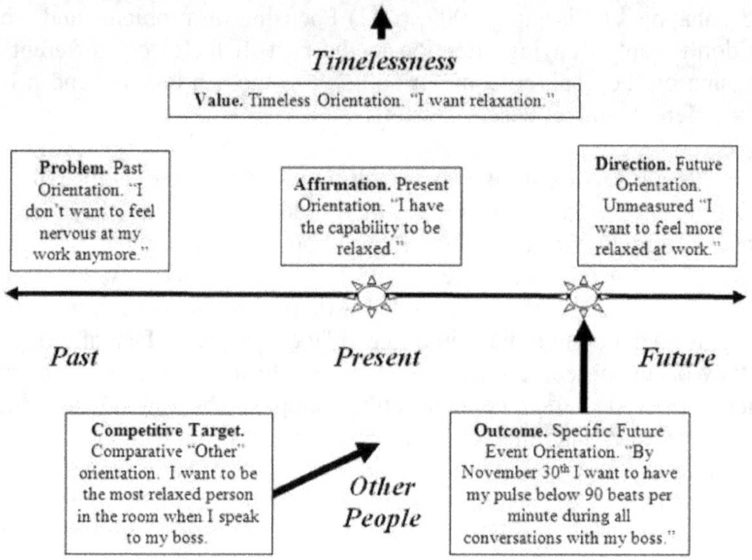

Values

The next most common response when I ask a new client about their goal, is for them to tell me a single word for a state of mind that they enjoy and value. "I want happiness." they say. In Wiseman's research, the most successful people were able to list concrete, specific benefits they would get from their goal, rather than just say that they would "feel happy". They had what Wiseman calls "an objective checklist of benefits" and made these "as concrete as possible", often by writing them down. He notes "… although many people said they aimed to enjoy life more, it was the successful people who explained how they intended to spend two evenings each week with friends and visit one new country each year." (Wiseman, 2009, p 91- 93). To explain the difference, if a client tells me that their goal is to be happy, I usually explain that there are pills that can do that for them easily. When they tell me they want to be happy without drugs, I tell them that avoiding all activity may be a really safe choice. Usually by that time they begin to get specific and explain exactly what they will be doing and thinking and how they will feel about that.

"Happiness" is not an end result, a goal. It is a state of being, a valued experience that could be experienced in many different contexts. To be able to check that they have achieved a goal, we need to know what the person's target context is, and what specific evidence they would need to know that they had achieved this desired state of being. A goal is not a value, it is a specific event which expresses or allows the expression of a value. Values are immensely useful to understand. Knowing a person's values enables them to check whether their goal will allow them to embody those values or not. Since values are what motivates a person to action, knowing them enables us to know whether they will actually want to achieve their goals or not (whether they will value those goals). A goalsetting process is like a ladder that a person climbs to reach what they want. A value is a wall that they would like to get to the top of. Leaning the ladder of goalsetting against the wrong wall means that the person is wasting their energy. But just choosing the right wall does not get you far in the process of climbing. Values tell you where it is worth going. Goals tell you how you will know you are taking steps in that direction.

Affirmations

Psychologists Joanne V. Wood and John W. Lee from the University of Waterloo, and W.Q. Elaine Perunovic from the University of New Brunswick (Wood, Perunovic and Lee, 2009), first asked 249 research subjects to <u>fill in a short questionnaire</u> (the Rosenberg self-esteem scale) designed to analyse their self-esteem and to say how often they said positive things about themselves, on a scale from 1(never) to 8 (almost daily). 52% gave a rating of 6 or higher. These 52% of subjects, who already had high self-esteem, reported that they already often said affirming things to themselves. They reported using positive self-statements before exams (85%), before giving a presentation (78%), to cope with negative events (74%), and even sometimes as part of their everyday routine (23%). On average, they felt that such statements were helpful. Those with low self-esteem also claimed that such statements sometimes helped them, but they reported that affirmations more often made them feel worse. To find out why, the researchers did two follow-up studies.

First, they asked their subjects to write down anything they felt or thought in a four-minute period. The recruits included equal numbers of students with high or low self-esteem and half of each group were told to say to themselves, "I am a lovable person", every 15 seconds, on the cue of a bell rung by the researcher. Afterwards, they completed several questionnaires. Two of these were designed to assess their mood, including questions such as "What is the probability that a 30-year-old will be involved in a happy, loving romance?" and "Would you like to go to a party?" Another set of questions rated their current self-esteem by asking them to say which of two adjectives they felt closest to – e.g. valuable or useless, nice or awful, good or bad. As you might expect, the students with higher self-esteem had higher, happier scores on all three questionnaires than those with low self-esteem. After saying the affirmations, there was no statistically significant change in their scores. But for those subjects who already had low self-esteem, the effect of the affirmations was dramatic and negative. They felt worse after saying these words, had more negative beliefs, and had lower expectations of success. Their self-esteem scores were almost halved as a result of trying to use affirmations.

The researchers explain the result by saying that everyone has a range of ideas they are prepared to accept. Messages that lie within this boundary are more persuasive than those that fall outside it - those meet resistance and can even lead to people holding onto their original position more strongly. If a person with low self-esteem says something that's positive about themselves but is well outside the range of what they'll actually believe, their immediate reaction is to dismiss the claim and feel even worse. Statements that contradict a person's current self-image and basic model of the world, no matter how positive in intention, are likely to trigger mismatching thoughts.

Of course, as an NLP Practitioner, you have several interventions that can change self-image and model of the world so that these affirmations would work… and of course then the affirmations may not seem so important anyway. Wood concluded that affirmations only work in situations where people make very specific statements that are impossible to argue with, or where none of their major beliefs are challenged. For example, people may be better off saying "I choose good gifts for people" rather than "I'm a generous person". Put in the terms of my communication skills text Transforming Communication (Bolstad, 2002), positive statements are better worded as sensory specific "I messages" rather than as judgments. Wood and colleagues cautioned that "outlandish, unreasonably positive self-statements, such as "I accept myself completely," are often encouraged by self-help books. Our results suggest that such self-statements may harm the very people they are designed for: people low in self-esteem." (Wood, Perunovic and Lee, 2009, p 865)

In the third study, subjects were asked to consider the statement "I am a lovable person" and either to focus only on ways in which it's true, or to consider ways in which it is and isn't true. After the task, people with high self-esteem benefited from focusing only on the positive side of the statement, but those with low self-esteem felt worse about themselves if they dwelled only on positives, and better if they were asked to take a more balanced approach. Wood suggests that if people with low self-esteem are asked to think only positive thoughts, and find it difficult to block out negative ones, that merely certifies their belief that they aren't measuring up to standards.

NLP developers Richard Bandler and John Grinder did not include "affirmations" in their list of NLP techniques. Robert Dilts and Judith DeLozier in their Encyclopaedia of NLP (Dilts and DeLozier, 2000, p 24) do champion affirmations, saying "Affirmation is a method for creating, strengthening and encouraging positive 'self-fulfilling' processes. "Affirmation" essentially involves the verbal assertion and reinforcement of empowering beliefs. The process of affirmation involves the repetition of a series of belief statements. In many ways, affirmations represent a fundamental example of "neuro-linguistic programming". They employ the use of language to establish and encourage positive mental "programming"." However, Dilts and DeLozier's examples of affirmations are all current reality based. Put another way, Dilts and DeLozier's examples are all process oriented e.g. "It is possible for me to be healthy and well," "I have the capabilities to be healthy and well," rather than outcome based "I am healthy and well." The above research suggests that since their affirmations don't challenge the client's "reality" they are more likely to be received positively.

Bandler and Grinder did develop methods for transforming internal beliefs, and they seem to have been very aware of the risk of contradicting a person's experience of reality. Bandler, for example, describes creating a new belief as creating a new focus of attention, rather than contradicting the evidence that a person has collected about "reality". Describing the construction of new beliefs, Richard Bandler says (1985, p 105-109) "Do you know what belief you'd like to have in place of the belief you have now?... Start thinking about it now, and be sure you *think about it in positive terms*, not in terms of negations. Think of what you do want to believe, not what you don't want to believe. I also want you to frame that belief not in terms of an end or goal, but in terms of a *process* or *ability* that would result in you getting that goal.

For instance if you'd like to believe that you know NLP, change it so that you believe you can pay attention, and learn and respond to feedback in order to learn NLP…. We want to mobilize new abilities, not install new delusions!" To the extent that "Every day in every way I am getting better and better," (to quote one traditional affirmation) is inconsistent with reality, it is of course a delusion. No wonder many people in the research resist it.

In relation to goals, what this research shows is that stating your goals (what you want to happen in the future) as affirmations (what you appreciate about what is happening now) is counterproductive. Affirming your current strengths, resources, achievements and gratitude is very useful, but it cannot replace goalsetting.

Although focusing on the problem you have had does not lead to success, neither does merely fantasising about the future success. Lien Pham and Shelley Taylor at the University of California did a study where a group of students were asked to visualise themselves getting high grades in a mid-term exam that was coming up soon. They were taught to form clear visual images and imagine how good it will feel, and to repeat this for several minutes each day. A control group was also followed up, and the study times of each student as well as their grades in the exam were monitored. The group who were visualising should, according to proponents of "The Secret" DVD and the "Law of Attraction", have a clear advantage. Actually, they did much less study, and consequently got much lower marks in the exam (Pham and Taylor, 1999).

This result is very consistent. There are now a large number of research studies showing that "The secret" or "The law of attraction" (visualising your outcome and then letting go and trusting that the universe will provide it) impedes success. Gabrielle Oettingen at the University of Pennsylvania has done a number of studies showing the same result. In one study, women in a weight-reduction program were asked to describe what would happen if they were offered a tempting situation with food. The more positive their fantasies of how well they would cope with these situations, the less work they did on weight reduction. A year later, those women who consistently fantasised positive results lost on average 12 kilos less than those who anticipated negative challenges and thus put in more effort (Oettingen and Wadden, 1991). Oettingen followed up final year students to find out how much they fantasised getting their dream job after leaving university. The students who fantasised more reported two years later that they did less searching for jobs, had fewer offers of jobs, and had significantly smaller salaries than their classmates

(Oettingen and Mayer, 2002). In another study she investigated a group of students who had a secret romantic attraction, a crush, on another student. She asked them to imagine what would happen if they were to accidentally find themselves alone with that person. The more vivid and positive the fantasies they made, the less likely they were to take any action and to be any closer to a relationship with the person 5 months later. The result is consistent in career success, in love and attraction, and in dealing with addictions and health challenges (Oettingen, Pak and Schnetter, 2001; Oettingen, 2000; Oettingen and Gollwitzer, 2002).

Directions

The last two types of non-goal are at least moving in a useful direction. However they measure themselves not against a desired future success, but against some aspect of the present situation. As it implies, a direction only tells you the direction, and not how far the person wants to get to by a certain time. A person may say, I want to earn more money next year than this year (meaning that if they earn one cent more, their goal has been achieved) or I want to be more relaxed when talking to my boss (meaning that a pulse rate just 5 beats per minute below their current level of anxiety would be goal success). In some ways this is very valuable information. A positive "towards" motivated direction is a generative plan (i.e. it keeps generating new actions) rather than one that leads only to one specific point. Some people would benefit by having more direction, rather than only specific targets. In that sense, directions are similar to values; they give an ongoing check that you are doing something useful. They are not goals.

Competitive Targets

Imagine that a client tells you that their problem is that they want to remain relaxed while they talk with their boss (problem), and they value calmness (value), and they know they have the ability to relax (affirmation). Then they explain "So my goal is that when I am speaking to my boss, I will be the most relaxed person in the room." Probably, you would immediately identify that even if they can measure their bosses relaxation (and they need to be able to do so to know if they achieved this "goal", in order to check that they are even more relaxed than the boss) this "goal" has some unhelpful consequences.

Firstly, it divides their attention, because usually a person measures their own success. In this case they must measure both their own success and the success of the others in the room, and then effectively compare these. It divides their attention between the two competitors. Secondly, the goal is almost worthless, because technically they will still have achieved it if they find that they are (for example) fractionally less than the psychological mess that their boss is. They are setting a goal and allowing their bosses level of success to decide how much they will reach for. The same two problems occur with all competitive goals – being "the highest earning person in my business", having "a closer relationship than any of my family" etc. Given the obvious ineffectiveness of such competitive goals, why do new clients choose them?

The answer is a social mythology around the value of "Competition." The belief many parents, teachers and team leaders have is that trying to do better than someone else leads to success, and even "builds character." David and Roger Johnson (in Kohn, 1986, P47) reviewed 122 research studies on how co-operation or competition affect success. In only 8 of these studies did competition seem to help. In most of the studies, people co-operating were far more successful, <u>and</u> felt better about their achievement at the end. Airline pilots who are competing against each other fly less safely than those who co-operate. Scientists who are competing for honours make less scientific advances. A study of business people showed that the most successful business people were the least competitive, dramatically contradicting what was being taught in business training. John Simmons and William Mares (in Kohn, 1986, p213) review studies of co-operatively run workplaces showing that they produce more than hierarchical and competitive ones. The reason is very simple. Competition requires paying attention to how the other person is doing. Success requires paying attention to how <u>you</u> are doing. The competitor is like a person running a race while looking over their shoulder to check the others (a problem which actually obstructs even sports success, and feeds what is known as competitive anxiety, where the sportsperson can perform better in practice than in the actual sports "competition". If you want to succeed - personally <u>and</u> in your group - the answer is to focus on your own achievements.

But doesn't business success, and thus economic survival, depend on the competitive, dog eat dog system of capitalism? The truth is surprising. Like everywhere else, competition and win-lose solutions simply obstruct economic success. One person who was very clear about that was W. Edward Demming, the business adviser famous for his central involvement in the economic miracle in post-war Japan. Asked whether competition wasn't the factor that made America great, Demming replies "No; it was co-operation. Competition is our ruination. We've been on the decline for decades; we're on the decline. The decline will continue till we learn." Business consultant Edward de Bono calls competition a "dangerous and seductive trap that limits and restricts business thinking." He gives specific examples. "When Kodak ventured into the instant camera business a few years ago, analysts marked down Polaroid stock. But in fact, Polaroid's sales increased because Kodak now had to advertise instant cameras....The more antique shops, the more the area will be visited by antique buyers...."

Goalsetting – The Secret Of Success?

Goals, then, are stated in the positive, they are sensory specific, they are measurable, they are time-specific and the time they refer to is in the future, and they refer specifically and only to the unique achievements of the person setting the goal.

The complete inventory of successful strategies that Richard Wiseman's research found fits neatly into my NLP-based SPECIFY model for outcome or goal setting (Bolstad, 2002).

Sensory Specific: Firstly, the most successful people did imagine achieving their goal, and were able to list concrete, specific benefits they would get from it, rather than just say that they would "feel happy". They had what Wiseman calls "an objective checklist of benefits" and made these "as concrete as possible", often by writing them down. He notes "… although many people said they aimed to enjoy life more, it was the successful people who explained how they intended to spend two evenings each week with friends and visit one new country each year." (Wiseman, 2009, p 91- 93)

Positive: Secondly, they described their goal positively. Wiseman says "For example, when asked to list the benefits of getting a new job, successful participants might reflect on finding more fulfilling and well-paid employment, whereas their unsuccessful counterparts might focus on a failure leaving them trapped and unhappy." (Wiseman, 2009, p 92)

Ecological: That's about as far as the research results coincide with the "Secret". For example, one surprising result of the research by both Gabrielle Oettingen and Richard Wiseman is that it pays to think about challenges you may face in achieving your goal (even though that may feel unpleasant at the time). After thinking about the positive benefits of achieving their goal, the most successful participants would "spend another few moments reflecting on the type of barriers and problems they are likely to encounter if they attempt to fulfil their ambition…. focusing on what they would do if they encountered the difficulty." (Wiseman, 2009, p 101) Oettingen trained people to do this process, which she calls "doublethink" and NLP would call checking "ecology". She was able to increase their success dramatically just with this step.

Choice Increasing and Celebrated: Related to this NLP concept of ecology is the fact that successful goal-setters made sure that they felt as if their progress was bringing them rewards rather than limiting their choices and creating work. They did this most of all because "As part of their planning, successful participants ensured that each of their sub-goals had a reward attached to it" so that it "gave them something to look forward to and provided a sense of achievement." (Wiseman, 2009, p 93)

Initiated by Self: Successful goal-setters have a plan. They do not leave their goal up to "the law of attraction" or to someone else who will save them. Wiseman notes "Whereas successful and unsuccessful participants might have stated that their aim was to find a new job, it was the successful people who quickly went on to describe how they intended to rewrite their CV in week one, and then apply for one new job every two weeks for the next six months." (Wiseman, 2009, p 91)

First Step Identified: Wiseman found that it was particularly important to break the goal down into small steps and manage one step at a time. "Successful participants broke their overall goal into a series of sub-goals, and thereby created a step-by-step process that helped remove the fear and hesitation often associated with trying to achieve a major life change." (Wiseman, 2009, p 90-91)

Your Resources Identified: In NLP we encourage people to identify both internal and external resources. Wiseman's research studied only external resources, most especially friends, colleagues and family. "Successful participants were far more likely than others to tell their friends, family and colleagues about their goals.... Telling others about your aims helps you achieve them, in part, because friends and family often provide much needed support when the going gets tough." (Wiseman, 2009, p 91)

Bibliography:

Andreas, S. (2010) <u>Help With Negative Self Talk</u> Real People Press, Moab, Utah

Bandler, R. (1985) Using Your Brain For A Change, Real People Press, Moab, Utah

Bandler, R. and Grinder, J. (1975) *The Structure of Magic*. Cupertino, California: Meta Publications

Bolstad, R. (2002) RESOLVE: A New Model of Therapy. Carmarthen, Wales, Crown Publishing

Bolstad, R. (2002) Transforming Communication Pearsons, Auckland

Bolstad, R. (2010) "The How Behind The Secret" Acuity the ANLP Journal, Issue 1

Byrne, R. (2006) *The Secret.* New York: Atria Books,

Canfield, J. and Hansen, M.V. (1993) *A 2nd Helping of Chicken Soup For The Soul.* Deerfield Beach, Florida: Health Communications Inc

Crum, A.J. and Langer, E.J.,\ (2007) "Mind-Set Matters: Exercise and the Placebo Effect" p 165-171 in *Psychological Science*, Volume 18, Issue 2, February 2007

De Bono, E. Surpetition Harper Collins, London, 1995

Dilts, R. and DeLozier, J. (2000) Encyclopedia of Systemic Neuro-Linguistic Programming and NLP New Coding, NLP University Press, Scotts Valley, California (Available at http://www.nlpuniversitypress.com/)

Dilts, R.B., Epstein, T. and Dilts, R.W. (1991) *Tools for Dreamers.* Capitola, California: Meta Publications

Erickson, M.H. (1980) The Collected Papers of Milton H. Erickson Vol I (ed Rossi, E.L.) Irvington, New York

Ericsson, K. A. (2003) "How the expert-performance approach differs from traditional approaches to expertise in sports: In search of a shared theoretical framework for studying expert performance." In J. Starkes and K. A. Ericsson (Eds.) *Expert performance in sport: Recent advances in research on sport expertise.* (pp. 371-401). Champaign, Illinois : Human Kinetics.

Ericsson, K. A. (2003) "The search for general abilities and basic capacities: Theoretical implications from the modifiability and complexity of mechanisms mediating expert performance" In R. J. Sternberg and E. L. Grigorenko (Eds.) *Perspectives on the psychology of abilities, competencies, and expertise.* (pp. 93-125). Cambridge: Cambridge University Press.

Ericsson, K. A. (2004) "Deliberate practice and the acquisition and maintenance of expert performance in medicine and related domains" in *Academic Medicine.* 10, S1-S12.

Goodkin K., Blancy N.T., Feaster D. et alia (1992) "Active coping style is associated with natural killer cell cytotoxicity in asymptomatic HIV-1 seropositive homosexual men" *Journal of Psychosomatic Research* 1992, 36:635-650

Hall, L.M. (2000) "A Few Secrets About Wealth Building" p 25-31 in *Anchor Point journal*, Vol 14, No. 4, April 2000

Kasser, T. and Ryan, R.M. (1996) "Further Examining The American Dream: Differential Correlates Of Intrinsic And Extrinsic

Goals" p 280-287 in *Personality and Social Psychology Bulletin*, Vol 22, No. 3, 1996

Kelly, K. (2007) *The Secret Of "The Secret"*. Sydney, Australia: Pan Macmillan

Kohn, A., No Contest, Houghton Mifflin, Boston , 1986

Langer, E.J. (1989) *Mindfulness*. Reading, Massachusetts: Addison-Wesley

Maruta, M., Colligan, R., Malinchoc, M. and Offord, K. (2000) "Optimists vs. Pessimists: Survival Rate Amongst Medical Patients Over A 30 Year Period" p 140-143 in *Mayo Clinic Proceedings*, Vol 75; Number 2, February 2000

Monterosso, S., Lyubomirsky, K., White, K. and Lehman, D.R. (2002) "Maximising Versus Satisficing: Happiness Is A Matter Of Choice" p 1178-1197 in *Personality and Social Psychology*, No 83 (5), 2002

Nightingale, E. (2009) "The Strangest Secret" published on line at http://www.innovationtools.com/Articles/SuccessDetails.asp

Oettingen, G. (2000) "Expectancy Effects on Behaviour Depend on Self-Regulatory Thought" p 101-129 in *Social Cognition*, No. 18, 2000

Oettingen, G. and Gollwitzer, P.M. (2002) "Self-Regulation of Goal Pursuit: Turning Hope Thoughts into Behaviour" p 304-307 in *Psychological Inquirer*, No 13, 2002

Oettingen, G. and Mayer, D. (2002) "The Motivating Function of Thinking About The Future: Expectations Versus Fantasies" p 1198-1212 in *Journal of Personality and Social Psychology*, No. 83, 2002

Oettingen, G. and Wadden, T.A. (1991) "Expectation, Fantasy, and Weight Loss: Is The Impact of Positive Thinking Aways Positive?" p 167-175 in *Cognitive Therapy and Research*, No. 15, 1991

Oettingen, G. Pak, H. and Schnetter, K. (2001) "Self-Regulation of Goal Setting: Turning Free Fantasies About the Future Into Binding Goals" p 736-753 in *Journal of Personality and Social Psychology*, No 80, 2001

Pham, L.B. and Taylor, S.E. (1999) "From Thought to Action: Effects of Process Versus Outcome Based Mental Simulations on Performance." P 250-260 in *Personality and Social Psychology Bulletin*, No. 25, 1999

Prime Time Productions, (2006) *The Secret DVD*

Rindfleisch, A., Burroughs, J. and Denton, F. (1997) "Family Structure, Materialism and Compulsive Consumption," p 312-325 in *The Journal of Consumer Research*, Vol 23, No. 4, March 1997

Schwarz, N., Bless, H., Strack, F., Klumpp, G., Rittenauer-Schatka, H.,

& Simons, A. (1991). Ease of retrieval as information: Another look at the availability heuristic. Journal of Personality and Social Psychology, Vol 61, No. 2, page 195-202

Senay, I., Albarracín, D. and Noguchi, K. (2010) Motivating goal-directed behavior through introspective self-talk: the role of the interrogative form of simple future tense Psychological Science Vol 21, No. 4: p 499-504, April 2010

Slater, P. (1980) *Wealth Addiction*. Dutton, New York

Slavik, D.J. (2003) "Keeping your eyes on the prize : outcome versus process focused social comparisons and counterfactual thinking" Thesis (Ph. D.), Fayetteville: University of Arkansas Timpany, L. (2005) "Building Outcome Bridges" p 3-4 in *Trancescript* Number 36, October 2005

Waltman, S.(2006) http://integrationcoach.wordpress.com/2006/08 "Integration Coaching"

Wattles, W. (2006) *The Science of Getting Rich*. Rockford, Illinois: BN Publishing,

Wiseman, R. (2009) *59 Seconds: Think A Little, Change A Lot*. London: Macmillan,

Wood, J., Elaine Perunovic, W., & Lee, J. (2009). Positive Self-Statements: Power for Some, Peril for Others. Psychological Science Psychological Science July 1, 2009 vol. 20 No. 7, pages 860-866

Zeigarnik, A.V. (1927) "Über das behalten von erledigten und unerledigten Handlungen" (The retention of completed and uncompleted actions) p 1-85 in *Psychologische Forschung*, No. 9, 1927

Richard Bolstad and Julia Kurusheva

When Ecology Is Unecological

The Experiment That Explains Psychotherapy Theory

What if my coaching session doesn't work? It's one of the most common questions new coaches have. To answer it, they seek ever more complex theories and techniques. This chapter urges us to look for what is far simpler.

In the 1970s, Professor Alex Bavelas of Massachusetts Institute of Technology completed an intriguing series of experiments. Two subjects are in separate rooms studying photos of human cells. They have been told that some of these cells are healthy and some are sick. Each time a photo is shown they either press the "healthy" button or the "sick" button, and two signal lights tell them whether their guess was "right" or "wrong". The first subject gets correct feedback, and within half an hour he is able to guess correctly 80% of the time. The second subject, unknown to him, is getting almost random feedback, because he is getting the feedback from the first person's guesses. There is, therefore, no way the second person can find out what identifies healthy cells. However, this does not stop the second person from developing a theory and believing that they are learning to distinguish sick from healthy cells. Their theory is necessarily convoluted: e.g. "a cell is sick if it has this shape, unless it has this colour or two of these patterns" and so on. This second theory is of course a complete delusion. It has no basis in reality whatsoever.

After half an hour, the two subjects have a tea break, and invariably, they chat about the experiment and share ideas. The first person has worked out the simple distinctions that enable one to see which cells are sick and which are healthy most of the time. The second person also has a theory about how to tell healthy from sick, and it is a very complex one. Every time the experiment is run, the first person now becomes convinced that they have been naïve. The second person's theory seems absolutely brilliant to them. It has so many subtle nuances that they never noticed. They immediately accept it as true. When the two subjects go back to their experiment, the first person now performs as badly as the second person. They have been convinced by the delusions. Bavelas points out that once someone has a theory about what is going on, contradictory evidence does not actually cause them to abandon their theory; it causes them to elaborate that theory with more and more complex provisos. Furthermore, people are actually attracted to more complex, elaborate theories; they think they are somehow intrinsically more intelligent.

Paul Watzlawick   quotes Gregory Bateson's comment about such experiments. Bateson was interested in schizophrenia. He said that the schizophrenic would be the person who claimed "These buttons don't mean anything. Someone in the other room switches the light whenever he feels like it (Watzlawick, 1976, p 48-54) Watzlawick sites an important example of this research in real life. Freudian psychotherapists believed that their elaborate method of dealing with phobias, involving perhaps ten years of psychotherapy, was the correct approach, and explained that phobias had a very complex inner structure involving repressed childhood "Oedipal" fears of castration. In the 1960s, behaviour therapists showed that they could cure phobias in a few weeks using conditioning processes. Freudian psychoanalyst Leon Salzman explained that it was obvious that the behaviour therapist "defines the condition in a way that is acceptable only to conditioning theorists and does not fulfil the criteria of the psychiatric definition of this disorder. Therefore, his statements should not apply to phobias, but to some other condition." Since a phobia is defined as an oedipal fear, Salzman says, defining it as a simple anchored response means that some other condition is being treated. On the other hand, since a phobia represents repressed childhood fear by definition, then only psychoanalysis of that childhood fear can relieve it.

Applying The Experiment To NLP

Each time a new method of helping people change emerges, it tends to have a relatively simple explanation for what is happening with human beings. This explanation works *some of the time*. When it does not work, however, the practitioners do not abandon it, they elaborate it. They require students to spend more time studying it, they insist that there are many factors which only a very advanced practitioner can detect that need to be considered

We know, for example, that 80% of individuals suffering major depression will "spontaneously" cease to be depressed in between 4-10 months (Yapko, 1992, p 16). People normally find their own way out of depression. This also means that if any type of "assistance" continues for ten months it will seem to have solved the problem in 80% of cases. A new form of psychotherapy that involves chanting the nursery rhyme "Humpty Dumpty" once a day will cure 80% of depressed people over the first ten months. But the practitioner of "Humpty Dumpty" therapy won't stop there. Over the next few years they will go on to elaborate the theory for those 20% who do not recover. Other nursery rhymes may be needed for more advanced cases. What they will not do is abandon their basic model. Especially, it is not likely to occur to them that the results they are seeing may (as in the case of the second person in the experiment above), be entirely random.

Sometimes, stuff just happens. That possibility seems never to occur to the second person in Bavelas' experiment. It occurs only to the schizophrenic in Bateson's hypothesis. Our brains are not built for accepting randomness, because in evolutionary terms, it is always smarter to check in case there was a pattern and a reason for an event. Take a simple example. Imagine you are in a training group of 24 people. Then you discover something extraordinary: one of the people in the group has the same birthday as you. Wow! What are the chances! Well, actually the chances that *someone* in a group of 24 people has the same birthday as someone else are over 50% (Taleb, 2007, p 159). That is to say, it's normal. It doesn't mean that people with that star sign are attracted to this group, it doesn't mean that the two people are destined to be together… it just means the universe is working as usual.

How NLP Lost Its Way

NLP as a model of changework emerged out of the study of Fritz Perls, Milton Erickson and Virginia Satir (at least in the usual mythology of its beginning). Most NLP Practitioners know something of the contributions of Virginia Satir and Milton Erickson to NLP. Perls is a bit of a mystery though. By all accounts from people who knew him, he was a fairly difficult person to know. But his approach to psychotherapy (Gestalt) contains several very important distinctions, and the clarity of these distinctions has gradually been lost in NLP. I say that as a psychotherapist who began my psychotherapeutic career, like Steve and Connirae Andreas, like Richard Bandler, as a Gestalt therapist. I'll quote from a book written by Fritz Perls, and edited by Steve Andreas under his old name (John O. Stevens). The book is called Gestalt Therapy Verbatim.

Fritz Perls was of the opinion that the whole notion of the "subconscious" or "unconscious" mind was unhelpful, in much the same way that he considered theories about the past to be unhelpful. These notions attempt to explain what is happening at this moment by saying that it is caused by something else. They answer the question "Why?" by reference to something else. Perls' idea was that if you really notice what is happening in this moment and how it is happening, in your immediate awareness, then you have everything that is necessary to understand and respond to it. After all, if there really exists an unconscious mind or a past trauma, but it has no effect on how we experience life in this moment now, then it is not relevant to how we live right now. If it has an effect, then we can just as easily study how the events are occurring right now, which give us reliable evidence of what actually exists. Perls says "The great error of psychoanalysis is in assuming that the memory is reality. All the so-called traumata, which are supposed to be the root of the neurosis, are an invention of the patient to save his self esteem…. If you ask how, you look at the structure, you see what's going on now, a deeper understanding of the process. The how is all we need to understand how we or the world functions….I know you want to ask why, like every child, like every immature person asks why, to get rationalisation or explanation. But the why at best leads to clever explanation, but never to an understanding. Why and because are dirty words in Gestalt Therapy…. We are what we are. These are the two legs upon which Gestalt Therapy walks: now and how." (Perls, 1969, p 43-44).

A core element of the radical approach of NLP at the start was this focus on "how" things happen in the mind, rather than on "why". Bandler and Grinder (1979, p 7) say in one of their first books, "We call ourselves modellers. What we essentially do is to pay very little attention to what people say they do and a lot of attention to what they do. And then we build a model of what they do. We are not psychologists, and we are also not theologians or theoreticians. We have no idea about the "real" nature of things, and we're not particularly interested in what's "true". The function of modelling is to arrive at descriptions which are useful." Their attitude to the unconscious was close to Perls', and they urged "Don't get caught by the words "conscious" and "unconscious". They are not real. They are just a way of describing events that is useful in the context called therapeutic change." (1979, p 37).

However, in the same book, Bandler and Grinder introduce the Six Step Reframe, their most profound change pattern at that time, and they explain the idea of ecology. They say (1979, p 149) "The ecological check is very important. Many of you have done elegant work, and the client is congruent in your office. When he leaves, another part of him emerges which has concerns that are contextually bound. When he gets home, suddenly he doesn't have access to what he had in your office or in the group. There are other parts of him that know that if he goes home and simply changes in the way that he was going to change, he would lose the friendship of this person, or blow that relationship, or something like that. … Regression to previous behaviour isn't a signal of failure, it's a signal of incompetency, and you need to go back and fix it."

And here we have the source of decades of anguish by NLP

practitioners. "Why am I so incompetent?" "Why did the change not work?" "Why did the problem come back?" "What did I do wrong?" "What did we not discover yet that is unconsciously blocking success?" "What is the hidden positive intention of this behaviour?"… And here we are, back with Freud, elaborating and re-elaborating our theory of "why" the person is not healthy and what else we need to do to fix them. The client has an addiction, for example, and despite all the Time Line processes, all the Parts Integrations, all the Reframings, all the Core Transformations… it comes back. Maybe we need an even more elaborate process? Maybe we need an even more elaborate theory about which processes to use in which situations? Maybe we need something more powerful than NLP? This, to quote Perls, is just bullshit. In what goes on in the person's mind and body between the time they are in your office and the time when the "problem" recurs, in the "how", is the answer to what needs to change. If the door needs shutting, all the analysis of the secret reasons why the person is leaving it open are a waste of time. They need to shut the door. In shutting it, everything that they do to avoid shutting it will be revealed. Obsessing about "ecology" is just one more distraction from the reality of how they do what they do.

A really good example is the treatment of depression. In Sigmund Freud's view (1953), depression results from a fantasised or actual loss of an individual towards whom the patient experienced ambivalent feelings (such as the mother). To deal with the loss, the patient internalises an aspect of that individual. However, the anger at that person now becomes directed towards the part of the self identified with that individual, leading to self-criticism and depression. Of course, NLP is more "positive" and we might restate this in a much more encouraging way. Maybe we could say that depression occurs when a person has a parts conflict where part of them is angry, with the positive intention of self protection, and therefore being safe; and part of them is avoidant, with the positive intention of not being hurt and therefore being happy. And of course, when other people respond with empathy, which provides an ecology issue that needs dealing with before we can integrate the parts in the conflict fully. And when the person doesn't respond even to this, well, as John and Richard said, that just shows that we are incompetent and have missed some other factor. Whether you call this psychoanalysis or NLP, it sounds a lot like the elaborate theory of the person who gets random results when they are trying to identify healthy cells.

In 2010, New Zealand NLP Practitioner Des Shinnick developed a method for treating depression in one session. It doesn't require the person to explore their ambivalence towards their mother, or resolve all the ecology issues about their depression; just to do some very specific things differently, looking in a different direction and shifting their attention to different aspects of their experience, in an ongoing way, through the day. Weirdly, this is successful enough so that a clinical trial of the method is being done by medical practitioners and so far the method is successful in over 80% of cases, within a few days of the process being done!!! In such a situation, it is clearly unecological to waste the client's time discussing ecology issues.

A Better Frame Than Ecology?

What do we do when someone doesn't change in the way we anticipate in NLP, for example they do the NLP trauma/phobia process and after a couple of days they start to panic about mice again? The ecology model says that we go back and check what the positive intention of the person recreating the problem might be and resolve that issue. This presupposes that there is a particular reason why this change did not work. However, most NLP Practitioners actually working with clients will have noticed that some clients can use NLP processes and change almost anything, while others cannot seem to change anything at all in a lasting way. This phenomenon of the client who can't change anything is much more common than the one presupposed by the ecology model – the client who can change other things, but who has an ecology issue about changing this particular thing. Using the language of ecology, we might suspect that the person who can't change anything has an ecology issue that prevents them from experiencing any major psychological changes. Those of you who have studied logic will remember that once a theory explains everything, it risks explaining nothing in particular. If all of our problems are "ecology" problems, then "ecology" is just another word for "problems". In this case, if ecology explains why a person can't change anything, then everything we do will seem to be "incompetent".

NLP Practitioner Andy Austin has a different way of explaining this challenge. Some people, he says, think about all life situations in a way that creates and sustains problems. The details of the problem or issue itself are not really what stops them from changing. What stops them from changing is not some hidden higher positive intention or some misguided "part" of their mind. It is just a way of thinking that doesn't work. To understand his model you need to get over another NLP Practitioners' common accidental presupposition – the presupposition that any style of thinking is as good as any other. This is the notion that any "metaprogram" or personality style is OK and we just need to find out how to utilise it. Shelle Rose Charvet sums up this common NLP idea when she says "There are no good or bad patterns to have. You can judge the appropriateness of each pattern only in the Context of the activity that needs to be done." (Charvet, p 13).

The work of Martin Seligman, researching the structure of depression, show why this is true but often irrelevant (some thinking styles are useful only in very, very limited contexts, for very, very limited outcomes). Take the example of depression. The very thinking styles that cause depression are used by the depressed person to convince themselves that they cannot or should not change. In fact, depression could be defined as the a style of thinking that assumes that a person cannot or should not change! Professor of Psychology Dr Martin Seligman calls this belief a "permanent, pervasive explanatory style" or "learned pessimism" (1991, p 40-48). One important thing to understand about life, before we move on to considering the learned pessimism style, is that life is cyclical. That is to say, challenges happen every so often. Rejection, disappointment, loss, and embarrassment do occur in any life. When they do, a person with a "learned pessimism" style of thinking will get depressed.

In one of Seligman's studies (1997, p 78-79), he followed a group of 400 school students through several years of their life. Those who started out with a pessimistic style were the ones who, when an event like a divorce happened, were likely to get depressed. The divorce (i.e. the life event) did not cause this depression by itself, and those with an optimistic style rebounded quickly from such events. What caused depression was the combination of painful life events plus a style of thinking. Because such events happen every so often, the person will appear to have a cyclical mood problem. In fact, it is not depression that is cyclical; it is life. Believing in "the cyclical nature of depression" is part of the permanent pervasive explanatory style of certain psychiatrists (Yapko, 1992, p 124). This style itself is part of the cause of depression. The person with depression is using a metaprogram that works only when things are going well. As soon as things are not going well, this style of thinking reveals a major flaw – it prevents them getting to feel any better.

Resilience, Recovery and Chronicity

The study of traumatic events such as war and tsunami offers another frame for thinking about these unhelpful thinking styles. When a traumatic event occurs, a neural network is set up in the brain with memories of the event (VAKOGAd), instructions about attempted responses (K), a time/place coding (Hippocampus) and an emergency rating (Amygdala). If the emergency rating is low enough, a pattern of **Resilience** occurs, where the person is distressed by the event but able to keep functioning normally. If the rating is high enough then at least for some time a PTSD-style response will occur and the person will have severe difficulty performing normal daily functions. The neurotransmitters which connect the new neural network are those present at the time, which is likely to include a lot of transmitters such as noradrenalin and adrenaline. The aim of the Amygdala connection is so that in any future similar events, the neural network will have override priority and be able to stop the Frontal Cortex (Conscious Goalsetting etc) from endangering life by thinking through a planned response. While this mostly saves lives, occasionally it results in a panic response which is triggered accidentally by sensory stimuli that are themselves not dangerous. In that case most people will gradually edit the neural network over the next couple of months so that it no longer interferes with everyday functioning, a pattern called **Recovery**. Some people have a pre-existing thinking style which makes recovery difficult (e.g. a pattern of constantly checking in case something bad is about to happen again) and they will then continue to have problems long term, a pattern called **Chronicity**. Which of the 3 patterns will occur is determined by the pre-existing thinking style and model of the world, previous experience of similar trauma, the severity of the current traumatic events, and the social support available at the time of the current trauma.

The resilience of a population varies culturally, but is generally high. "Epidemiological studies estimate that the majority of the U.S. population has been exposed to at least one traumatic event, defined using the DSM--III criteria of an event outside the range of normal human experience, during the course of their lives. Although grief and trauma symptoms are qualitatively different, the basic outcome trajectories following trauma tend to form patterns similar to those observed following bereavement. Summarizing this research, Ozer et al. (2003) recently noted that "roughly 50%-60% of the U.S. population is exposed to traumatic stress but only 5%-10% develop PTSD" (Bonanno, 2004, p. 54). "It is well established that many exposed individuals will evidence short-lived PTSD or subclinical stress reactions that abate over the course of several months or longer (i.e., the recovery pattern). For example, a population-based survey conducted one month after the September 11th terrorist attacks in New York City estimated that 7.5% of Manhattan residents would meet criteria for PTSD and that another 17.4% would meet the criteria for subsyndromal PTSD (high symptom levels that do not meet full diagnostic criteria; Galea, Ahern, et al., 2002). As in other studies, a subset eventually developed chronic PTSD, and this was more likely if exposure was high. However, most respondents evidenced a rapid decline in symptoms over time: PTSD prevalence related to 9/11 dropped to only 1.7% at four months and

0.6% at six months, whereas subsyndromal PTSD dropped to 4.0% and 4.7%, respectively, at these times (Galea et al., 2003 quoted in Bonanno, 2004, p 24)

The American Psychological Association says research suggests that research supports several "Ways to Build Resilience", in order to cope with traumatic events. Note that many of these are presupposed in the structure of coaching:

* to maintain good relationships with close family members, friends and others;
* to avoid seeing crises or stressful events as unbearable problems;
* to accept circumstances that cannot be changed;
* to develop realistic goals and move towards them;
* to take decisive actions in adverse situations;
* to look for opportunities of self-discovery after a struggle with loss;
* to develop self-confidence;
* to keep a long-term perspective and consider the stressful event in a broader context;
* to maintain a hopeful outlook, expecting good things and visualizing what is wished;
* to take care of one's mind and body, exercising regularly, paying attention to one's own needs and feelings and engaging in relaxing activities that one enjoys.
* to learn from the past
* to maintain flexibility and balance in life

In the research (Schnurr et alia, 2004), Japanese ancestry Americans had only 14% of the incidence of PTSD that European ancestry Americans had. That beats any PTSD treatment success rate! Polynesian (in the research, specifically Hawaiian; in many ways the same culture as New Zealand Maori or Samoan) ancestry also reduced PTSD rates to 35%. Resilience is pretty much the core successful human response to disaster that NLP seeks to remedially create (in fact NLP goal-setting, reframing and dissociation are all listed in the 10 points above). Note that research show that resilience is not a set personality trait so much as a set of actions you can choose to take. Also note that in the same research, a past history of being a survivor of violence almost doubles the risk of PTSD (177%). Good relationships buffer us from harm, bad ones signal a need for extra support.

Patterns of Chronicity

The thinking styles that obstruct change and recovery after a traumatic event are of course ones that were learned earlier in a person's life. The simplest way to deal with them is to show the person how they are operating and have them practice an alternative. It's not very glamorous compared to ten years of psychotherapy, but it's a lot cheaper. Andy Austin lists several of these "patterns of chronicity" and here we have adapted his categories as a reminder.

The Big "What If…" Question. "Yes, but, what if… which means…(an impossible to manage scenario)?" The positive intention of negative "What if?" questions is to attempt to anticipate and find solutions to future challenges, but by running it on impossible scenarios, the person is locked in panic. Happy people don't spend all day asking "What if I die horribly?"

The Big "Why…?" Question. "Why did this happen to me?" The positive intention of past-related "Why?" questions is to find new meanings, but the person rejects each possible future-oriented meaning and keeps searching as if trying to find a meaning which can change the traumatic event or recreate the past.

The Big Maybe Response. When asked to scale their current experience of an emotion, or give any report on their internal experience, the person says they are not sure, or prefaces their answer with "Maybe". The positive intention of "Maybe" responses is to avoid mistakes such as false hope, but by refusing to commit to any specific data, the person can never measure change and can never experience success.

Testing for Existence of The Problem Rather Than Testing for Change. Even though 99% improvement might be made, if the person with chronicity is able to locate just 1% of the problem existing, this will generally be seen as representative of 100% of the problem existing. The positive intention of "Can I still do it?" responses is to detect and respond to danger effectively, but by failing to notice improvement the person continuously reinstalls the entire problem.

Negative Nominalisations. The person talks about their traumatic responses as if they were "things" rather than actions. "I have Trauma", "I have PTSD", "I have a Wounded Inner Child", "I have a Clinical Depression.". The positive intention of Negative Nominalisations is to explain what is happening by labelling it, but the result is that the processes being discussed seem permanent, damaged and even become personified as malevolent, and so are unable to be simply changed.

Being "At Effect" rather than "Being At Cause". By being "at effect" the person experiences emotional problems happening <u>to</u> them, rather than being something that happens by them. A person "at effect" will seek treatment rather than seek change. Questions such as "Will this work for me?" or statements such as "It didn't work for me." And "It worked for a day and then the problem came back." Presuppose that the problem and the NLP process are 100% responsible and the person themselves is 0% responsible for their own results. The positive intention of "At Effect" responses is to explain what is happening without being at fault, but by not allowing for the possibility of their responses affecting their internal experience, the person makes it impossible to change their experience.

Three Stage Abreaction Process. The person has a "nocebo" (I will not please; the opposite of placebo) response to NLP processes where they have an "uncontrollable" negative response to all interventions designed to actually help them change, although they permit interventions which maintain their problem. A small percentage of all medical clients in clinical research trials will complain that they get headaches etc due to an inert "pill". This nocebo response also occurs with psychological interventions. "Abreaction" is a term from Freud's work, referring to the re-anchoring of an old traumatic response. The positive intention of "Abreaction" responses may be to protect the person from feared results of the change process, but it blocks all change. It is of course perfectly possible to explain that abreaction-nocebo responses are simply accidental anchored responses and of little psychological significance (a view closer to Carl Jung's view of them).

Stage 1. Signal (Implied Threat of Emotion) e.g. "This is making me feel ill."
Stage 2. Increased Amplitude of Signal (direct Threat of Emotion) e.g. "Now I really feel sick. Your process is harming me. Stop or I will start screaming!"
Stage 3. Abreaction (what Andy Austin calls Punishment of the Practitioner) e.g. vomiting, convulsing, running out of the room screaming, uncontrollable crying.

Just pointing out these patterns and encouraging clients to create more useful foci for their attention is the solution to these patterns. The search for a special magic that will make the patterns go away is part of the problem. Like any new behavior, developing more resilient patterns of responding to challenges takes time and attention. The Key Questions

Changing Someone's Life
in a Single Session

The possibility of a client achieving their outcomes for coaching or psychotherapy in a single session has been understood since Freud's one session treatment of the client he calls "Katarina". By 1976, research showed that 51% of clients who had only a single session of psychotherapy experienced significant improvement, and that this improvement was still obvious 8 years later (Hoyt et alia 1990). This chapter by Julia Kurusheva looks at how to create major changes in a single NLP session and covers:

- A 'sprint' version of the RESOLVE model of coaching
- A range of solution focused questions to be used at each step
- Common 'obstacles' and some ways of clearing them
- Other observations of what works

In his 48 page study "Structure de Changement en PNL", New Caledonian NLP Trainer Damien Raczy reports on his research into the success of coaching in more than 100 coaching sessions spread over 50 weeks. He took several variables in his work as a coach and investigated the extent to which each variable was correlated with client success (measured by the speed of them solving their problems, their success in completing real life tasks between sessions, and their own opinion of the their progress and of the coach). The coaching variables which he compared with this success included the extent to which his session correlated with several overarching session models:

- The RESOLVE model developed by Dr Richard Bolstad
- The SPRINT version of the RESOLVE model developed by Julia Kurusheva and explained here
- The Clean Language model developed by Penny Tompkins and James Lawley
- The Autocoaching model developed by Ian McDermott
- The 6 Step Coaching model of Michael Hall
- He also assessed his use of a number of NLP techniques such as identifying positive client resources before starting, setting client tasks between sessions, checking the ecology of any change carefully and setting clear outcomes.

His conclusion is that achievement of tasks between sessions is extremely significant (93% correlation with client success) and alignment with the SPRINT model is extremely significant (90% correlation with client success). Identifying resources is also very significant (89%) but many factors were only minimally correlated with success. He found that "The usage of SPRINT is certainly the factor that that most strongly is correlated to successful performance from the standpoint of the customer and from the standpoint of the practitioner." (Raczy, 2011, p 22, translated by Richard Bolstad)

The Origin of the SPRINT Model

As an NLP practitioner I usually recommend my clients to arrange from 2 to 4+ sessions to resolve their life challenges. Very rarely I would see a client for only one session. When discussing with other NLP practitioners how realistic one session change was, I had had an opinion it was a fairly unreasonable expectation. Until recently, when during one month I had the experience of running 50 single sessions with some amazing results.

Most of my clients were participants on the overseas NLP trainings run by Richard Bolstad and I, and they ranged from first-time NLP students to those at the trainer level. Because of the limited time we were staying in their city, I could only see each client for one session of 75 minutes. In most cases I worked with an interpreter which cut the actual time by about half. So, how much can you do in 30-40 minutes?

Of course we know from NLP that change is instant, and it's not **changing** that takes time. It is **not-changing** that takes time. And certain steps, followed consistently, create the optimum conditions for someone to change quickly. In fact, the change can happen at each of these steps. Fast reliable changes is what I experienced, and now I'd like to share with you what I learned about making it possible.

'Sprint Version' of Resolve and Specify Models

I used the RESOLVE and SPECIFY OUTCOME models as the basis of my sessions.

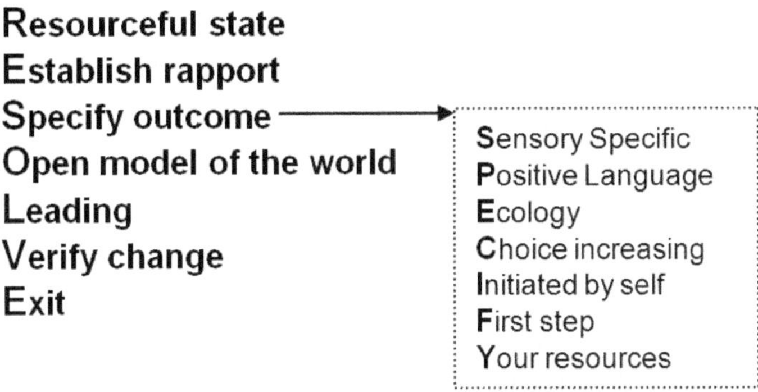

Working without manuals or taking notes, I soon discovered that my unconscious mind created a simple chart which I was mentally checking throughout a session. Not using notes allowed me to more fully concentrate my attention with clients and use sensory acuity more efficiently. Below is the chart – the 'Sprint Version' - I was using.

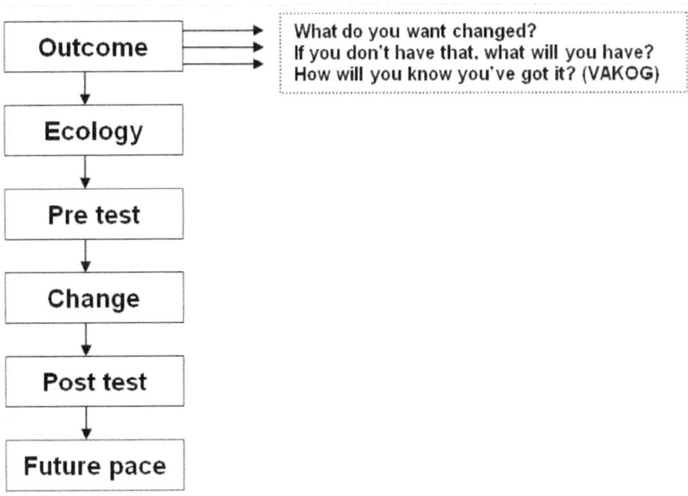

Any session would start with me being in a Resourceful State and with Establishing Rapport – the first steps of the Resolve model. Being a foreign consultant and an assisting trainer, I already had credibility with my clients and most of them were 'pre-qualified', meaning that they knew about NLP and had trust in it. This allowed us to save time explaining NLP and pre-framing change i.e. doing the Pointing Exercise (see Appendix), which most of my clients had already done during their training.

For rapport I would match my client's posture, tone and speed of voice, predicates, gestures and breathing. The session would start without my normal practice of taking contact details so that the Establish Rapport part was trimmed down to a wide smile, a traditional bow and a greeting "Hello [their name in native language]". Their name was all I could say in their language. The rest was up to my interpreter.

Outcome

"What would you like to change today?"
"What would you like to get out of this session?"

I would ask the second question if my client was not very clear about the first one.

Then they would explain their concerns and I would **Reflective Listen** to them. This would be a very important step not only for rapport, but especially in acknowledging and validating my client's experience. Sometimes a person had never previously talked to anyone about their challenge or had not had an experience of actually being <u>heard</u>. Just this simple step, not even solution focussed yet, allowed them to accept the change much easier.

"During the session I had the feeling that Julia understood not only what I said but also what I did not express in words. This was the first session that felt so warm." N.Y., Counsellor

"... I knew that I was not expressing my feelings freely. I thought it was important to do this in a safe environment. During the session I was able to express my feelings and felt quite relieved." Y.M., Counsellor

Clearing Obstacles

"I don't know my outcome. I don't know how it could be."

- "That's right, you don't. This is exactly what we are doing now."
- "Of course you don't know, but *if* you *knew*, you know."

"I can't think of/see my outcome until I'm out of this stuckness."

- "Of course you can't, but *if* you *could* see it?"
- "Right, so you haven't been able to see it. How would you know that this has changed for you so that you were out of it? What would you see/hear/feel that would let you know you are out?"

Positive Language - "If you don't have that, what will you have INSTEAD?"

In most cases people described problems rather than outcomes, and it was essential to help them "convert" those into positive language by following this simple formula:

$$\text{PACE} \longrightarrow \text{LEAD}$$

Reflective Listen   *Ask Solution Focused Question*

"So, this is want you'd like to change, and if you change that, then what will be there instead?"
"And if that was not there anymore, what would be there instead?"
"So, if you didn't feel that, what would you feel then?"

An actual representation of the 'desired' state in positive language allows recognition of **it** after the change happens. It is still possible to 'clear the problem' without knowing the 'desired' state, but clients would more likely feel confused and not know what to expect.

This is an incredibly important part of the change. So often people know really well what it is they don't want, but they never imagined what it would be like when it's over. This new way of thinking about what they want (rather than don't want) and what it would be like, gives them a completely different perspective, alters the habitual thinking and teaches them to "look outside of stuckness" to see what's on the other side of it.

"How will you know that you've got it?"
"What will you see, hear, feel, and say to yourself when you've got it?"
"What will others notice different about you?"

These questions would create a new experience in the body-mind system, and every new experience would be stored as a body "memory".

This is one of the functions of our unconscious mind to store memories.

In this way we create a **'future memory'** by fully, with our five senses, associating into an experience that hasn't happened yet. This process has been used by shamans and healers for a long time. Serge Kahili King, the teacher of the Hawaiian shamanism-based model Huna, says:

"... an intensely imagined experience is just as good as the real thing, at least as far as memory-based behaviour is concerned. Hawaiian and other shamans have used this bit of wisdom for untold ages as a tool for healing and self-development. Recently this ancient shamanic understanding has been put to modern use by Olympic athletes, among others, with extremely effective results. By using full sensory imagination in which they perform perfectly every time, the athletes create body memories which make the physical performance easier and better. The same process can be used to train yourself in any skill, state, or condition whatsoever."

Practising to set up sensory specific outcomes in this way is like training a muscle in the gym. It is especially useful for people who are not very clear with what they want. Once they started specifying their goals, even smaller ones first, their body-mind system would soon generalise this skill into other areas and into the larger goals which ultimately will strengthen their sense of clarity, direction and purpose in life.

"For a long time I have wanted to restore a relationship with someone, yet was not willing to do something about it. During the session, Julia guided me through the process and let me know how I would feel if the relationship was restored. She also let me understand the purpose of this restoration. When everything was so clear, I made up my mind to take action." Y. H., Social Welfare, Japan

"During the session, Julia helped me correct all my colours so that I could see and experience "What I really want" and "What had been stopping my success". " H. A., Okinawa

Another fascinating thing happened several times after setting the outcome in this way. When I checked how my client felt about their initial concern, they would say: "Well, now that I have this outcome and the future is looking bright, my problem is irrelevant and not worth paying attention to." It was as if suddenly the initial problem deconstructed and disappeared from their focus.

When working with people, it is vital to remember and pay attention to the fact that your client may feel really different about their problem after each of your questions. I found it really valuable to allow for the possibility of spontaneous change at any step, validating any changes and shifts throughout the session and talking to clients as if "the problem is changing".

"After about an hour I was surprised to find that what I thought was a problem seemed like a situation where I was just stepping on the brake. I realized that problems do not actually exist. We create them." M. S., therapist

Specify Outcome – other steps

Occasionally, to increase motivation, I would ask these two questions, but mostly used them at the end when future pacing:

- "What do you **personally** need to do to achieve / maintain this?"
- "What is your **first step** (next steps)?"

The final step - **Your Resources** to achieve this outcome - proved to be effective when tackling doubts that changes would be possible:

- "Some time in the past you may have had an experience in your life when you did/overcame/achieved something similar. Remember this time now and step right in." (**associate into** a past time of achieving a goal)

This step by itself is so powerful that several times I skipped an official NLP change process and used it to produce a change. I got my client to remember a time when they achieved something and to step right inside their body in that memory. Then, as they were feeling it fully, to fly inside their outcome and bring all these feelings with them and feel what that feels to be inside the outcome with these feelings of success. Then I asked them to step outside and see themselves in that picture and adjust anything so that it became so attractive and appealing they couldn't wait to get back in and be that person.

"I no longer feel depressed. Instead I feel wonderful. I do not quite understand what happened in me, but I feel like a completely new person." Y. W., student, Japan

Clearing Obstacles

"It looks good but I don't believe I can achieve it."

- "What would make it easier to believe you can achieve it?"
- "Remember a time in your life when something didn't seem achievable and yet you've done it and felt great! Step right inside that time and feel it fully (associate in). As you're feeling these resources now, fly out of that memory and into that future picture and into your body and feel how it feels now…. Now step outside and see yourself in that picture and adjust anything you need to so that it becomes so attractive and appealing that you can't wait to get back in and be that person"
- Clear a limiting decision using Time Line Therapy™ (see Appendix).

Observations

I noticed occasionally at trainings, after learning about conscious and unconscious minds, some people would get upset at their conscious mind for "being so controlling or rational". The Specify Outcome model demonstrates the relationship between them.

With our conscious mind we choose an outcome, we decide what it is we want. The conscious mind plays a role of a decision maker. Our unconscious mind gets these instructions and aligns its inherent unlimited potential to achieve it. Another function of the conscious mind is to get feedback and to check whether or not we are on track with our outcome. The unconscious mind aligns our actions in response. For example, if we are hungry we make a decision what to eat. The unconscious mind can simply imagine that we ate and feel full, but the conscious mind will keep tracking whether if happened or not.

Understanding and appreciating the role of each helps to feel at ease and maintain rapport between conscious and unconscious minds.

Ecology

1. **"What will change as a result of your getting your outcome?"**
   "What are the other benefits/advantages?"
   "How does this outcome increase your choice?"

2. **"Are there any situations/circumstances in which this change**

wouldn't be OK / you wouldn't want to be affected by this change?"

3. **"Is there anything you will lose?" "What's important about that?"**
"How can you achieve this differently?"
"What are the other ways to ensure you are [...]?"
"How are you already doing/being [...] now?"
"Is there any part of you that wouldn't like this change (ask yourself?)"

Ecology plays crucial part in *not-changing*. Once the 'objections to change' are discovered and new ways of meeting them ecologically are generated, the change is only a moment away. With these 3 sets of questions above I would be checking:

1. What are the benefits of this change? (to build up the positive expectation of their outcome)
2. Contextualisation of the outcome (i.e. a person may set a goal to be more enthusiastic, but they cannot be enthusiastic 24/7, they also need sleep).
3. What will you <u>lose,</u> if anything?

In most cases my clients were afraid of losing something as a result of the change:

Protection / Safety -
- e.g. *"If I stop being angry in these situations, I won't be safe"*

An important value of theirs such as being respectful, humble, gentle, etc. -
- e.g. *"If I assert myself, I won't be respectful"; "If I become very rich, I may become arrogant"*

Attention from others -
- e.g. *"If I recover from this condition, I won't get any understanding and sympathy"*

A subject for discussion with friends –
- e.g. *"If my life is not difficult, what would I talk to my friend about?"*

In addressing these I used **open solution focussed questions**, such as:

- What are the other ways to ensure you are safe?
- How are you already protecting yourself now?
- How can you be protecting yourself in other ways when this behaviour is let go off?
- In what ways could you get attention from others, once this problem is solved?

"The session also made me realize that my attitude, which caused some misunderstanding, had a purpose of protecting me as a young child. This clarification made me feel so peaceful." Yoshimi H., Social Welfare, Japan

- Language patterns connecting two states that are opposing each other:

  - "How could you be respectful *while* being assertive?"
  - "In what way can you be humble *while* being rich?"

These are very powerful questions and immediately connect two split experiences so you need to be careful using them. Check that it does in fact seem acceptable to be or have both states together.

The ecology check would always take a good chunk of the session. I would keep reflecting each of their answers in their exact words weaving them together into a 'Conditional Close' statement:

"So, if you could protect yourself in this way, <u>and</u> you could ensure that you stayed respectful, <u>and</u> if you could discuss other things with your friends, would it be then all right to make this change?"

Each time their precise words were reflected back to them, clients would get immersed in their own internal experience of having and/or being all these things.

Memorising clients' words without writing them down is an invaluable skill in change work. Several years ago I attended a workshop on Clean Language by Sue Knight, an NLP trainer from UK I highly respect, in which she modelled and emphasised the importance of being fully present for your client and **training** yourself to **memorise** their words. I cannot emphasise enough how much I benefited from this skill. I believe that this part of rapport building is at least as powerful as visual mirroring and really works as an "Ad mirroring".

Pre Test

Open Model of the World

Normally I would do the Pointing Exercise (see appendix 1) to demonstrate how NLP can help change (i.e. "your body responds to your thinking"). This time most of my clients already had that experience.

Where necessary, I would explain the Time Line Therapy^{TM} process by drawing a picture and using the frames from Lynn Timpany's article "Preframing Time Line Processes".

Then I would pre-test the problem:

- **"Can you do it now? Will you know if/when it changed?"**
- **"Think of it now, you'd know if that changed, wouldn't you?"**
- **"When you think about that old problem now, can you get enough of a sense of that problem, so that you'd know if it changed?"**

By answering this question the client accepts the hidden presupposition that change is possible. I have never had anyone say "No" to this question.

Change

I selected a change process by using the Personal Strength Model by Richard Bolstad (see Appendix 2).

Because my aim was to help my client reach a major/significant transformational experience in one session, I found that two processes generated particularly notable results: Time Line Therapy^{TM} (Tad James, see appendix 4) and the Core Outcome process from Core Transformation^{TM} (Connirae Andreas, see appendix 3).

Frequently I used two additional pieces in these otherwise standard processes:

- Growing Up A Part
- Spreading Change into the Future Timeline

Growing Up a Part

(used in Time Line Therapy™ after checking inside the healed event that it feels balanced and emotions have disappeared or after the Core Outcome process) -

Step outside that earlier person or part and ask her/him if they want to evolve forward through time so that they can benefit from your experiences, learnings and wisdom. If they do, imagine them surrounded with the light, love and healing and allow them to evolve forward through time all the way up to your current age, so that they also learn from each of your experiences while enriching each of your experiences with their own energies, qualities and wisdom. When the part has arrived at your current age, invite it to move inside your body, merging with you. Let this new wholeness spread into every organ of your body, every cell, every molecule, every atom, becoming a part of your being so fully that it can radiate right through your body. As it spreads through your body, you can allow it to integrate with the core of your being, enriching your experience of your inner essence.

Spreading Change into the Future Timeline

(used after healing the subsequent events and floating above now looking into the future) -

Create a symbol for these positive qualities you are developing and put it on a card. Now notice that you have a huge deck of cards in your hands all with the same symbol on one side and you don't know what's on the other side (because you don't know yet who you're going to get these qualities from). Float up above now and throw them out across your future Timeline, and see them sparkling like stars falling into your future Timeline lighting it up.

Straight after the process I'd say: "Welcome back. What was your experience like?" and then go to the Post Test.

"In the same way that one suddenly becomes aware that music must have been playing only at the very moment that it is turned off; in the same way I suddenly became aware that "guilt" has been a permanent feature of my entire life, just at that very moment when you helped me heal it during our session. I'm talking about a permanent, underlying feeling of guilt, or obligation, in relation to every woman I had any relationship to for my entire life! This discovery is making an astonishing difference in my life now. I feel so much more relaxed, so

much freer, and so much more able to be myself! I am very grateful that you allowed me the time I needed to access that force and focus that energy and love, and pour it into the moment of my birth, until I really felt that I had completely healed that event! A real transformation took place in me at that moment." C.V., Japan

Post Test

Verify change: "Try and think of that old problem and notice what's different now?"

This question "seals" the change. Occasionally, clients may have doubts that the change really happened or will last.

Clearing Obstacles

"I feel OK now but how can I be sure it won't come back?"

- "Try and feel that same emotion? Try again. Try again. That's right, it changed."
- "What would make it easier for you to believe it's changed now?"
- "That's right, there is no guarantee, and 'yes', you could re-create it if you wanted it. It is your brain and you are in charge of it. But why would you spoil such a good change? It's like dragging up a newly planted flower to see how the roots are growing."

"It's kind of upsetting to realise that I had this problem for XX years, and now it took one hour to change it. What about all these years?"

- "Yes, it is a bit like that, isn't it?
    - So much greater is the joy of you getting it now.
    - And what about all the things that you learned about this issue?
    - Imagine how you could use your learnings from this experience, and if someone in a similar situation will ask for your advice, you could confidently assure them that it is possible."

Future Pace

"Think of a time in the future, where in the past you would have had that old response, and notice how it is different now. Think one

week/ month/ year from now and notice what's different then?"

To finish up the session I'd ask: "How are you feeling now?"

- If they said "Great", I would congratulate them and say "Great work!"
- If they said "Confused", I'd say "That's right. It may appear/feel confusing. It's used to be a reliable response and now it's changed. So, be alert to all the other changes that will be happening from now."

There were some sessions after which clients did not feel they achieved much. However most of them reported during next several days that they were experiencing incredible changes in the way they felt about their issue, improvement in their health conditions and well-being, reconciliation in relationships, clarity, enthusiasm, and peace. The consistency with which this would happen was amazing.

Other Observations

I believe that the following factors also help in change work:

- **Beliefs.**

Believe that change is possible and demonstrate this by all aspects of your behaviour.

- **Assumption.**

Assuming that inherently people are good helps me to help stay away from judgements and assist everyone who comes to reach their goals.

- **Utilise.**

Utilise everything - clients' words, gestures, behaviours, "resistances".

- **Trust your feelings.**

If you feel confused, trust this feeling and honestly ask your client to clarify things for you. I used to think, if I was feeling confused, that I must not have understood my client. I learned the value of confronting my clients with what seems inconsistent or incongruent to me, i.e. "Could I please check, you are saying that you are OK with it, and at the same time you are frowning" or "Could I please clarify with you, just 5 minutes ago you said that you feel like this most of the time, and now you say that it only happened twice."

- **Energy.**

When I work I imagine that every client is connected with the Source of Energy and Love (I see it as a stream of white energy surrounding them and connecting to the sky above and the earth below). By doing so, in energy terms I affirm their own connection with the Source, i.e. their spiritual freedom and autonomy; and in NLP terms I believe my clients have all the resources they need. This helps me stay clear in terms of the problem ownership and know where my client is and where I am. It also helps to stay objective and neutral, regardless of how "hard or devastating" someone's problem may appear to me.

- **Observe.**

Change can happen at any of these steps so it's useful to be alert to and validate any shifts that occur and frame them as changes. With each step I am 'stacking the deck' so that change becomes inevitable.

Of course, I still see great value in having more than one session. And also now I can confidently say that a single session change is possible and can be achieved consistently.

Summary - 'Sprint Version' of Resolve and Specify Models

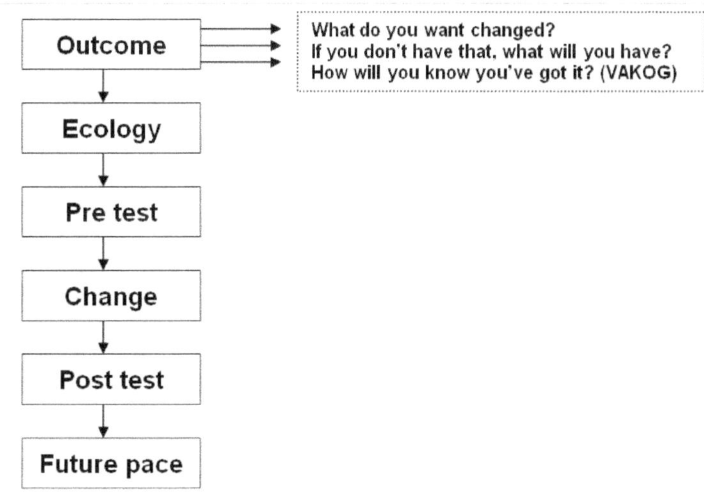

Outcome
What do you want changed? (reflective listen)
If you don't have that, what will you have? (positive language)

How will you know you've got it? (sensory specific language VAKOG)

Ecology
What will you gain?
What will you lose?
When is it not OK?

Pre Test / Open Model of the World
Explain NLP (if needed)
Pre-frame change process
Pre-test "Can you do it now? Will you know if it changed?"

Change
Change work process

Post Test / Verify Change
Try and think of that old problem and notice how it's/what is different now?

Future Pace
Think of a future time, where in the past you would have had that old response, and notice how it is different now? Think 1 week/month/year from now and notice what's different then?

"This summer, I had the privilege to attend NLP sessions in Japan by Julia Kurusheva, as her interpreter, and I was able to witness the dedication and mastery with which Julia conducted her sessions, accompanying her clients in their journey with so much caring love until a tremendous shift occurred and they reached their goal and were transformed in a single session. I also had a session as a client for chronic migraines and haven't had a single one since then!" Christine de Larroche-Kodama, teacher and therapist, Tokyo

I'd like to finish by saying how incredibly rewarding it was for me to have worked with these many unique extraordinary individuals; how moved and inspired I was by the power and courage of their spirit. At times I was so excited to hear my client's positive learnings that I thought of writing "The Book of Positive Learnings"!

And I am learning every time I help someone change, not only how to be a better change agent, but most importantly, more central than any skills, how to live and love.

With admiration of human spirit,

Julia Kurusheva, Auckland, New Zealand, September 2007

Bibliography

Andreas, C. and Andreas, T. 'Core Transformation: Reaching the Wellspring Within", Real People Press, Moab, Utah, 1994

Bolstad, R. RESOLVE A New Model of Therapy Crown Publishing, Bancyfelin, Wales,, 2002

Hoyt, M.F., Rosenbaum, R. and Talmon, M. "Planned Single Session Psychotherapy" p 59-86 in Budman, S.H., Hoyt, M.F. and Friedman, S. The First Session In Brief Therapy Guildford Press, New York, 1992

King, S.K. Urban Shaman, Fireside, New York, 1990

Raczy, D. "Structure de Changement en PNL", Noumea, 2011

Timpany, L. 'Preframing Time Line Processes', www.lynntimpany.co.nz

Transformations International Consulting & Training, Mastering Success Manual, Christchurch, New Zealand, 2005

Appendices

Appendix 1: Pointing Exercise

Get your client stand with their feet slightly apart. Ask them to bring their left arm straight up in front so it's parallel with the floor. Emphasise the importance of keeping their feet in the same place throughout the exercise. Now say: "Keeping your feet still, turn your body to the left, pointing with the finger as far as you can turn, until it <u>gets tight</u>. Notice, by the point on the wall, how far round you are pointing. Now turn back to the front. Close your eyes and make a picture of yourself turning again, but this time going much further. What would you be looking at if you went 30 centimetres further? Sense what it would feel like to be that much more supple and turn that far easily. Also, what would you say to yourself if you could do that easily. Would you be surprised? Now open your eyes, and, using that same arm, physically turn again to the left, and see <u>how far you go now</u>."

Check how much further your client has turned and mark it with the words "That's right". Explain the difference as due to programming the brain to achieve: "The same process we call 'goal setting'. When people don't achieve in life, it's not 'laziness'. It's just a lack of adequate, compelling goals. When you turned the second time, you had given your unconscious mind (the part of your mind which runs your body) a set of instructions: by making pictures of your goal, feeling what that goal would feel like, and listening to my voice and your own internal voice talking about the goal. These "internal representations" (internal pictures, sounds and feelings) are treated by the unconscious mind as if they are real."

Appendix 2: Personal Strengths Model

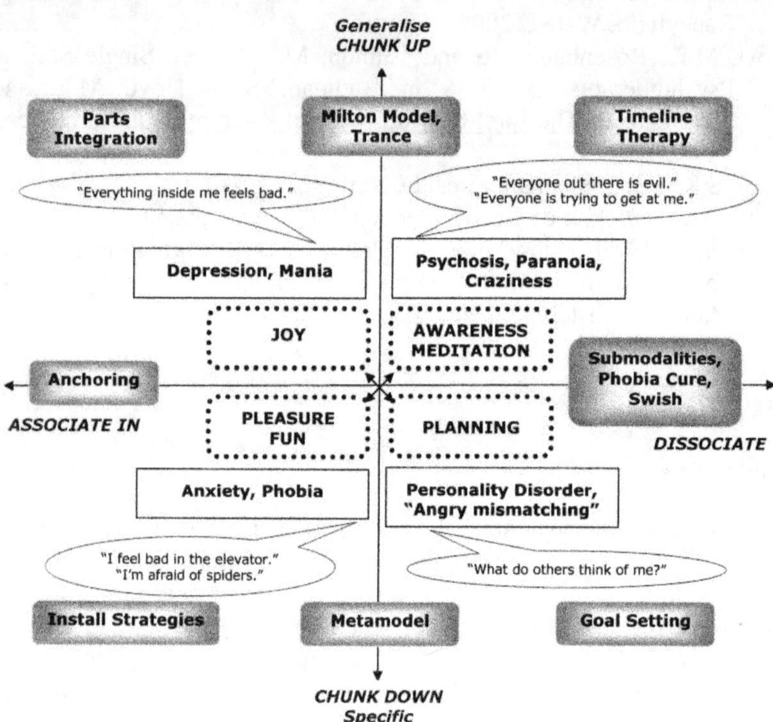

Appendix 3: The Core Outcome Process (Simplified version included for reference only; from Core Transformation™ by Connirae Andreas. This process should not be done without adequate training by a certified trainer of Core Transformation™)

<u>Phase 1</u>: Eliciting the Outcome Chain

1. "What feeling, behaviour or thought [X] do you want to change?"… "Where, when and with whom do you have this [X]?"… (**Pre-test**)

2. "Take a moment to relax, turn inward… Think of a specific time that [X] occurred… Mentally step into the situation, seeing what you

saw, hearing what you heard, feeling what you felt at the time… As you relive this experience, notice your internal images, sounds and/or feelings… Since you didn't consciously generate [X], it's as if some part of you generated it. You may begin to sense this part of you, in your body or around you. Where do you sense this part 'lives'?"

3. "Even though you don't know what the positive intention of this part is, you can begin thanking this part for being there, because you can trust that it has some positive intention for you."…

4. "Ask this part of you, *'What do you want?'* After you ask this question inside, relax and notice what response you get back from that part of yourself.… Thank this part for its response."

5. "Invite this part to step/breathe into what it is like to already have [***Intended Outcome***] fully and completely. Ask this part, *'When you have [**Intended Outcome**], what do you want, through having [**Intended Outcome**], that's even more important?' "*… "Thank that part for its response."
   Repeat step 5 until the Core State.

6. When you get to what seems to be the Core State, say "Ask this part of you *'Is there anything even more important you want through having [**Core State**]?' "*

You can tell it's a Core State by the following clues:
1. It's a state of being (in contrast to doing, getting, having, relating), such as "Beingness," "Inner peace," "Love," OK-ness," "Oneness," "Wholeness," "Spiritual Connection.
2. It's not dependent on others (like "appreciation from others," "love from others").
3. It's not reflexive (like "loving myself").
4. It's not a specific emotion, such as confident, hopeful, satisfied, courageous, proud, etc.
5. They can go no deeper: either there is no answer or they describe consequences of having the Core State, such as "my whole life will be different."
6. The person often shows a major change of state: relaxation, skin colour changes, changes in breathing, changes in tempo.

Phase 2: Reversing the Outcome Chain with the Core State

7. "Somehow our inner parts get the idea that in order to experience Core States such as [*Core State*], we have to first do and get certain things. Unfortunately, this doesn't work very well. We don't get to experience our Core States very often when we go about it that way. The only way to experience a Core State is just to step into it and have it; to be it, begin from it."

8. "Invite this part of you to step into [*Core State*] now, and ask this part, 'When you already have [*Core State*] in an ongoing way, how does already having [*Core State*] as a way of being in the world change and transform [*Intended Outcome*]?"
    Repeat Step 8 with each Intended Outcome before going on.

9. "Ask the part, 'How does already having [*Core State*], as a way of being, transform the situations in which you used to [X]?"

Advanced Options: Ways to Tailor Step 9
When an intended outcome is valuable in and of itself, such as "motivation" or "feeling good about myself," say: "Ask the part, 'How does already having [this part's Core State] make it easier to have [intended outcome]?'" or "Ask the part, 'How does already having [this part's Core State] enhance and enrich [intended outcome]?'"
When an intermediate outcome is dependent on other people, such as "appreciation from others," say: "Ask the part, 'How does already having [this part's Core State] change your experience when you are getting [intended outcome]?… How does already having [this part's Core State] change your experience when you are **not** getting [intended outcome]?'"
When an intended outcome does not serve the person well, such as "revenge" or "being perfect," say: "Ask the part, 'How does already having [this part's Core State] affect your desire for [ill-formed outcome]?' or "Ask the part, 'How does already having [this part's Core State] transform this whole area of [ill-formed outcome]?'"
If an intermediate outcome involves physical safety (in contrast to emotional safety) say: "Ask the part, 'How does already having [this part's Core State] actually help you keep yourself physically safer?'

Phase 3: Growing Up the Part

1. "Inner parts are often much younger than we are. That means this part hasn't had the benefit of all of your experiences and learnings and wisdom that you have gained over the years. So now, turn inward and ask this part, "How old are you?" Now ask the part if it

wants to make its job a lot easier by having the benefits that come from evolving forward through time.”

2. “Now invite this part of you to begin by having [*CS*] fully present at its age, and then invite this part to evolve forward through time letting [*CS*] radiate through all your experience, all the way up to your current age. As it does this, it will learn from each of your experiences, and it will enrich each of your experiences with [*CS*]. Nod when the part has arrived at your current age.”...

3. “Where is this part now located?”
   If part is outside their body say: “Invite this part of you to move inside your body, bringing the full sense of [*Core State*] with it ... And now let the sense of [*CS*] spread into every cell of your body, becoming a part of your emotional coding. This [*CS*] is now available to all of you. ... As [*CS*] spreads throughout your body, you can allow it to integrate with the core of your being, enriching your experience of your inner essence.” …

4. “Now that this part of you is current age and fully throughout your body, you can notice what it’s like, now, to have [*CS*] as a way of being. You can notice how this changes your experience with [*Intended Outcome*]… and [*Intended Outcome*]…and [*Intended Outcome*]…” - list all Intended Outcomes.

5. __Ecology Check__ “Ask on the inside, ‘Is there any other part of me that is concerned with this issue or objects to my having [*CS*] in an ongoing way?’”
   If any part does, run the Core Outcome process with that part. Otherwise, continue (continue only after you’ve done the process with all parts involved).

6. “Now allow your entire past to be behind you in a line or pathway. Let your future flow out in front of you in a line or pathway… Now, float up over your timeline with [*CS*] fully present; and go back to the moment of your conception. Bring [*CS*] into your conception, through your birth and through all your experiences, all the way up to the present. When you have reached the present just give me a nod…Now, see yourself moving into the future, with [*CS*] in every experience you will have… You can take all the time you want, and when [*CS*] are fully integrated into your whole life, you can reorient to the here and now.” …

Appendix 4: Time Line Therapy® (Simplified version of removing a

negative emotion from the Time Line, included for reference only. Time Line Therapy™ is exclusively trademarked to Dr Tad James and the Time Line Therapy ® Association. This process should not be done without adequate training by a certified trainer of Time Line Therapy™)

1. *Elicit Time Line.* While observing all non-verbal behaviour, say..."If I were to ask your unconscious mind, where your past is, and where your future is, I have an idea that you might say, "It's from right to left, or front to back, or up to down, or in some direction from you in relation to your body. And it's not your conscious concept that I'm interested in, it's your unconscious. So, if I were to ask your unconscious mind where's your past, to what direction would you point?" [Observe] "And your future, what direction would you point if I asked your unconscious mind, where's your future?" "Now, would you bring to mind the directions that you pointed to. Do you notice that they imply a line?"

2. *Pre-test:* "Think of a time when *[the stressful emotion you are clearing]* was a problem. Notice that you can still feel some of the feeling in that event now. You'd know if that changed wouldn't you." "Is it alright for your unconscious mind for you to release this emotion today and for you to be aware of it consciously?"

3. *Identifying the root cause:* "What is the root cause of this problem, the first event which, when disconnected, will cause the problem to disappear? If you were to know, was it before, during, or after your birth?" If the person says "I don't know what the root cause is." Then say "I know you don't know, but if you did…. Take whatever comes up…. Trust your unconscious mind."
If before birth: "In the womb or before?"
    If in the womb:"What month, from one to nine?"
    If before the womb:"Was it a past life or passed down to you from your parents and ancestors?"
        Past life: "How many lifetimes ago?"
        Genealogical: "How many generations ago?"
        If both genealogical and past life, clear the earlier one first, then clear the other.
If after birth: "If you were to know, what age were you?"

4. *Removing a Stressful Emotion From The Time Line.* "Float up in the air, way above your Time Line." "Float all the way back so you are directly above the event looking down on it [*Position 2*]. Let me know when you are there…. Notice where the emotions are. Ask your unconscious mind what it needs to learn from the event, the learning of which will allow you to let go of the emotions easily and effortlessly. Your unconscious mind can preserve all the positive learnings. Tell me what some of those learnings are. (Check the learnings are positive, about self and future oriented). Whatever positive learnings you need to have learned from this event, preserve them in that special place you reserve for all such learnings." "Now float back to a position above the event and at least 15 minutes before any of the events which led up to that event [*Position 3*]. Turn so that you are looking towards now... Now… check that the emotions have gone?" *If they've gone say* "Great" *and go on to Section 7.*

5. If the emotion did not disappear yet then:

<u>First</u>, *check you're at the root cause event* "Are you before the first event?" *[If not go back to 5.)]*

<u>Second</u>, *check position is high enough and back enough.* "Get high enough and far enough back until the emotion disappears."

<u>Third</u>, *check the unconscious is totally agreeable to let go of the emotion. Reframe objections as follows...*

    a. Learning "I know that there's a part of you that may have been holding on to the emotions so as to learn something from this event. I'd like to ask that part to take responsibility for storing all the positive learnings from this event so it's okay to let go of the emotions now. What is there to have learned from this event, the learning of which will allow you to easily let go of the emotion? If you let go of the emotions and preserve the learnings, you will have learned what you needed to learn now."

    b. Safety: "And if there's any part of you that believed that storing those emotions could keep you safe, I'd like that part to notice now that holding onto the emotion hasn't kept you safe. Actually holding on to that emotion was dangerous for your health. Anything less than completely releasing it and preserving the learnings about taking care of yourself is not keeping you totally safe."

    c. Any Other Intention: "I'd like to talk to the part of you that thinks it would rather not let go of this emotion and I'd like to ask the part to tell me its highest intention." *Keep asking its intention for that until the intention is clearly one better served by letting go of the emotion. Then point that out (as in the two reframes above.)*

6. ***Generalising The Change.*** *The following statement can be made before* <u>or</u> *after the emotion is gone.* "Imagine an infinite source of love and healing above your head, and allow it to flow down to your heart and from your heart to the person in the event below until that person is totally healed." *The following statement must only be made after the* *emotion is gone.* "Now float down inside the event looking through the eyes of that earlier person [*Position 4*], and check on the emotions. Check that it feels emotionally balanced. Stay there as long as it takes to know that the emotions are fully cleared. Are the emotions there or have they disappeared now. ?" *If they've gone say* "Great" *and go on. If they're still there go back to 6).* "Float back up above and before the events leading up to that event [*Position 3*]. Now come back along your time line only as quickly as you can realise that your unconscious mind has preserved all the learnings, and let go of the similar emotions on all the related events all the way back to now…. Good. Floating above now, look out into the future, and notice that the changes spread out into the future opening up new possibilities and creating new happiness. Knowing that those changes will continue, float down into now and come back into the room…. That was a major shift wasn't it… Now try and think of that situation where that emotion used to be a problem; the one you thought of before we started. Notice that it's changed now!" "And when you think of a future time which in the past would have brought up that backlog of emotion, notice that now that's changed too!"

The Wheel Of Change

The Key Challenge Facing New Coaches Is Relationship-Based, Not Technique Based

For the last thirty years, I have trained counsellors, NLP Practitioners and coaches. I have also been a supervisor of these helpers, as they launch their new careers. Along the way I have developed my own models and change techniques to explain how to successfully help clients create the changes they want in their lives. But when I talk with new coaches about their work, the difficulties they have are rarely about how to do the specific processes that they learned in their trainings. The difficulties they have are about their relationship with their clients.

Understandably, those difficulties emerge out of the interaction between the coach's own relationship style and their clients' unique relationship styles. Increasingly, I have come to realise that **different stages of the change process require different relationship styles**. As a result, some practitioners are good at helping clients who are starting this process of change, some are good at helping clients who are good at finishing the process, and others are good at helping clients who are in the chaos at the centre of the process. If you understand this whole change cycle, you can recognise the strengths of your own helping style, and develop the skills you have previously found difficult. This will not only enable you to guide all your clients more effectively through the entire change process; it will also enrich your own personal life and enable you to make personal changes more effectively yourself. After all, what stops you helping your clients is the same thing that stops you changing yourself.

The Four Change Styles

The model I am presenting here emerged from an unusual source. Bill Moyer is a social change theorist. He works with organisations seeking social changes: organisations working for outcomes such as a more ecological and just society. Moyer has proposed that "There are four different roles activists and social movements need to play in order to successfully create social change; *the citizen, rebel, change agent*, and *reformer*. Each role has different purposes styles, skills and needs, and can be played effectively or ineffectively…. Both individual activists and movement organisations need to understand that social movements require *all four* roles, and that participants and their organisations can choose which ones to play depending on their own makeup and the needs of the movement." (Moyer, 2001, p. 21).

I want to first explain these roles in the social sense that Moyer uses them, and then apply them to individual change work. This will deliver you a model of change that makes sense whether you are working with an individual, a family, an organisation or a society. To make sense in more general terms, I will call Moyers' four styles:

- **The Auditor** (what Moyers called the Citizen)
- **The Rebel**
- **The Innovator** (what Moyers called the change agent)
- **The Reformer.**

The above sequence is the sequence in which the change styles are required, as a person, organisation or society shifts from their old state to their new state. This sequence is what I am calling "The Wheel of Change".

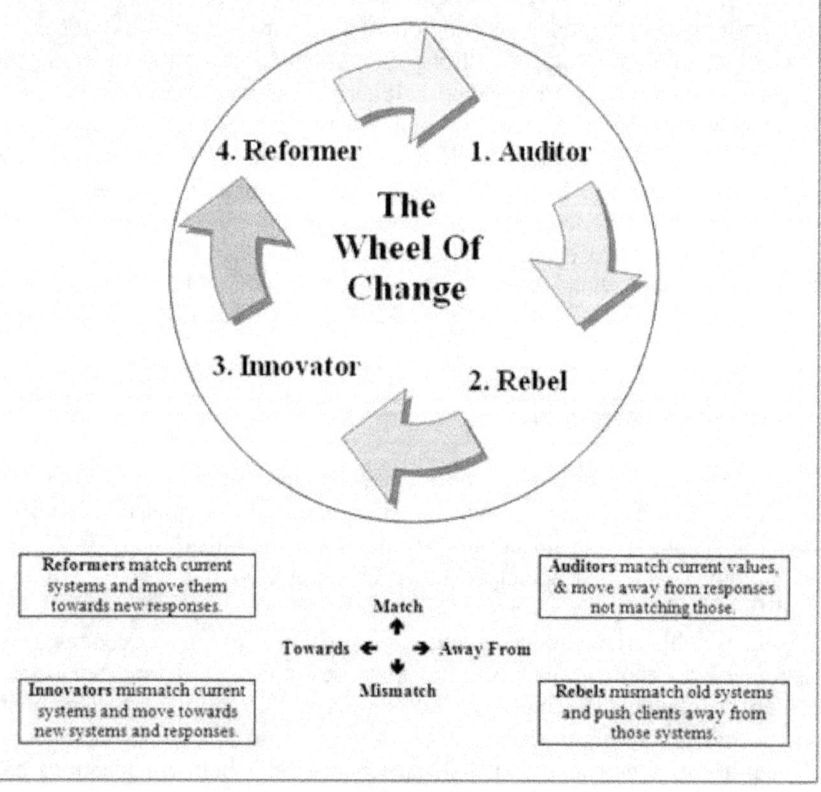

Moyer explains each style in general terms and with examples, and as an NLP Trainer, I notice that there is a structure behind the individual styles. These change styles differ in their relationship to two personality continua (metaprograms) described in NLP (see Charvet, 1997):

- **Preference for Sameness (Matching) vs. Preference for Difference (Mismatching)**
- **Towards Motivation vs. Away-From Motivation**

Matching and Mismatching refer to the extent to which a person pays attention to and appreciates the similarities (between two aspects of their experience, between their view and yours, between what has previously happened and what is happening now etc) or the differences. Sameness people notice similarities and prefer that things stay the same, whereas Differences people notice differences and prefer that things change. Towards and Away From refer to the "direction" in which someone is motivated to act. Some people are motivated mostly towards their goals and desired results, some mostly to avoid risks and problems.

The Four Styles In Social Change

First, I'll explain the four styles in the original context where Moyers observed them: social activism.

Auditors (Citizens) frame a new idea for social change as a necessary way to more fully express the true, underlying values that their society has already committed itself to. They feel part of their society and want it to be even more true to its own ideals. They describe their activism as being a way to be a good citizen and support the true needs of their society. They urge society to move away from those things that don't really fit with its own highest ideals. For example, the African American activist Martin Luther King described his aim as to "fulfil the American dream, not to destroy it." (Quoted in Moyer, 2001, p. 11). This is important at the start of a social change process. It raises issues in a way that those who fear change may find more acceptable, by suggesting that change will actually help stability. Auditors **match** their society and move **away from** its inconsistencies.

Rebels take action to get away from harmful social systems. They directly challenge society as it is. They describe their activism as a way to eliminate injustice and suffering. Often critical both of established society and utopian or reformist plans for a new society, they urge society first to confront and give up what is wrong. Rebuilding is for later. The Anarchist revolutionary Michael Bakunin stated a core Rebel value when he said "The urge to destroy is also a creative urge." This is important to give energy to the change process once it has begun, to ensure that things don't just settle down as they were. When successful, this rebel style provokes such a strong response that it becomes impossible to go back to the old order. Rebels **mismatch** their society and move **away from** its failures.

Innovators (Change Agents) organise and participate in community actions which are an alternative or a vocal opposition movement opposed to the established social systems. They urge society to create a new social order and see their movement as the kernel of this order. The creators of collective industries in the Spanish revolution were Change Agents, as were the creators of the first women's refuges, alternative schools, and eco-villages. This creation is an essential antidote to the rebel style, and it gives the first expression to positive action in the change process. It provides and tests real life models of what the future could be like. Innovators **mismatch** old systems and move **towards** new possibilities.

Reformers work within mainstream systems to get the movement's aims expressed in concrete terms and installed into accepted practice. They see social change as a process of convincing governments, community agencies and corporations to put new schemes into practice. They cooperate with existing agencies to build the new society. New Zealand suffragette Kate Sheppard described her work to get women the vote in these terms. Reform is essential to ensure that the new practices become universally accepted and incorporated into every facet of daily life. Reformers **match** their social systems and **match** the new ideas, and move **towards** a successful blending of these.

Moyer gives several examples of effective integration of these four roles in social change campaigns. One is the campaign to end apartheid style rules about where black people sat on southern USA buses in the mid twentieth century. On December 1st, 1955, African American Rosa Parks was arrested in Montgomery, Alabama, for refusing to give up her seat on the bus for a white person. For 381 days, the 50,000 strong black population of Montgomery boycotted the buses, until the United States supreme court overturned the Alabama segregation laws. Bill Moyer points out that in such a campaign all four of his MAP (Movement Action Plan) roles come into play. "The boycott effectively used all four MAP roles. The citizens [auditors] kept the campaign grounded in the nation's widely held values of democracy and freedom, and their demands were based on the civil rights guaranteed by the U.S. Constitution. Many of the citizens were based in the Christian church, which was revered by the large majority of whites in Montgomery and within mainstream America. The rebels brought attention to the movement with the non-violent bus boycott campaign. The entire black community of Montgomery filled the social change agent [innovators] role by its involvement in the boycott, mass meetings, and car-pooling. Finally, the reformers ultimately won the day through the court case, which was decided favourably by the U. S. Supreme Court." (Moyer, 2001, p. 120)

The Polish Solidarity Movement

We can see the same process at work in the monumental changes that shook Poland as a society in the 1970s and 1980s. In the midst of these changes, it was easy for people to think that there was one correct way to achieve change. We can now see that all four change styles worked together to shift Polish society into the twenty first century. Here I briefly give an example or two from each role.

Jerzy Popiełuszko (auditor)

Blessed Father Jerzy Popiełuszko (1947-1984) was a Roman Catholic priest who argued that the Socialist regime needed to be changed because it did not fit with the deeper Christian values that Polish society had been founded on. In his preaching he explained moral aspects of the painful reality of everyday life, in the light of the teachings of the Church. He did not try to change the Church to which he belonged, but simply to apply its message more congruently in the rest of society. He was thus able to say the unthinkable: that the "unchristian" aspects of Polish socialism needed to change. His voice was one of the first raised against the old regime, and he was one of the first to be silenced in his murder in 1984.

Lech Wałęsa, Anna Walentynowicz (rebels)

Lech Wałęsa (1943-) was an electrician and organiser of the Solidarity movement, famous for his charismatic and challenging style. The organiser of several strikes in the 1970s, he was continually laid off for his activism and was jobless for long periods. Accepting the Nobel Peace prize, he later said "When I recall my own path of life I cannot but speak of the violence, hatred and lies." This contrasts dramatically with Popiełuszko's patient approach. When the community needed this rebellious approach, he was a hero, but Wałęsa was later criticized for his confrontational style and for instigating "war at the top," whereby former Solidarity allies clashed with one another, causing annual changes of government. He agreed to stand for government only because he felt that he "had to". Anna Walentynowicz (1929-2010) was a welder and crane operator. Her firing in August 1980 was the event that ignited the strike at the Lenin Shipyard in Gdańsk that very quickly paralyzed the Baltic coast and a began giant wave of strikes in Poland. The Interfactory Strike Committee [MKS] based in the Gdańsk shipyard eventually transformed itself into Solidarity trade union. Early Solidarity pamphlets described her as a "thorn in the side" of the government, and she became known as the iron woman for her strength of opposition. Like many rebels, Wałęsa and Walentynowicz were the driving force of change, but found themselves dissatisfied with the results of their work. They continued to rebel against the new regime too.

Jacek Kuroń (innovator)

Jacek Kuroń (1934-2004) was a youth worker who gradually shifted from being a staunch defender of Marxism to being a left wing opponent. During the strikes of July and August 1980, Kuroń organized an information network for workers across the country, seeing this as the kernel of a future workers democracy. He launched his famous slogan, "Don't burn the committees [meaning the local party buildings], set up your own" in order to encourage workers to see Solidarity as a positive force rather than merely a rebellion. He organised groups to run their own communities as alternative societies, growing vegetables and self-managing their apartments etc. In 2000, after the changes in Poland, Kuroń and his wife Danuta founded the Jan Józef Lipski Common University in Teremiski. He subsequently became the first dean of this alternative university, continuing his innovator role rather than joining the new system or continuing to rebel.

Tadeusz Mazowiecki (reformer)

Tadeusz Mazowiecki (1927-) was a magazine editor who held government office under the old regime 1961-1972 and then ended up being Poland's first non-communist Prime Minister in 1989. Mazowiecki's government managed to carry out many fundamental reforms in a short period. The political system was thoroughly changed; a full range of civil freedoms as well as a multi-party system were introduced and the country's emblem and name were changed (from the People's Republic of Poland to the Republic of Poland). On December 29, 1989, fundamental changes in the Polish Constitution were made. In 1989, in his first parliamentary speech in Sejm, Mazowiecki talked about a "thick line" (*gruba linia*): "We draw a thick line on what has happened in the past. We will answer for only what we have done to help Poland to rescue her from this crisis from now on". Originally, as Mazowiecki explains, the phrase meant non-liability of his government for damages done to the national economy by previous governments. Media led by Adam Michnik's left-leaning Gazeta Wyborcza later rephrased the term as a "thick stroke" (*gruba kreska*), essentially crossing out the communist past and going easy on the misdoings of the communists. Mazowiecki was the quintessential reformer, fitting a system back together after the change, codifying the changes, and signalling that the time of major change was now over.

The Four Styles In Organisational Change

Now let's consider the four styles in a business organisation that undergoes major changes.

Auditors frame the organisational change needed as a way to more fully express the true, underlying values that the organisation has already committed itself to. They feel part of their organisation, and want to support the true needs of their organisation. They urge the organisation to move away from those errors that don't really fit with its own highest ideals. An example would be the Japanese textile manufacturer Sakichi Toyoda and his son Kiichiro Toyoda. In 1924 Sakichi Toyoda developed a device which automatically stopped his weaving loom when a thread breakage was detected. Kiichiro Toyoda created a car manufacturing company (Toyota) using Jidoka, a production system modelled metaphorically on this loom. Jidoka is a defect detection system that trusts any worker to stop production whenever they detect an error, and direct all attention to repair. When the design plans for the original loom were stolen, Kiichiro Toyoda commented on the benefits of constantly monitoring a system and improving it, saying "Certainly the thieves may be able to follow the blueprints and produce a loom. But we are modifying and improving our looms every day. By the time the thieves have produced a loom from the plans they stole, we will have already advanced well beyond it." (Morgan and Liker, 2006, p 333). This is the Auditors approach to change and indeed it was Kiichiro Toyoda himself who set up what he called the Audit Improvement Committee within Toyota in 1943. Auditing is the essential first step in demonstrating to the organisation that change is necessary. Auditors **match** their organisation's core values and outcomes, and move **away from** its inconsistencies.

Rebels take action to get away from and eliminate what they believe are harmful systems. They directly challenge the organisation as it is. They describe their action as a way to eliminate mistakes, injustices, failures, bureaucracy and waste. Often critical both of established organisational systems and reformist plans for a new system, they urge the organisation first to confront and give up what is wrong. Rebuilding is for later. An example would be Anita Roddick, founder of the Body Shop, who said

"I have always been an activist, an agitator and an entrepreneur rather than a conventional business leader.... Far too much conventional business thinking is about finding out what your competitors are doing and copying them. At The Body Shop, we looked at the opposition and did exactly the opposite. That meant constantly following unmapped paths." The book this quote comes from is fittingly called "Business As Unusual". (Roddick, 2008, front and p 284). Rebels shake up an organisation so that change is pushed onto the agenda and cannot be avoided. Rebels **mismatch** their organisation as well as their industry, and move **away from** the established rules.

Innovators organise and participate in processes which are an alternative or an opposition movement opposed to the established systems. They urge the organisation to create a new system and see their own actions and their own team, department or organisation as the kernel of this order. An example would be Mary Kay Ash, founder of Mary Kay cosmetics, who said "After making a long list of the qualities of the dream company I would have wanted to work for, I thought "Instead of writing a book about how a good company should run, wouldn't it be great if someone ran one." And so the idea of Mary Kay Cosmetics was born." (Williams and Williams, 2003, p 334). In her own book she says "Real leaders... set examples for others by demonstrating good work habits, displaying positive attitudes and possessing a team spirit. True leaders establish success patterns that make everyone think success." (Ash, 2008, p ix). Innovators generate the first successes for a new change process and provide models for an organisation to study the new ideas. Within an organisation, they may set up a project team which test drives the new system, or create trainings where new procedures are role-played. Innovators **mismatch** old systems and move **towards** and create new models.

Reformers work within the mainstream organisational systems to get their vision of a better future expressed in concrete terms. They see organisational change as a process of convincing governments, community agencies and corporations themselves to put new schemes into practice. They cooperate with existing agencies, authorities and systems to build the new structures into what is there. An example would be John H. Johnson, who first published an African American magazine in 1942 at a time when, as a "negro" he was not even allowed to stay at most business hotels across America. By 1995 he was America's leading African American business owner and ran a range of companies that included cosmetics producers, life insurance providers and magazine printers, almost all directed primarily at the African American market. Johnson said "I don't want to destroy the system; I want to get into it."

(Gross, 1996, p 153). "We try to seek out good things, even when everything seems bad," Johnson said in explaining the purpose of his *Ebony* magazine. "We look for breakthroughs, we look for people who have made it, who have succeeded against the odds, who have proven somehow that long shots do come in." His pride in achieving success within the established system is demonstrated by the fact that when his magazines first came out they had difficulty getting any advertising by white companies. By 1995, 80 of the 100 largest advertisers in the USA advertised in Ebony. Reformers spread organisational change through the system, ensuring that all practices are aligned with the new vision. They create operating manuals for actioning the principles that the Rebels demanded and the Innovators test drove. Reformers **match** their organisation and **match** the new ideas, and move **towards** a successful blending of these.

The Four Styles In Personal Change

Now let's consider the styles in a personal coaching or counselling situation. In coaching and counselling, we are assisting people to make changes, which means assisting them to move through the wheel of change. Our clients may have a strong preference for one or other of the change styles: if they compulsively use that style alone they will seem to be "stuck" at that stage in the change cycle. Often a coach or counsellor has a strong preference for working with one of the change styles. They understand the strengths and weaknesses of that style (perhaps because it is their own style) and find it easier to successfully help people with that style. As an example, in 1965 a fascinating film was made demonstrating the work of three very different psychotherapists: Carl Rogers (Client Centred Therapy), Fritz Perls (Gestalt Therapy) and Albert Ellis (Rational Emotive Therapy). The film was produced by Dr Everett L. Shostrom, (Actualizing Therapy) who had been Gloria's principal therapist for some years and helped her integrate the three sessions afterwards. Each of these four therapists focused on a different stage in the wheel of change. Each of them had skills for working with Gloria at one of the four steps in particular.

Auditor: Gloria begins her first session (with Carl Rogers) by stating "Ah, the biggest thing I want, the thing that keeps coming to my mind I want to tell you about is I have a daughter, nine, who at one time I felt had a lot of emotional problems ... and I wish I could stop shaking ... and ah, I'm real conscious of things affecting her. I don't want her to get upset; I don't want to shock her. I want so bad for her to accept me. And we're real open with each other, especially about sex ... and the other day she saw a girl that was single but pregnant and she asked me all about "Can girls get pregnant if they're single?" And the conversation was fine, and I wasn't un-at-ease at all with her, until she asked me if I'd ever made love to a man since I've left her daddy. And I lied to her; and ever since that it keeps coming up to my mind, 'cause I feel so guilty lying to her; 'cause I never lie, and I want her to trust me. And I want, I almost want an answer from you; I want you to tell me if it will affect her wrong if I told her the truth, or what."

At this point Gloria wants her behaviour to be more consistent, to match better. She is moving away from the experience of lying and wants that sense of trust again. She has framed the issue in Citizen/Auditor terms. Carl Rogers matches Gloria's core value of open relationship (even more strongly than Gloria has) and notes that she wants to move away from the harm that has been done to it. He says "And it's this concern about her, and the fact that you really aren't; that this open relationship that has existed between you, now you feel is kind of damaged." She agrees.

As their session moves on, to help her reframing the challenge she faces, Rogers tells her "I guess; I am sure this will sound evasive to you, but it seems to me that perhaps the person you are not being fully honest with is you; because I was very much struck by the fact that you were saying, "If I feel alright about what I have done, whether it's going to bed with a man or what, if I really feel alright about it, then I do not have any concern about what I would tell Pam, or my relationship with her. Gloria agrees and replies "Right. Alright. Now I hear what you are saying. Then alright, then I want to work on accepting me then. I want to work on feeling alright about it. That makes sense. Then that will come natural and then I won't have to worry about Pammy."

Carl Rogers is, in Moyer's terms, a citizen (in my terms an auditor), and he has great skill working with clients at this stage of change in particular. He matches Gloria and helps her move away from what does not work in her own behaviour. He aims to help her be more fully who she is by avoiding incongruity.

Rebel: Gloria's second session is with Fritz Perls. Gloria opens the session with the words, "Right away, I'm scared." and Perls immediately responds "You say you're scared, but you are smiling. I don't understand how one can be scared and smile at the same time." Perls develops this theme a bit further a few minutes later when he remarks, "Are you aware of your smile, you don't believe a word of what you are saying... You are a phony." Gloria argues "Oh, I resent that very much!... I most certainly am not being phony. I will admit this; it's hard for me to show my embarrassment and I hate to be embarrassed. But boy I resent you calling me a phony. Just because I smile when I am embarrassed or I'm put in a corner doesn't mean I'm being a phony!" Perls leans forward to shake her hand and says "Wonderful! Thank you. You didn't smile for the last minute." Gloria comes into this interaction in quite a different state to the one she was in at the start of her session with Rogers. She intuits that this is related to the way Perls looks and sounds, and she may be right. Whatever the cause, she begins in the Rebel style, and Perls is completely at ease with this. In fact, he says nearer the end of the session "Well Gloria, can you sense one thing. We had a good fight." Instead of gently helping Gloria notice that it is she who is being dishonest with herself, as Rogers did, Perls mismatches and challenges her to stop this "being phony". By his own mismatching he then provokes the response that he wants to support (her being congruent, albeit congruently angry). Gloria, in fact, is surprised at how at ease Perls seems in this mismatching and away from exchange. She says about his fighting comment "But you seem so detached. You don't even seem to care that I'm mad at you."

Innovator: Gloria's third session is with Albert Ellis, and again she raises the issue of her dishonesty, this time in relation to the men she dates. Gloria begins by explaining that she has read Dr Ellis' book and she wants to apply his model in her interaction with men. In terms of my model, she announces that she is in Change agent/Innovator mode. After exploring her current thinking patterns (which he calls catastrophising), Ellis encourages Gloria to install a new strategy of thinking, to enable herself to be more "up-front" with the men she dates. He tells her that change doesn't just happen as a result of knowing what is wrong though. It involves her being willing to "work and practice, work and practice how to be yourself." Gloria agrees "I want a step towards working towards this." He says "If you were one of my regular patients I would give you this homework assignment and then check up on you to see whether you can force yourself to <u>open your big mouth and be you</u> for a while…. After a while if you took the risks and forced yourself to, as I said, open your big mouth now (and even though you thought, "Maybe it will come out badly, maybe he won't like me, maybe I'll lose him completely, and so on and so forth.") then you'd start swinging in the groove and being what you want to be, and I would almost guarantee that you'd become more practiced and less inefficient, especially in terms of the shyness, because you wouldn't be focusing on "Oh my God, is this awful. How bad I am." Because you would be focusing on "What a nice individual this is, and how can I enjoy him?" which is the focus of a relationship." Ellis focuses Gloria on the alternative thinking pattern that she could begin putting in place to create a new future. He is very clear about how to help her move towards this different way of behaving, which is to say, he is familiar with the Innovator style. He has little interest, for example, in the "fight" that Perls co-created with her, or in just empathising with her dilemma and helping her clarify her choices the way Rogers did.

Reformer: After the three sessions, Gloria is interviewed by Everett Shostrom and she reviews what she has learned from the three very different encounters. Shostrom's task is of course to help her make sense of the encounters and think about where she goes from here. He knows, in that sense, that he is going to assist Gloria to move through the Reformer phase of change. She explains "First of all, I found I was the most relaxed and the most comfortable with Dr Rogers, and I enjoyed talking to him, and I felt free. And I was afraid of Dr Perls and I wasn't near as comfortable with him. And Dr Ellis I couldn't keep up with. I had to think more with him and I didn't feel as sharp with him. It took me a while to sink in what he was saying.... I felt my more lovable, soft caring self with Dr Rogers, and I even felt more real, even about sex, and I was surprised with that. And Dr Ellis I just ah, I will say I felt cold towards Dr Ellis. I didn't have enough feeling; I was so busy trying to think with him, but I didn't have enough feeling there. And I feel the most, the biggest amount of emotions came up with me in Dr Perls"

So far, Gloria has suggested that only Roger's session was of value, and Shostrom aims to help her find what will be valuable in all of her experiences. Shostrom prompts her "Let's think about each of them again, in terms of what you learned." Gloria explains "I found that if I would just see a man like Dr Rogers, it would be harder for my anger and my spitfire self to come out, so I don't think it would be as full balanced therapy, for me anyway. I'd tend to lean on him too much maybe. And Dr Perls I can see that I'd want to get in there and fight. Especially with Dr Perls and Dr Rogers they're almost a perfect combination for me, because I can be so much more my one side with Dr Perls and the opposite with Dr Rogers. And I felt unfinished especially with Dr Perls. I wanted more; I wanted to go on more. I felt real let down." Shostrom asks her "Would you say you felt your feeling self with Dr Rogers, your fighting self with Dr Perls and your... " and she completes "...my thinking self with Dr Ellis. Exactly." Gloria indicates that she understands that each therapist's style linked to a particular stage of therapy. She says "I feel that if I were to go into therapy, especially being brand new, I would choose someone like Dr Rogers because it wouldn't frighten me so. But I think at the stage of the game I am right now, Dr Perls could be the most valuable to me. So he isn't quite as coddling, but I think I could really get a lot from him... although I'd want to battle with him too."

Gloria, reflecting some 13 years later on her sessions, had extra comments about Fritz Perls. She said that she had now changed her mind, and realised that after the session with Perls, she felt "small, belittled, unimportant, confused and lacking wholeness. In a sense then, I felt a bit of myself destroyed in that short session." (Dolliver, Williams, and Gold, 1980). These comments demonstrate the dangers of the Rebel style when it is not effectively followed by more positive processes. As Gloria said at the time, she felt that her process with Dr Perls was incomplete. Understandably, the risks of this are greater when the interaction is mismatching and away from.

However Dr Shostrom's role itself is also important in the therapeutic process. He helps her link the therapeutic experience into her daily life and think about what she would choose to do next as a result of it. He is not, at this time, attempting to push more change in terms of her honesty with herself, but merely to check how she will use and integrate what she has learned into her future daily life. This is the function of the Reformer.

Using The Four Styles As Steps Of NLP Based Coaching

Gloria observes, in the quotes above, that there is a sequence in which these four styles of coaching are useful. We could consider the whole coaching or therapeutic process, then, as having four stages represented by the four change styles in sequence. To explain this more fully, I will explore a therapy session run by Richard Bandler, identifying these four stages and relating them to my previous model of therapy (RESOLVE).

Auditor: In this example session from 1984, Bandler works with Susan, who suffers panic attacks where she imagines that people in her family may have died in a car accident (Bandler, 1984, p 1-31). Bandler begins the session by asking Susan to tell him what she wants him to do (p 5). He says "Okay Susan. Now why don't you tell me what it is that you would like? I don't know. We just got brought here and wired up, so you have to give me a hint." Bandler matches Susan's experience and checks what she wants to move away from (Bandler, 1984, p 7).

Susan: It's a fear of losing friendships or close relationships. Even when I anticipate a loss that isn't even real I get a panic attack.
Richard: The situation that you are worried about being in is the one of anticipating and thinking about the loss?

Bandler's initial question, notice, is a towards question ("What is it that you would like?" He is well aware that she may be thinking about what she wants to avoid, rather than what she is moving towards. In order to assist Susan to change though, he needs to take her understandably "away from" concern and help clarify her outcome. She is thinking about her problem; he is wanting to assist her to find a solution. To bridge the gap in their styles, Bandler asks Susan to get clearer about what she is moving away from. She tells him she wants some distance from her problem (still an away-from statement), but (paradoxically) also begins to define a more towards-style outcome. He asks her (p 16):

Richard: If you were to have distance how would you know you had it?
Susan: Well I believe I wouldn't feel those feelings. I'd have confidence, some self confidence and I think I could say to myself, well, just because they're not here now doesn't mean that you've lost them and it really doesn't matter. Maybe something happened. And also you can go on. So what if they don't show up. You can go on.

At this "Auditor" stage, Richard Bandler is asking what needs to change so that Susan's life is more fully the way she wants it. The Auditor stage encompasses what my previous model of coaching (RESOLVE) would call Resourceful State, Rapport and Specify Outcome.

Rebel: So far, Richard Bandler has elegantly matched and "reframed" Susan's concerns. He now does a number of things which mismatch Susan's model of the world, in order to show Susan the possibility of change. He asks her to explain to him the strategy she uses to create her problem and plays "devil's advocate" asking how she creates the problem (1984, p.9). Doing this, he evokes, or even *provokes* an understanding that the situation can change.

Richard: But how do you do it? How do you know, how do you get the panic?
Susan: Do you mean what feelings do I get?
Richard: Let's say I had to fill in for you for a day. So one of the parts of my job would be if somebody was late I'd have to have the panic for you. What do I do inside my head in order to have the panic?
Susan: You start telling yourself sentences like ..."
Richard: I've got to talk to myself?
Susan: So and so is late, look they're not here. That means that they may never come.
Richard: Do I say this in a casual tone of voice?
Susan: No

Now Bandler is deliberately mismatching Susan, so that she needs to disagree with him. This particular pattern that Bandler is using to mismatch has been modelled by NLP trainer Tad James and called The Logical Levels of Therapy. It is one example of the provocative styles of coaching that are so effective dealing with a client using the Rebel style. It utilises what other therapies would have called "resistance" and uses their mismatching to create positive responses. James points out that in using this process, Bandler has achieved, by linguistic presupposition, a number of positive shifts in Susan's experience:

- Susan agrees that she causes the panic: she is "at cause".
- Susan agrees that it takes a specific strategy to cause her panic.
- Susan agrees she is expert enough to teach Bandler how to do it; she is not just a helpless victim of panic, but a skilled practitioner of panic.
- Susan describes the process in second person, as if someone else does it, thus getting some sense of distance from it.
- Susan, in order to answer Bandler's last question above, has to consider what would happen if she ran her strategy differently to the way she usually does. She has to mismatch herself.

Bandler continues asking her in similar detail about the visual aspects of her strategy for producing panic. He checks that, by bringing the pictures up close, she can bring on a feeling of panic, and then he compliments her on her success, again drawing her attention to mismatching, this time between what she does and what others do (p 16-17).

Richard: You've obviously mastered this. By the way, do you know that this is an accomplishment?
Susan: You mean to master the panic?
Richard: I bet you a lot of people here couldn't panic.
Susan: Probably not. Not like I do I'm sure.

As a Rebel himself, Bandler provokes mismatching and away from responses. The Rebel stage encompasses what my previous model of coaching (RESOLVE) would call Opening Up the Model of the World.

Innovator: Bandler now shows Susan explicitly what she needs to do to create the distance she wants. He starts off with a simple experiment. He tells her to take the pictures she frightens herself with and alter them (p 18-19):

Richard: Let me show you something else. Go back and look at it again from a distance. Now make the picture darker. Have you ever seen the brightness knob on the television? Turn the brightness down. What happens?

Susan: It creates more distance. Makes it fade away.

Richard: Makes it fade away. Turn the brightness up. Make it brighter. You do this real good. You're fast. And brighter. Now make it closer. What happens now as you make it closer and brighter at the same time?

Susan: I start getting feelings of tension and anxiety.

Richard: It works. Now the only difference is, is this time you did it deliberately.

Bandler has now set her a very sensory specific goal to work towards. In his work with Susan, Richard Bandler guides her through the NLP Swish technique, which installs a more resourceful way of responding to the situation. The process gets her to alter her picture rapidly, shifting to what NLP calls a dissociated viewpoint (giving her the distance she has been asking for). Repeating this several times "installs" the new perspective in her brain. This is a classic Innovator coaching process, creating a model of what Susan could do when her entire response has changed.

Richard: Go ahead and make the picture bright and focus on it. Close your eyes again, move right in and as you approach very closely to it you begin to feel the panic. What I want you to do is to see in the small, lower left hand corner a little tiny dark square that has a picture of you the way you would be if you had made this change. It's real darkened in the corner but suddenly the big picture begins to get darker and the other one begins to expand and become brighter until it fills the whole screen. But you can do it faster than that. There you go. Hurry up. Until you can see yourself the way you would be. Now I want you to do the exact same thing. I want you to do it five times real fast.

In this Innovator stage, Bandler is helping Susan move towards an innovative new response to the situation. The Innovator stage encompasses what my previous model of coaching (RESOLVE) would call Leading.

Reformer: Next, Bandler ensures that Susan is fully convinced that she has changed. His aim is to show her how this new response is going to work for her. He tells her (p 24-25):

Richard: You go ahead this time and go back and look at that panic. See if you can hold it. I want you to try as much as you can in vain.

Susan: It's hard. I just keep getting white.

Richard: What do you mean?

Susan: I'm having trouble doing it.
Richard: I thought you'd mastered that.
Susan: I am a master at panic. Right now all I'm getting is white....
Richard: Try it once more. Just to be sure.
Susan: I really just can't do it.

Once he has this clear, unequivocal statement verifying the change, Bandler moves on to what NLP would call "futurepacing" (planning for the future effects of the change). He is checking that the new response "fits" with Susan's current life, and that it matches what she has wanted. He wants her to think about how this will move her towards the life she has wanted (i.e. he wants to guide her through the Reformer phase of change). He gives her a real world task to do to test her experience (to meet him in 10 minutes – he never turned up!). He says (p 25-26):

Richard: You've got to keep your promise. You said it would change your whole life.
Susan: Yeah.
Richard: Now you have to keep your end of the bargain.
Susan: Well I think if I don't have this problem that it is going to change. Because it's going to affect everything.
Richard: You're not going to be able to do it.
Susan: That would be wonderful.
Richard: Try it
Susan: I've tried it.
Richard: Try it now.
Susan: I just can't get it. I just can't get it.
Richard: Well if it was so easy before and it's so hard now, that's an indication. You can go try it in the real world. I tell you what. Why don't you go outside by the coffee machine and I'll meet you there in ten minutes?

Eight months later, Susan was interviewed by Michael Saggese about her experience. She told him (p28-30):

Susan: When I left the studio that day I knew I felt really good but I was still a little sceptical of what had happened because my panics are so bad and so painful to me. I went home that evening and the same situation occurred. Someone was supposed to come and they didn't show up for several hours. And I didn't get upset at all. I was able to lie down and take a nap. It didn't upset me at all. I was just truly amazed....
Michael: And that change is still holding up more than eight months down the road now.
Susan: Right.

Michael: How do you feel about that?
Susan: You don't know what a relief it is!

As the Innovator stage matches and moves towards the future, it encompasses what my previous model of coaching (RESOLVE) would call Verify Change and Ecological Exit.

Developing Your Flexibility With The Metaprograms

To be able to do effective coaching, it is useful to have the flexibility to match and mismatch, and to move away from as well as towards. As you guide your client though these different styles, your own ability to use each style facilitates their progress. It is also useful to know how to respond to each style in order to ensure the person is not limited by that style. For example, it is useful to be able to respond to someone who moves away from problems in such a way as to enable them to also reach their desired outcomes.

Next I want to review in more detail what I mean by matching, mismatching, towards and away from. I want to give some general suggestions about responding to these styles (based on the work of NLP Trainer Shelle Rose Charvet, 1997), and then come back to thinking about how to work therapeutically in a coaching situation with each style.

Sameness and Difference

When people pay attention to the world, they can either notice mostly the similarities or mostly the differences (or some of each). People who notice sameness most (matchers) will also like things to stay the same, and they like to agree with others. Reformers and Citizens (Auditors) tend to use matching more. People who notice differences more (mismatchers) will also like to change, and they like to clarify differences with people. Change agents (Innovators) and Rebels tend to use mismatching more. To the sameness person, a friend is someone who shares your views and does things together in the same way as you. To the differences person, a friend is someone who tells you "where they stand", opens your life up to new things, and respects your uniqueness. Using NLP questionnaires, we have found that most of the population identifies sameness and then notices the exceptions or differences within that (i.e. they are in the middle of the continuum).

Certain careers (the military, empathic counselling, factory process work, and nursing, for example) encourage paying attention to sameness.

Other careers (such as accounting, legal work, quality control, university lecturing and political activism) encourage attention to differences. People who sort mostly for differences will feel interested when a project is described as "revolutionary", "new", "totally unique", "unheard of", and "a complete turnaround". People sorting for sameness will prefer projects described as "maintaining", "identical in style", and "like earlier projects". People sorting for sameness and then noticing the exceptions to that will enjoy projects described as "better", "more advanced", "improved", "a further development"

To find out whether someone mainly pays attention to differences or to similarities, you'd ask them, "What is the relationship between what you're doing in this context this year and what you were doing last year?" There are three main possible results of asking the question:
1)   Sameness: It's exactly the same.
2)   Sameness with exception: There's a lot of similarity except that it has developed.
3)   Difference: It's totally different. OR What do you mean by "relationship?"

In an organisational change context, Auditors (Citizens) and Reformers are sameness focused. Rebels and Innovators (Change Agents) sort mainly for differences. How can you get people with these two different personality types to work together in a group or get an individual with a "compulsive pattern" to have more flexibility? There are several things you can do to help others to get their pattern to work better for them, for example:

For working with sameness people:
•   Build markers of familiarity into change processes for similarities people. Show them how to detect what will be the same or be preserved over the course of the changes.
•   Give sameness people the task of monitoring ongoing processes needed for stability, and identifying what works already.

For working with differences people:
•   Build differences and variations into any repetitive task for a differences person.
•   Give differences people the task of identifying flaws, and thinking up new ideas.
•   Give differences people something to disagree with that leaves the things they want stable.

- Invite differences people to consider a decision from the other side, using phrases such as: "Maybe you **don't** want to do it this new way?" "It's a good idea, **do you not think so?**"
- Do *not* use the words "have to" and "must" with differences people, unless you want them to disagree. Use "could".

Much of change depends on the ability to mismatch. As George Bernard Shaw said in his 1903 "Maxims for Revolutionists", "The reasonable man adapts himself to the world; the unreasonable one persists in trying to adapt the world to himself. Therefore, all progress depends on the unreasonable man." On the other hand, there is an important effect of matching that people in organisations or one-to-one relationships benefit from understanding. Matching is the basis for keeping people working together, because matching is what creates "rapport". Rapport is the sense that you have a common bond with someone, that you're on the same wavelength, that you see eye-to-eye. It's the feeling of shared understanding that happens between old friends.

Double Handshake: A Sameness-Differences Exercise

Stand in a pair and look at the person in front of you. Realise that you could recognise this person as different, compared to any of the 7 billion people of the planet. They are different to all humans who have ever lived, and different to all who ever will live. There is no-one else who has exactly the same appearance, life experiences and opinions as this person. Meeting them is a unique moment in your life. As you realise this, reach out and hold their right hand with your right hand.

Look at them again, and realise that the shape of their face, the colour of their eyes and the type of hair they have has been inherited from their parents. When you look at them, you see into their family of origin. The way they speak and even their gestures are learned in a social context. Looking at them, you are looking at their culture and their social group. Their DNA is mostly the same as that of every other human being on the planet, including you. Looking into their eyes you look into the eyes of all humanity, and your brain recognises your common ancestry with them. As they breathe, notice that they breathe in air that is produced by the plants on this planet, and as they breathe out they nourish those plants. They have co-evolved with all the other living things on this planet and could not have emerged outside it. When you look at this person, you look at one of the fruits of the ecosystem of the whole planet. Their body is made of atoms from the sun, and looking into their eyes, you see the structure of the universe revealed. As you understand their inseparability from all that exists, reach out and hold their left hand with your right hand.

Now, without needing to think of any particular meaning, reach out and take their right hand in your right hand, and reach out over the top of this and take their left hand in your left hand. Allow your body to understand them as simultaneously unique in all history, and one with all that exists.

Towards And Away From

When people motivate themselves to act, they can either notice mostly what they are wanting to change or move *away from* (the problems), or mostly the things they want to create or move *towards* (the solutions), or some of each. People who move Towards their desired outcomes are energized and excited by their goals, and may at times seem to naively not notice the problems they may face. Reformers and Change Agents or Innovators (using Moyer's model of social change roles) tend to be motivated Towards more. People who move Away From undesirable problems more will be energized by challenges, and may at times seem to get "stuck" complaining about the various crises, challenges and unacceptable events they want to draw attention to. Citizens (Auditors) and Rebels tend to be motivated Away From more.

To the Towards person, what matters is the vision, the result that we are moving towards. They can explain in detail what results they want, but may be unclear about what the current situation is. To the Away From person, what matters is the challenge in the current situation. They can explain in detail what must be changed and why, but may be unclear exactly what they want instead. Using NLP questionnaires, we have found that about 40% of the population mainly uses Away From motivation, about 40% mainly uses Towards motivation, and about 20% uses both equally.

Certain career paths (medicine, insurance, and policing, for example) encourage paying attention to what is wrong and moving away from it. Other career paths (such as tourism, artistic design and) encourage attention to desired results and moving towards these. People who are motivated Towards will feel interested when a project is described with words such as "achieving", "benefits", "advantages" and "what you've wanted". People who are motivated Away From will prefer projects described with words such as "solve", "avoid", "get rid of", "prevent", and "find out what's wrong".

To find out whether someone mainly motivates themselves Towards or Away From, you'd ask them, "Why is this important to you?" There are

three main possible results of asking the question:
a) Towards: Because it gets me what I want.
b) Away From: Because it helps me avoid what I don't want.
c) Towards and Away From: Because it get me what I want and avoids what I don't want.

A fully "towards" person gets up in the morning by thinking of all the things they want to achieve. The "away from" person gets up by thinking of all the problems they'll have if they don't get up soon. A towards motivated entrepreneur wants to earn money because of all the thing they can do with it. An away from motivated entrepreneur is more interested in avoiding bankruptcy and poverty.

Anthony Robbins tells of a business disagreement he and his partners had with a man who'd done some work for them. Robbins began their meeting by telling the man that he wanted to create an outcome that would work well for both of them. The man said that didn't interest him - he just wanted Robbins attorney to stop calling and hassling him. Puzzled, Robbins suggested that at least in a basic way they were all committed to helping both themselves and others experience better quality of life. The man disagreed.

At this point, Robbins says, a light bulb finally lit up inside his head and he changed gears. He told the man that if they didn't sort out the issue within the next sixty seconds, Robbins was not going to carry on negotiating. He suggested that the man check inside to see "if you're willing to pay the price that you're going to have to pay...Because I'm going to continually tell people about how you behaved here and what you did...You can decide now that you want to work this thing out or otherwise you're going to lose everything... Check me out. See if I'm congruent" .It took him twenty seconds to jump up and say to Robbins "Look guys, I always wanted to work with you. I know we can work this out." Robbins points out that the man didn't do it grudgingly. "He got up enthusiastically, as though we were true pals. He said "I just wanted to know we could talk."

Robbins had recognised the man's "away from" motivation. Finding a co-operative solution just didn't mean anything to him. Avoiding conflict and embarrassment did. If Robbins had used such threatening language with a "towards" person they'd have left the room. But for this man, reminding him what he could lose actually motivated him to co-operate fully. Robbins NLP training enabled him to create rapport with someone others might have considered a lost cause. In doing so it saved him a costly court case <u>and</u> won him a useful ally (Robbins, 1986, p 270).

On the day Nelson Mandela became president of South Africa, he revealed his ability to use both towards and away from language, saying "My government's commitment to create a people-centred society of liberty binds us to the pursuit of the goals... [Towards language] ... of freedom from hunger, freedom from deprivation, freedom from ignorance, freedom from suppression and freedom from fear. [Away From language]" (Quoted in Charvet, 1997, p 39)

How can you get people with these two different personality types to work together in a group or get an individual with a "compulsive pattern" to have more flexibility? There are several things you can do to help others to get their pattern to work better for them, for example:

For working with Towards people:
- Show them how checking for possible safety and resistance issues will help in reaching goals more effectively.
- Give them the task of identifying and designing the progress towards goals.

For working with Away From people:
- Explain the problems that setting a clear goal will help solve.
- Describe goal-setting as creating deadlines for solving the problems.
- Give them the task of identifying, monitoring and solving the problems in a plan.
- Have them do something (anything) and then "fix it" as a way of reaching the outcome they are aiming for.

Aligning Neurological Levels (An Away-From and Towards Exercise) From Robert Dilts

1. Choose a problem you've had, and would like to change in a fundamental way.

2. Stand somewhere with plenty of space in front of you (enough to step forward six times). Think of the environment where the problem (that you want to move away from) occurs. Notice what you see, and listen to the sounds there.

3. Take a step forward. Consider what you actually do and say in the problem situation. Just run a movie of what happens with that problem.

4. Take another step forward. When you do those things, what capabilities, what skills are you using (perhaps habits that you wish you didn't use, but that happen automatically, or skills that don't seem to work for you)? And what skills are you not using?

5. Take another step forward. Consider what beliefs you are acting on in that situation. What is important to you when you are in that situation (it may be just changing the situation)? What do you find yourself believing about your potential or lack of it, and about the situation that you want to change?

6. Take another step forward. Who are "you" in this situation? What kind of person are you in this situation and what would you like to change about that?

7. Take another step forward, and remember that you are here for a reason. You only got yourself into that situation because, in a wider sense, you're here on earth for a reason. You may not know in words what that reason is, but notice it now. Realise that this "reason" connects you to something vast. You may think of it as God, as the universe and the laws of nature, as consciousness or beingness, or just as humanity. But it is a vast source of energy, in front of you now.

8. Take another step forward, into that source of energy. Feel its power.

9. As you feel that power, take a step back and notice how that power gives renewed strength to your mission, your reason. Take another step back and feel how that power transforms your sense of who you are. Take another step back and feel how that power changes what you believe about that situation you were considering; changes what seems important there. Take another step back and notice how it changes what skills you can use there, gives you new choices. Take another step back and be aware of how using those skills, with that vast power, changes what you will do and say there. Take another step back and be aware how those actions, done with that power, will change the situation itself.

10. Thank that power.

Coaching Processes That Focus On The Change Style At Each Stage

Now that we have covered all the core background information about this model, I will introduce four core models of coaching that I believe are particularly suited to these four stages of change. In each case I will discuss how to use that methodology to deal with clients who seems stuck in the cycle of change at their usual and preferred style of operating. The aim of these models is both to meet the client where they are (in their current change style) and to assist them to move on through the change process rather than becoming stuck in that style. The coaching models I will introduce are just examples of working with each stage. I have chosen them because they all emerged from the same basis (largely the work of Milton Erickson and the collection of change models associated with Neuro Linguistic Programming) and form an easily integrated unit. In each case, my aim is not to cover fully how to use each model (a subject that would take at least four books) but simply to frame the model in terms of the wheel of change. Previously, most writers have described these very different models of coaching as a result of therapists/coaches having different styles themselves. One of my hopes is that coaches can now identify different styles of coaching as effective responses to <u>clients</u> using different styles in their attempt to change. The models I will review are:

- Solution Focused Coaching (For dealing with the Auditor style/stage)
- Provocative Coaching (For dealing with the Rebel style/stage)
- NLP - Strategy Creation (For dealing with the Innovator style/stage)
- Tasking (For dealing with the Reformer style/stage)

Dealing With The Client Who Matches and Moves Away From: Reflective Coaching

Over 50% of the clients who come to me in counselling, and many coaching clients present with comments that are matching and away from. They know that they want things to change, but when I ask them what they want instead, their mind keeps going back to what they have already. Their internal representations have not changed in content (they still imagine the <u>same</u> thing they have been doing for the last several years) but the feeling response to it is now away-from.

To get the away-from oriented client to think towards their goals, I utilise pacing (creating similarity, letting them know that I can "walk alongside them") and then leading (inviting them to consider things differently). The extent to which I convey the feeling that I understand them is the extent to which they will feel safe next to consider my new "towards" frame. Again, we have a great deal of evidence backing up the value of both non-verbal and verbal pacing.

Psychology researcher Lawrence Rosenblum notes that numerous studies now show that matching someone else's behaviour non-verbally enables them to be more open to considering your suggestions. He lists the following examples "Being subtly imitated by a "negotiator" would make you more likely to agree with his or her opinion (Maddux et alia, 2008). Being imitated by a pretend cola salesman would make you more likely to rate the soda favourably and drink more of it during your interaction. You'd give a higher tip to a waitress who imitates your order verbatim rather than paraphrasing (van Baaren et alia, 2004). And you'd even rate a computer animated "interviewer" as more persuasive and positive if it subtly imitated your own head nodding (Bailenson and Yee, 2005). Finally, when GPS driving directions are conveyed by a voice that matches your own vocal emotion, you're less distracted than if provided directions by a voice not matching your emotion (Jonsson et alia, 2008)." In Lawrence Rosenblum's book "See What I'm Saying" (Rosenblum, 2010, p 211) he lists several other examples of this research. People who sing in time with each other (as opposed to singing the same song but not in unison) or walk in step with each other for a few minutes (as opposed to simply walking beside each other) are then much more cooperative with each other. They also report "a feeling of connectedness and trust with their partner subjects" after doing this (Wiltermuth and Heath, 2009).

Research identifying the effectiveness of *verbal* pacing (often called "reflective listening"; restating what the person said in similar words) first emerged in 1950, and a summary of the 50 years of continuing evidence for this core helping skill is presented by Allen Bergin and Sol Garfield (1994) in their Handbook of Psychotherapy. It is the core skill used by Carl Rogers. Building rapport in NLP terms also includes pacing the person's core metaprograms (personality style) and values as these are revealed. Clients have been shown, for example, to prefer a counsellor whose word use matches their own representational system (visual, auditory, kinesthetic or auditory digital) by a ratio of three to one! (Brockman, 1980). The type of reflective statement which will be useful varies depending on how fully the Practitioner has succeeded in establishing rapport already. Early on, replies which match the client's conscious experience (as expressed in their words) will be most acceptable. Later on, replies which match the client's semi-conscious values, beliefs and evolving sense of identity will be accepted and may be more powerful (Carkhuff, 1973). Consider the following client situation and statement.

A mother is talking about her relationship with her 17 year old son. She has discussed his use of illegal drugs and her attempts to caution him about the dangers of these. She has teary eyes and looks down, shaking her head as she speaks. "He knows he can get away with it; that's the thing. If he just stays in his room and sulks for a couple of days, I just about go crazy with worry. Eventually, he gets whatever he wants - permission to go out with his friends, use of the car. In the end, I give in, and I know it's my own fault. I can hardly blame him, when I'm so inconsistent."

Reflective listening to this message could acknowledge:
- Key words stated by the client e.g. "Inconsistent." Or, emphasizing the second person personal pronoun "You worry."
- Simple facts reported by the client e.g. "So at the start you tell him he can't have what he wants, but if he continues, that concern leads you to give in and let him have it." You can enhance the separation between the way the client experienced the facts (their "map" of what happened), and the actual events ("the territory") by using perceptual verbs e.g. "So it seems to you at those times as if you have no choice but to give in."
- The internal emotional state of the client as surmised from behaviour and statements e.g. "You feel so worried, and you feel upset and guilty; is that right?"
- The facts and the internal emotional state that they have triggered e.g. "You feel worried about what he's up to, and you feel disappointed in yourself for giving in to him too; is that it?"
- A summary of the client's story so far e.g. "So there are several levels to this problem. There are things like the drug taking that you've been concerned about. And then there's the interaction between the two of you as you try to stop those other problems and end up giving in to him. Right?"
- Dilemmas or incongruities implied by the client's statements and/or behaviour. e.g. "Let me check this then. Sounds like an internal conflict. On the one hand, you worry about him and want him to be happy. On the other hand, you'd like to be more assertive and stick to your own decisions, even if that results in conflict. Does that make sense to you?" This kind of reflecting of incongruity is a core auditor skill.
- The deeper significance or meaning of the experiences reported by the client, in terms of their basic values, beliefs, and sense of identity. e.g. "I get the impression that the person that you feel *most* disappointed with at those times is actually yourself. The issue you're dealing with sounds like it's also about you taking charge of your *own* life and being more certain about what you want. Is that close?"

♦ The client's positive outcome e.g. "Are you saying you'd like to find some way that you can be more consistent, and less swayed by his behaviour?"

While the later replies in this list invite a deeper response, any of these replies has a good chance of communicating to the client that she is understood and that the Coach recognises her own positive intentions. The purpose of reflective listening is partially to reassure the person that they are not being blamed, judged, or controlled by the consultant. This meta-communication creates a safe environment for the client to explore their dilemmas and begin to identify their own outcome. At the same time, these replies are far from "non-directive". They all share a similar focus or "frame". Part of this "frame" is the focusing on the client's own responses, rather than the behaviour of other people (such as her son). A metacommunication of this client-centred focus is that the aim of consulting is to help her change her *own* responses; to take charge of her *own* maps and state, to be "at cause".

Dealing With The Client Who Mismatches and Moves Away From: Provocative Coaching

At the away from and mismatching phase of the change cycle, one of the most significant challenges is for the client to begin to blame the "failure" of the change process on the coach and the model of change being used. This shifts their attention away from their own control of events, and reduces their motivation to act on their own. Clients who believe that they are in charge of their own responses ("At cause", to use the NLP jargon) do far better in numerous research studies with a variety of different models of therapy (Miller et alia, 1996, p 319, 325). Furthermore, research shows that this sense of being in control is not a stable "quality" that some clients have and others do not; it varies over the course of their interaction with the helper. Successful therapy has been shown to result first in a shift in the "locus of control", and then in the desired success (Miller et alia, 1996, p 326). When my client presents using mostly mismatching and away-from language, I want to "pace" that style and <u>then</u> provoke them into creating their own strong towards motivation.

Frank Farrelly was the author of a book called Provocative Therapy focusing on radical therapeutic moves intended to jolt the client out of the helpless, blaming mindset. This approach was modelled by <u>Richard Bandler</u> during the early years of <u>Neuro-Linguistic Programming</u> and Bandler later commented "If you think I'm crazy, you should meet Frank!" Farrelly says "Provocative Therapy is a system of psychotherapy in which the therapist plays the devil's advocate, siding with the negative half of the client's ambivalence toward his life's goals, his relationships, work and the structures within which he lives."

Farrelly initially worked with Carl Rogers' model but began to have problems with the two metaphors of therapy that Rogers found most useful. "Two images that seemed to have real meaning for Carl at this time, when speaking of the role of the therapist, were the roles of midwife and horticulturist. The horticulturist, I remember his saying a number of times, merely provided the appropriate conditions for the seed's growth. In the same way he felt this was what the therapist did to provide growth for the client. And the midwife, another analogy he used a number of times, did not create the person but merely assisted in his birth. I was becoming increasingly frustrated in my work with patients and clients using the client centered approach and waiting for the client to initiate most if not all actions and behaviors. And I remember distinctly the meeting in which finally I vented my frustration and told the project clinical meeting, "I'm sick and tired of trying to be a horticulturist or a midwife. I'm not any good in either role. What I want to do is to pry apart these people's shells, penetrate through to their core, and inject some *LIFE* into them." (In saying this I was pulling my hands apart, throwing my fist forward, and suddenly opening my hand with splayed fingers to indicate "injecting some life in them") Allyn Roberts, who was listening, chuckled and stated, "Frank, you're so phallic!"' " (Farrelly, 1974, p20)

This story itself is shocking in the way that Provocative Therapy is shocking. Farrelly says he starts from a base of warm-hearted humour and aims to call out (the original meaning of pro-voke) five responses from the client. The client will:

1.   Affirm his self-worth, both verbally and behaviourally.
2.   Assert himself appropriately both in task performances and relationships.
3.   Defend himself realistically.
4.   Engage in psycho-social reality testing and learn the necessary discriminations to respond adaptively. Global perceptions lead to global, stereotyped responses; differentiated perceptions lead to adaptive responses.
5.   Engage in risk-taking behaviours in personal relationships, especially communicating affection and vulnerability to significant others with immediacy as they are authentically experienced by the client.

We have already considered two examples of provocative approaches in this article: Fritz Perls use of the accusation that Gloria is "a phony", and Richard Bandler's use of the temporary employment agency process (called Logical Levels of Therapy by Tad James) with Susan. NLP Trainer Nick Kemp has modelled the provocative coaching style (http://www.provocativechangeworks.com/) and lists the following types of intervention:

- **Confusion:** The coach may deliberately mishear the client, or may suggest insane solutions to their problem in order to break them out of their sense of certainty about the choices available. After a time in this confusion, it may be impossible for the client to congruently return to their old behaviour.

- **Digital Choices:** The coach may present the client with two polarised and exaggerated choices, and alternate between arguing for one and arguing for the other.

- **Detail, Detail, Detail:** The coach may keep asking the client for more and more irrelevant detail about their problem, until the client shift to seeing a larger picture in reaction.

- **Devil's Advocate:** The coach may point out the many advantages of not solving the problem, so that eventually the client more and more strongly defends their need to do whatever it takes to change.

- **Going Global:** The coach may discuss the problem as if it is an example of a much larger and more exaggerated issue, such as their general failure as a human being or their destiny, forcing them to see it as the smaller and easier issue that it is.

- **Interrupting:** The coach may interrupt the client's flow of thought by asking a series of questions and not giving the client time to reply, by talking about irrelevant subjects and so on, thus breaking the rigid thinking strategy that the client has evolved.

- **More of the Same:** The coach may prescribe the problem, recommending other places that the client could create the same difficulty, and giving more and more reasons why they should continue with their current responses to it.

- **Other People's Eyes:** The coach may ask the client to explain what their boss, spouse, or mother would think and suggest, thus requiring them to shift to a whole new (possibly bizarre) way of thinking about the problem. Often the client will then have new understanding of how others' behaviours affect them and how their behaviour affects others.

- **Time:** The coach may ask the client how this problem fits in the larger perspective of time, checking how old the client is, or how long they have been acting in the same way, and thus create a new sense of the importance of changing in this moment.

- **Here and Now:** the coach may focus completely on what is happening in this present moment and ignore any comments about other times and places when the client believes the problem occurs.
- **Trance:** The coach may take advantage of the shock produced by any of the previous techniques by suggesting that the client go into a trance and make changes at the unconscious level.

The temporary employment agency process of Richard Bandler has 5 steps:

1. Restate the client's problem "So you say…"
2. Ask them to be precise "How specifically…?"
3. Ask them how they do the problem "So how do you…?"
4. Ask them how I would do the problem "So if I come from a temporary employment agency and I want to do this, how do I…?"
5. Ask them if it would still work when I change it "So would it still work if I…?"

Dr Milton Erickson, who was one of the original models studied in the development of NLP, considered psychotherapy to be first and foremost a naturalistic phenomenon. He told an interesting story about how he decided to become a psychotherapist himself (Gordon and Meyers-Anderson, 1981, p 167-172). When Milton was ten years old, and living in a small town in Wisconsin, a notorious criminal named Joe was released into his community after a long jail term.

Within four days of Joe's return, three of the town's stores were broken into at night. Everyone in the village was terrified, as Joe had a history of uncontrolled violence, both in and outside of jail. At this time, there was a young unmarried woman named Susie, whose father was a very wealthy farmer near the town. Susie was in town on an errand for her father, when Joe wandered out onto the sidewalk and blocked her path. Joe looked Susie up and down very slowly, and she responded in kind. "Can I take you to the dance next Friday?" Joe asked. Susie, considered the most "choosy" woman in town, thought for a moment, and said "You can if you're a gentleman." Joe stepped out of her way and she went on down the street.

The next morning, boxes with all the stolen goods were left outside the three stores. Joe walked out to Susie's farm that day and got himself hired as a labourer. He went to the dance with her, that Friday and every Friday for some time. And he behaved in every way like a gentleman.

The two of them were married the next year, and Joe began helping manage the farm. When Milton considered what to do with his future at the end of Elementary school, it was Joe who encouraged him, as he did many other children, to go on to High School and then to University. By then, Joe was on the school Board and was one of the "pillars" of the community.

Milton said about this "And all the psychotherapy Joe received was "You can if you're a gentleman." ...Psychotherapy has to occur within the patient, everything has to be done by the patient, and the patient has to have a motivation." Erickson's interest was in how to create this motivation within the client, and allow them to solve their own problems. From observing Joe, he had a strong belief that even the most "hopeless case" could change if this was achieved. Provocative therapy focuses entirely on creating this motivation.

Dealing With The Client Who Mismatches and Moves Towards: Solution Focused NLP Coaching

Neuro Linguistic Programming (NLP) has already been utilised significantly in the field of coaching. Most of the change processes in NLP assume that the client is operating largely from a towards and mismatching style. At this stage, the client is moving towards new responses; new strategies for responding to the cues that used to trigger their problem states of mind and problem strategies. They are ready to create something new. The cases of Post Traumatic Stress Disorder I worked with in Bosnia-Herzegovina provide a good example situation to explain the range of choices NLP offers. In persons with PTSD, memories of a traumatic event such as a motor vehicle accident may be reactivated by any future events that involve motor vehicles or any events that generate high levels of adrenaline in the body. The person has of course had many other mildly disturbing experiences that they have coped with effectively in their life before (by "reframing" the meaning of the event, and by distancing themselves as they review the event, for example). But in the case of their memory of the motor vehicle accident, they find themselves unable to use these healthy skills or "resources". This is because as soon as they begin to re-experience the traumatic event, they are operating from a neural network (a brain system storing the memory of the original challenge) which has inadequate connection to their "healthy" state. When reliving the accident, they are unable to remember their usual skills. They can only run the strategies that are associated with the neural networks laid down at the time of the crash. The strategies and the state of mind they were in at that time are linked together.

Using NLP-based techniques, we have several choices for getting the resources from where they reside in the person's other neural networks, and shifting them into the neural network where the accident has been coded. The following categorisation of these methods is not intended to be comprehensive. NLP is a vast and constantly evolving field, and these are merely some of the models in use within that field. NLP change processes tend to assume that the client knows their outcome (towards) and is ready to do something new and different (mismatching). On NLP-based coaching trainings, of course, most of our coaches are operating in this stage as we work with them, and the challenge for new practitioners is that often their clients in the real world are responding to change with a very different style.

To summarise the hundreds of NLP change choices, I group the NLP interventions in ten categories:

1. Anchoring (in the PTSD example, having the person remember a time they felt relaxed, get back that feeling, and associate that relaxation with the situation they want to change their response to)
2. Installing a new strategy (rehearsing the person through a new sequence of responses to use each time they experience discomfort related to the original challenge or each time they are in situations that remind them of the challenge)
3. Changing submodalities (having the person alter the qualities of the memory they have trouble with, for example by distancing themselves from it visually in their mind)
4. Trancework (relaxing the person and asking their unconscious mind to deal with that type of situation more resourcefully)
5. Parts Integration (connecting the part of their brain that is trying to protect them from further danger by panic, with the part of them that wants to relax)
6. Time Line changes (going back to the time in their memory storage where they first experienced the problem and changing the way they recall that memory)
7. Linguistic reframing (changing their understanding of the <u>meaning</u> of the events they went through, so those events no longer trigger panic)
8. Changing interpersonal dynamics (teaching them interpersonal skills to get support and meet their needs in other ways in their daily life)
9. Changing physiological contexts (changing the body posture they use to recall the events, for example having them recall the events while doing rapid side to side eye movements or while doing some enjoyable and challenging physical activity)

10. Tasking (Giving the client a task to complete in their own time, in order to produce one of the above results)

All these techniques presuppose that the client knows what they want (has a solution or outcome to move towards). It is possible to guide someone into a solution or towards framework by simply reflecting their problem statement as a goal. Simplistically, if a person says "I'm hungry." I can restate "You'd like something to eat." Similarly, if they say "I feel really lonely in my life. I don't get to meet new people and it seems like I'm always by myself." I could reply "You'd like to learn new ways of meeting people and create a life where you feel more in contact." If the person responds to this statement by talking more about how they want to move away from their problem, then I may simply accept that we have not fully established rapport yet. In NLP terms, any "resistance" to my leading onward is an indication of inadequate pacing or rapport.

Another choice at this point is to use Solution focused questions. Research on the Solution Focused Coaching model (a model closely allied with NLP) confirms that clients improve after questions from their helper which focus on what outcome the client has. Also, the amount of discussion of solutions and outcomes in the first session is strongly correlated to the chances that the client will continue with the change process (Miller et alia, 1996, p 259). William Miller has done an overview of the research into successful psychotherapy, in which he identifies that enabling the client to set their own goal for therapy significantly increases their commitment to therapy and enhances the results (Miller, 1985). Solution focused coaches focus their entire intervention on eliciting the client's own outcomes and solutions. As de Shazer reports, this results in 75% success over four to six sessions (Chevalier, 1995). That is to say, setting an outcome is itself a change process.

Fundamentally, I ask core "towards" questions which help the client shift from thinking about problems to thinking about solutions; for example:
- "What has to be different as a result of you talking to me?"
- "What do you want to achieve?"
- "How will you know that this problem is solved?"
- "What would need to happen for you to feel that this problem was solved?"
- "When this problem is solved, what will you be doing and feeling instead of what you used to do and feel?"

If the person presents an issue about someone else (i.e. they want me to "fix" someone else or help them to "fix" someone else), I help them refocus on what they personally can change; for example by asking:

- "How can you change your own behaviour so that this person would choose by themselves to make the changes you want them to make?"
- "What would <u>you</u> need to change in yourself to make this person more likely to change?"
- "What would changing that person get for <u>you</u> that is important?"
- "What can you change about yourself so that you respond more resourcefully to this person with the problem they have?"

If the person presents multiple issues, I help them to clarify which is the most important issue to work with; for example by asking:

- "What are these problems an example of?"
- "Which of these issues will, when you solve it, let you know that all the others can be solved?"
- "Which of these will be the easiest for you to change first?"
- "For which of these issues do you already have a sense of what your goal is?

If the person talks unstoppably about their problem/s, I help them pause their running of the tape-recording of thought. I interrupt them; for example by asking:

- "I realise that this is really important. Can I just check… What would you like to get by telling me this story?"
- "I understand that this is important and so can I check; what are you telling me by telling me this story?"

If the person cannot think of an outcome or is confused about what an outcome would be, I ask about real or hypothetical times when the problem doesn't occur (the "exceptions") and about the opposite of the problem; for example by asking:

- "Think of a time that you noticed this problem wasn't quite as bad? What was happening at that time? What were you doing different?"
- "Suppose one night there is a miracle while you are sleeping, and this problem is solved. Since you are sleeping, you don't know that a miracle has happened or that your problem is solved. What do you suppose you will notice that's different in the morning, that will let you know the problem is solved?"
- "What is the opposite of this result that you have experienced so far? Is that something that you want?"

If the person says that they have no outcome but that they have been told to come and see me, I treat that situation as the real problem and focus on that; for example by asking:
- "What do you need to be doing differently so that they don't tell you that?"
- "What would you like to change in your response to them, so that you don't end up feeling pressured to come here?"

SPECIFY

In NLP terms, the outcome I am seeking will meet certain criteria. I list these with the acronym SPECIFY: Once I have a general statement of an outcome, I ask:

Sensory Specific. "What, specifically, will you see/hear/feel when you have this outcome?"

Positive Language. Asked only if they describe their goal in negative terms (e.g. saying what they want NOT to do or have) "If you don't have the old problem, what is it that you will have?"

Ecological. "What else will change when you have this outcome?", "What situations do you want this outcome in and what situations do you not want it to affect?"

Choice increases with this outcome. "Does this outcome increase your choices?"

Initiated by Self. "What do you personally need to do to achieve this?"

First step identified and achievable. "What is your first step?"

Your Resources Identified. "What inner resources do you have which will help you to achieve this outcome?" OR "Tell me about a time when you had the feeling state you need to know you can achieve this, for example, a time when you achieved something else that seemed in the same way, challenging before you started" (may need to remind them about learning to talk etc). As they recall that time, place your hand on their shoulder or "anchor" the experience in some other way, and then use this anchor as you ask them to "Now think about this new goal and notice how good it will feel to know you have achieved this too now." This is simple **anchoring** in NLP terms

If we identify ecological challenges with their outcome (for example they say that reaching this outcome could harm something else important to them, or cause them to lose advantages that they want to keep) I help them think with an "and" frame about this; for example by asking:
- "How can you keep what you have that is important to you now, at the same time as gaining this outcome?"

- "In what ways could gaining this outcome actually <u>increase or enhance</u> the availability of these other things that are important to you?"

Dealing With The Client Who Matches and Moves Towards: Task-Based Coaching

A series of significant change patterns can be used after the client already has a sense that they have done the change process, and as they think about how to apply their new ideas positively in their daily life. At this point they are moving towards a more positive future and thinking about how to match their new responses to the other processes occurring in their life. Solution focused Coaches have studied the difference in the way the coach asks about the results of change processes afterwards (for example when the client returns to the next session). In studies replicated several times, they have found that if the coach asks questions which imply the possibility of failure (e.g. "Did the change process work?") they get a different result than if they ask questions which presuppose success (e.g. "How did that change things?"). When asked a question that presupposes change, 60% of clients will report success. If the question presupposes possible failure, 67% will report that their situation is the same as it was before (Miller et alia, 1996, p 255-256).

A number of studies have led helpers to recognise the importance of futurepacing the changes their clients initiate (having the client imagine themselves back in their actual life using their new skills). This process functions both to check out the appropriateness of their plans, the "ecology" in NLP terms, and also to install the expectation of success in the person's future (Mann et alia, 1989; Marlatt and Gordon, 1985). Allen Ivey and others have their clients write a "future diary" of their success a year into the future. Alan Marlatt has clients step into the future and fully consider what might make them change their mind about their changes, and then has them plan to prevent that. Both approaches have been shown to deliver far more robust change than parallel programs which skip this futurepacing stage.

On the other hand, one of the significant risks of being towards motivated and matching is that the client naively thinks that everything will be easy now. They assume that since they feel good now, they will always feel good and everything will go as they imagine it. Clients who have been influenced by the DVD "The Secret" frequently come to coaching strongly matching and towards, and with no reality testing. Although focusing on the problem you have had does not lead to success, neither does merely fantasising about future success. Lien Pham and Shelley Taylor at the University of California did a study where a group of students were asked to visualise themselves getting high grades in a mid-term exam that was coming up soon. They were taught to form clear visual images and imagine how good it will feel, and to repeat this for several minutes each day. A control group was also followed up, and the study times of each student as well as their grades in the exam were monitored. The group who were visualising should, according to proponents of "The Secret" DVD and the "Law of Attraction", have a clear advantage. In fact, they did much less study, and consequently got much lower marks in the exam (Pham and Taylor, 1999).

This result is very consistent. There are now a large number of research studies showing that "The secret" or "The law of attraction" (visualising your outcome and then letting go and trusting that the universe will provide it) impedes success. Gabrielle Oettingen at the University of Pennsylvania has done a number of studies showing the same result. In one study, women in a weight-reduction program were asked to describe what would happen if they were offered a tempting situation with food. The more positive their fantasies of how well they would cope with these situations, the less work they did on weight reduction. A year later, those women who consistently fantasised positive results lost on average 12 kilos less than those who anticipated negative challenges and thus put in more effort (Oettingen and Wadden, 1991). Oettingen followed up final year students to find out how much they fantasised getting their dream job after leaving university. The students who fantasised more reported two years later that they did less searching for jobs, had fewer offers of jobs, and had significantly smaller salaries than their classmates (Oettingen and Mayer, 2002). In another study, she investigated a group of students who had a secret romantic attraction, a crush, on another student. She asked them to imagine what would happen if they were to accidentally find themselves alone with that person. The more vivid and positive the fantasies they made, the less likely they were to take any action and to be any closer to a relationship with the person 5 months later. The result is consistent in career success, in love and attraction, and in dealing with addictions and health challenges (Oettingen, Pak and Schnetter, 2001; Oettingen, 2000; Oettingen and Gollwitzer, 2002).

Richard Wiseman (2009, p 88-93) did a very large study showing the same result. He tracked 5000 people who had some significant goal they wanted to achieve (everything from starting a new relationship to beginning a new career, from stopping smoking to gaining a qualification. He followed people up over the next year, and found firstly that only 10% ever achieved their goal. Dramatic and consistent differences in the psychological techniques they used made those 10% stand out from the rest. Those who failed tended either to think about all the bad things that would happen or continue to happen if they did not reach their goal (what NLP calls away from motivation, and what other research calls counterfactual thought) or to fantasise about achieving their goal and how great life would be. They also tried to achieve their goal by willpower and attempts to suppress "unhelpful thoughts". Finally, they spent time thinking about role models who had achieved their goal, often putting pictures of the role model on their fridge or other prominent places, to remind them to fantasise. These techniques did not work! And the most successful people did not waste their time doing them.

Wiseman warns that visualising what it will be like to have achieved your goal has become a popular tactic. "This type of exercise has been promoted by the self-help industry for years, with claims that it can help people lose weight, stop smoking, find their perfect partner, and enjoy increased career success. Unfortunately, a large body of research now suggests that although it might make you feel good, the technique is, at best, ineffective." (Wiseman, 2009, p 84). This is because, as Wiseman notes, whether you achieve your goals is primarily a question of motivation; of getting yourself to do certain things. Fantasising that everything has already been done reduces motivation. It is fantasising that you are doing and achieving things that works!

Giving the client real-life tasks to do in their daily life is an important way of futurepacing, presupposing success and preparing for the realistic challenges of daily life. The client needs to be in a motivational state to undertake the task you set. Solution Focused Coaching, developed by Steve de Shazar based on Milton Erickson's work, utilises this tasking very fully. de Shazar (Steve de Shazer, 1985) suggests you use a "scaling question" to ascertain how committed they are to changing. You might say, "On a scale of one to ten where one means you are only willing to hope and pray that this issue is resolved, and ten means you are willing to do anything at all; where would you rate your current motivation?" Note that this question developed by Solution Focused Coaching rates "The Secret" at "1 out of 10" for motivation.

The results can be considered in three categories, which I'll illustrate here with examples of tasks set by Milton Erickson. If the client rates themselves at 1-3 (such clients are called "Visitors" in Solution Focused Coaching), then my only task will be that they come back to see me another time, when maybe they will be more interested in change. Erickson was very willing to allow this, rather than to try and force cooperation. For example, in one discussion (Erickson, 1992, p264) he describes his initial session with a 29 year old man who wet his bed each night: "He wanted to know if I could do something about it. I told him, "Yes, I can, but I don't think you will like it. But you can listen to me anyway." I held his attention, and I told him what I could do about it, and he said "Uh-huh." About three months later he came to me and said "What was that you were going to do about my bedwetting. I think I want you to do it now."

If the client rates themselves at 4-7 out of 10 in terms of their motivation, then the task I give them will involve basically doing what they have already been doing, and noticing what is happening. Erickson points out that such tasks themselves cause change. He says about uncontrollable gagging, as an example "In this matter of gagging, why not be perfectly honest with your patient by telling him, "You really do gag." I know it and he knows it. Then I can ask the patient to really study that gag: where does the gagging really start -in the abdomen, in the thorax, in the pharynx?; where do you get that feeling first? You ask the patient to focus on his gagging.... Ogden Nash wrote a very nice poem about the centipede. The centipede was walking along perfectly happily one day, with all of his legs going in proper order, until along came so-and-so who asked the centipede which leg came after which. Now that poor centipede lies in a ditch wondering which comes after which." (Erickson, 1992, p118).

If the client rates themselves at 8-10 (called a "Customer" in Solution Focused Coaching), then they are ready for somewhat more challenging tasks. In setting such tasks, I tell them that my proposal may seem strange or even contrary to reason, but we are not aiming for reason; we are aiming for change. There are four types of task that I may set clients:

a)   Tasks which prescribe practise of a skill, subskill, metaprogram, or of a change process itself.

These are the most obvious form of task. Such tasks are useful when your client is motivated to change, but has no practical experience using the strategies needed to achieve their goal or to live the way they intend. You may set tasks which build on the skills a client has already and extend them in a small specific area. You may break the main change desired into small manageable chunks (with or without giving the client/student the big picture at the start) and set each chunk as a task. You may identify mental sortings (personality styles) which are essential to change, and set tasks which require those sorts. You may rehearse the person through a therapeutic or learning process in the session and have them repeat it at home (what used to be called homework).

In education, this process is understood very well. If someone has a difficulty, you get them to practise the sub-skills which will help them resolve that difficulty and achieve their goal. In coaching, surprisingly, this has not seemed so obvious, but it is just as true. NLP Trainer Tad James tells the story of a woman who came to see him because of difficulty planning her life. He told her he would help her as soon as she could beat him at a game of chess. What do you have to do in order to play chess? Anticipate several steps ahead and plan! One of the most obvious personality trait differences between our more distressed clients and those people who are really enjoying their life is whether they sort their experiences looking for problems or for solutions. Steve de Shazer (1985) and the Solution Focused Coaching school have made an art form of developing tasks which require clients to rehearse themselves through the process of sorting for success. They have them do this even before the first interview, by asking the client on the phone to "Notice anything, however small, which improves between now and your first session with us."

Milton Erickson tells the story of his work with an alcoholic street person named Harold, who came to his first interview suffering from suicidal thoughts and anxiety. Harold announced that he was a "Dumb moron" and could expect to achieve very little in therapy. Erickson agreed with him that they should not attempt too much. However he pointed out that even a tractor needs regular cleaning.... Harold came back the next week having had a bath. Erickson agreed that the best they could hope for was to get Harold a labouring job, and he pointed out that labourers need physical balance. He assessed Harold's physical balance and found it inadequate. So dance classes were prescribed to rectify this. Shorthand and typing were skills that Erickson suggested might help with the fine motor coordination Harold was lacking, and needed for his labouring work. Bit by bit, Harold acquired all the basic skills Erickson suggested he needed to reach his own limited goals. But by then Harold had begun to suspect that he was in fact not so much of a moron, He graduated from college, began dating women, and got himself a more responsible job than he had ever imagined.

b)   Tasks which prescribe a solution for the underlying problem.

These tasks can be given to clients in situations when there is an ecology issue preventing the giving of the first type of task. The client wants to learn new skills consciously, but has some unconscious reason for preserving the behaviour used previously. Solving this underlying reason will free the client up to be able to practise the desired strategies. To identify tasks of this second type, ask yourself and the client "What is the intention behind the behaviour that is a problem?" and identify a more useful behaviour which would meet that intention even better than the problem behaviour used to. Set this new behaviour as a task, and leave the old problem behaviour to disappear.

In education, such traditional responses as giving an attention seeking school student a monitor job fit in this category. As a trainer I often require students to "check in" with another student and tell them how things have been, before we start the session. This meets that need to share experiences and build friendships, which might otherwise result in more challenging behaviour once the session has started. Other tasks to set students for similar reasons could include having them write "affirmations" to each other. When students feel respected and valued, they have less need to prove their value in ways that could disrupt the group learning process. Much of what Solution Focused Therapy does fits into this category too, because when people find a successful solution, they no longer need the problem that brought them to therapy. For example, a task often set by Solution Focused Therapist Steve de Shazer (1985) is to require the client to "Pay attention to what you do when you overcome the urge to ....[do the problem]"

Milton Erickson also focused much of his attention on the underlying issues, rather than on the "problem" identified by the person. A twenty one year old woman once came to visit Erickson complaining that she was suicidal. She had never had a boyfriend, and had all sorts of imagined personal defects. A young man showed up at the drinking fountain at work whenever she did, but she couldn't believe that he liked her. Erickson suggested first that, as she was considering suicide, she should take all her money out of the bank and have one last "fling", getting new clothes, having her hair done etc (Haley, 1986, p71). This fling, of course, dealt with some of the woman's problem (her unkempt appearance) without her having to try to achieve anything. But it also let her nurture herself, thus approaching the underlying issue. Finally, Erickson had her practise squirting water through the gap in her front teeth (one of her "worst" defects), thus turning the problem into a skill (see the fourth type of task, below). She was then instructed to go back to work and squirt water through her teeth at the young man, then run away. The man ran after her and kissed her, and two days later they had their first date.

The story of the African Violet Queen is another example (Gordon & Anderson, 1981, p18). In this case, Erickson visited an elderly woman with severe depression. She stayed at home in a large dreary empty house, going to church each week but communicating with no-one. In one room of her house she kept a few flowers -African Violets. This was the only room that didn't have the curtains drawn when Erickson visited her there. His solution was to get her to buy a couple of hundred potting plants and grow more of the flowers. She was then to note all the births, deaths, weddings etc in her church notices, and send an African Violet to the family concerned. This simple task did far more than resolve the depression. When this woman died twenty years later, she had hundreds of friends at her funeral, and was known as the "African Violet Queen of Milwaukee".

c)   Tasks which prescribe a metaphor or a puzzling but potentially symbolic action.

Metaphorical Quests are particularly useful for clients who have some motivation, but who would resist a direct request to practice new strategies. The therapist need not have any notion of the underlying reason for this resilience. Almost any task can be given as a metaphor. You may tell the person the symbolic meaning of the task, or (even better) you may ask them to generate their own meaning (known in mythology as setting a riddle). In the latter case, you tell them to let you know next session what meaning they have discovered. You can then agree that they are right about the meaning of the task (after all, it's their metaphor!)... but there's another meaning also hidden in the task. Perhaps they will have found that second meaning by next week.... This process causes the client to search inside for the meaning (a process called in NLP "transderivational search"). As you listen to the results of this search, you can learn more about how they have utilised the metaphorical potential of the task. This process can be diagnostic (it may help you understand their problem more) and therapeutic (it may help the client find new solutions).

Milton Erickson once had a visit from an alcoholic who said that his parents, grandparents, wife and in-laws were all alcoholic. Erickson sent him to the Botanic Gardens, to visit the Cacti house and think carefully about how cacti could survive three years without water. The man's daughter came to visit Erickson years later and said both her parents gave up alcohol after that one visit.(Rosen, 1982, p81). Having a client carry round a photo of the person who set a rule they have been reluctantly following, or having a person who needs to grieve go to the airport and wave goodbye to five planes also use this principle.

However, often Erickson would prescribe a task which he seemed not to know the meaning of himself, and then wait to find out what meaning the client discovered in that. Jeffrey Zeig suggests giving a stone to a client to carry round for a week. The client is then asked why the coach gave the stone to them. After their initial comments, the therapist says "Yes, that's right; and there is another meaning too. Think on it over the next week and tell me then." Many of the tasks that traditional heroes perform are metaphorical in this sense.

d) Tasks which prescribe the symptom or problem strategy, often with a small change.

If you reach the end of a session and find that the person is still not convinced that they have achieved anything useful, you may give them a paradoxical task. The nice thing about this fourth group of tasks is that they can be given to clients with fairly low levels of motivation, because they do not ask the client to change in any obvious or dramatic way. These tasks can also be given in situations where the client's previous attempts to find a solution have become part of their strategy for doing the problem, or have apparently worsened the problem (e.g. a binge eater whose dieting enhances their craving).These tasks merely invite the person to continue doing what they always did... with a tiny variation. Any energy that was going into "resisting" change is thus converted into energy supporting the task. Simply requiring the person to repeat their problem on demand changes the problem (puts it under conscious control). You may require the person to alter the behaviour in some small way, for example:

1) by specifying a time and place for it. An overanxious student may be required to worry about their grades for 15 minutes at 5pm each day (no more and no less). Someone anxious about meeting people may be told to meet five people in the next week and make a mistake in the first sentence they say, each time.
2) by requiring them not to do the desired behaviour but only the "problem" (which at times means it loses its "problem" status, because it was only a problem when they were trying to do something else). In sex therapy, a couple having orgasmic difficulties are often required to have sex for one hour each night and not attempt to orgasm. Milton Erickson's favourite cure for insomnia was to have the person stay up all night doing jobs around the house that they had been meaning to do but hadn't gotten round to.
3) by adding some humorous or otherwise emotionally incongruent element to it. One time (Haley, 1973, p178) Erickson dealt with a couple where the husband was running the house by threatening that he'd have a heart attack if he didn't get his way. Erickson had the wife get a

collection of advertisements from funeral services and place them around the house whenever he complained thus. She also would add up their insurance policies and discuss the best way to use them. Quickly the husband shifted to dealing with the issues that really concerned him in the marriage, which were then able to be sorted out. Prescribing ritualistically sequenced argument procedures for couples can be an example of this type of task. Another is having students list 10 reasons why they could never learn some new material (that they've been claiming is too hard) before doing it.

4) by specifying the problem behaviour in such a way that it causes the solution to occur as well (a double bind). Fritz Perls was famous for dealing with clients who claimed they could not say "no" to someone, using this type of task. He'd tell them that they had to say "No" to him immediately. Telling a student to make sure they don't think about an assignment they have been avoiding, and be careful not to think of it for the next 24 hours, is another example.

The Wheel of Change: Summary

Clients who seek change present four very unique change styles, sometimes with one predominating and sometimes in a sequence that matches the process of effective change agents in a community or organisation. The four styles, given below in that sequence, are each characterised by a combination of four personality styles (Towards, Away-from, Matching and Mismatching):

- The Auditor (what Moyers called the Citizen) style is Matching and Away from. Clients using it will benefit by careful pacing and leading, in the way that Reflective coaching invites change.
- The Rebel style is Mismatching and Away from. Clients using it will benefit by playfully drawing attention to the fact that they could take charge of creating a better life, in the way that Provocative coaching invites change.
- The Innovator (what Moyers called the change agent) style is Mismatching and Towards. Clients using it will benefit from focused techniques that build new strategies and responses which become models of their future action, in the way that NLP change techniques often invite change.
- The Reformer style is Matching and Towards. Clients using it will benefit from being asked to go out into their real life and take action, facing both desired and undesired results of their behaviour and

realistically responding to both, in the way that Ericksonian Tasking often invites change.

The wheel of change provides a radically new frame for thinking about change styles and techniques. It suggests that these techniques can better be evaluated by their match to the style of the client than by their match to the preferred style of a coach or therapist. This new frame confirms that whichever style you have intuitively preferred has indeed been successful with those clients who match its strengths, and the frame invites you to expand the skill you have into the other three areas to achieve the same success there. The model answers the most frequent questions that I hear from new coaches after their training, as they struggle to understand why what worked so well in the training room is sometimes failing in their clinical practice. It dramatically enhances the range of choices that you can elegantly and congruently incorporate into your own skill as a coach, giving you a sense that whatever stance the client brings to their session, you can enjoy utilising it to create amazingly swift and elegant outcomes. At the same time, it gives us:

- A model for selecting coaching responses
- A model for assessing where we are in the steps of the coaching process
- A model for understanding each client's unique style of changing
- A model for cooperating in the change process in a group or organisation
- A model for changing the world

Unfortunately, it does not yet give us a grand theory that unites both Relativity and Quantum mechanics, such as physicists have been searching for. Otherwise, it pretty much explains everything. Doesn't it?

Author's Thanks:

I hope it is clear that "the wheel of change" idea emerges out of numerous other people's work. I'm grateful to the developers of NLP such as **Richard Bandler, John Grinder, Steve Andreas, Shelle Rose Charvet** and **Tad James,** to the developers of Solution focused therapy such as **Steve de Shazer,** to the developers of Provocative therapy such as **Frank Farrelly** and **Nick Kemp,** to the developers of Ericksonian therapy especially **Milton Erickson** and **Jeff Zeig,** and to **Bill Moyer.** I want to thank **Tomasz Kowalik** for posing the question of how apparently contradictory models of coaching such as the Client Centred Approach and Provocative Coaching can be integrated. I also want to thank my partner **Julia Kurusheva** for the session at which I conceived the fusion of all these trends.

Bibliography:

Ash, M.K. <u>The Mary Kay Way: Timeless Principles from America's Greatest Woman Entrepreneur</u> Wiley, New York, 2008

Bailenson, J. N. & Yee, N. "Digital chameleons: Automatic assimilation of nonverbal gestures in immersive virtual environments." Psychological Science, 16, 814-819, 2005

Bandler, R. <u>Magic In Action</u>, Meta Publications, Cupertino, 1984.

Bolstad, R. <u>RESOLVE: A New Model Of Therapy</u> Crown House, Bancyfelin, Wales, 2002

Bolstad, R. <u>Transforming Communication</u> Pearsons, Auckland, 2004

Brockman, W.P. "Empathy revisited: the effects of representational system matching on certain counselling process and outcome variables", Dissertation Abstracts International 41(8), 3421A, College of William and Mary, 167pp., 1980

Charvet, S.R. <u>Words That Change Minds</u> Kendall/Hunt, Dubuque, Iowa, 1997

Chevalier, A.J., <u>On The Client's Path</u>, New Harbinger, Oakland, California, 1995

de Shazer, S. <u>Keys to Solution In Brief Therapy</u>, Norton, New York, 1985

Dolliver, R.H., Williams, E.L. & Gold, D.C. "The art of gestalt therapy or "What are you doing with your feet now?"" in Psychotherapy, 17, 136-142., 1980

Dilts, R. <u>Modelling With NLP</u> Meta Publications, Capitola, California, 1998

Erickson, M.H. <u>Healing In Hypnosis</u>, Irvington, New York, 1992

Farrelly, F. and Brandsma, J. <u>Provocative Therapy</u> Meta Publications, Cupertino, California, 1974

Gordon, D. and Meyers-Anderson, M. <u>Phoenix</u>, Meta Publications, Capitola California, 1981

Gross, D. <u>Forbes Greatest Business Stories Of All Time</u> John Wiley & Sons, New York, 1996

Haley, J. <u>Ordeal Therapy</u>, Jossey-Bass, San Francisco, 1984

Haley, J. <u>Uncommon Therapy</u>, W.W.Norton & Co, New York, 1986

Jonsson, I. M., Nass, C., Harris, H., & Takayama, L. "Matching in-car voice with driver state: Impact on attitude and driving performance." Proceedings of the Third International Driving Symposium on Human Factors in Driver-assessment, Training and Vehicle Design. 173-180, 2008

LaFrance, M. "Nonverbal synchrony and rapport: Analysis by the cross-lag panel technique." Social Psychology Quarterly 42, 66-70, 1979

Lakin, J. L., Chartrand, T. L. & Arkin, R. M. "I am too just like you: Nonconscious mimicry as an automatic behavioral response to social exclusion." Psychological Science, 19, 816-822, 2008

Lakin, L., & Chartrand, T. L. "Using nonconscious behavioral mimicry to create affiliation and rapport." Psychological Science, 14, 334-339, 2003

Lankton, S. and Lankton, C. The Answer Within, Brunner/Mazel, New York, 1983

Maddux, W. W., Mullen, E., & Glainsky, A. D. "Chameleons bake bigger pies and take bigger pieces: Strategic behavioral mimicry facilitates negotiation outcomes." Journal of Experimental Social Psychology 44, 461-468, 2008

Mann, L., Beswick, G., Allouache, P. and Ivey, M. "Decision workshops for the improvement of decisionmaking: Skills and confidence" in Journal of Counselling and Development, 67, p 478-481, 1989

Marlatt,G. and Gordon, J. Relapse Prevention: Maintenance Strategies in the Treatment of Addictive Behaviours Guilford, New York, 1985

Miller, S. D., Hubble, M.A. and Duncan, B.L. Handbook of Solution Focused Brief Therapy, Jossey-Bass, San Francisco, 1996

Miller, W. "Motivation for treatment: a review with special emphasis on alcoholism." In Psychological Bulletin, Vol 98 (1), p 84-107, 1985

Morgan, J.M. and Liker, J.K. The Toyota Product development System: Integrating People, Process and Technology, Productivity Press, New York, 2006

Moyer, B. with McAllister, J., Finley, M.L. and Soifer, S. Doing Democracy New Society, Gabriola Island, Canada, 2001

Oettingen, G. "Expectancy Effects on Behaviour Depend on Self-Regulatory Thought" p 101-129 in Social Cognition, No. 18, 2000

Oettingen, G. and Gollwitzer, P.M. "Self-Regulation of Goal Pursuit: Turning Hope Thoughts into Behaviour" p 304-307 in Psychological Inquirer, No 13, 2002

Oettingen, G. and Mayer, D. "The Motivating Function of Thinking About The Future: Expectations Versus Fantasies" p 1198-1212 in Journal of Personality and Social Psychology, No. 83, 2002

Oettingen, G. and Wadden, T.A. "Expectation, Fantasy, and Weight Loss: Is The Impact of Positive Thinking Aways Positive?" p 167-175 in Cognitive Therapy and Research, No. 15, 1991

Oettingen, G. Pak, H. and Schnetter, K. "Self-Regulation of Goal-

setting: Turning Free Fantasies About the Future Into Binding Goals" p 736-753 in *Journal of Personality and Social Psychology*, No 80, 2001

Palubeckas, A.J. "Rapport in the therapeutic relationship and its relationship to pacing" Dissertation Abstracts International 42(6), 2543-B 2544-B, Boston University School of Education, 127pp, Order = 8126743

Pham, L.B. and Taylor, S.E. *"From Thought to Action: Effects of Process Versus Outcome Based Mental Simulations on Performance."* P 250-260 in *Personality and Social Psychology Bulletin*, No. 25, 1999

Rizzolatti, G., & Craighero, L. "The mirror-neuron system." Annual review of Neuroscience, 27, 169-192, 2004

Robbins, A. Unlimited Power, Fawcett Columbine, New York, 1986

Roddick, A. Business As Unusual Anita Roddick Publications, Chichester, England, 2008

Rosen, S. My Voice Will Go With You, W.W. Norton & Co, New York, 1982

Rosenblum, L.D. See What I'm Saying WW Norton & Co., New York, 2010

Shostrom, E. (Ed). Three Approaches to Psychotherapy (Film No I). Orange, California: Psychological Films, 1965.

Slavik, D.J. *"Keeping your eyes on the prize: outcome versus process focused social comparisons and counterfactual thinking"* Thesis (Ph. D.), University of Arkansas, Fayetteville, 2003

van Baaren, R. B., Holland, R. W., Kawakami, K & van Knippenberg, A. "Mimicry and prosocial behavior." Psychological Science, 15. 71-74, 2004

Williams, P. and Williams, R. How To Be Like Women Of Influence, Health Communications Inc, Deerfield Beach, Florida, 2003

Wiltermuth, S. S., & Heath, C. "Synchrony and Cooperation", Psychological Science, 20, 15, 2009

Wiseman, R., *59 Seconds: Think A Little, Change A Lot*, Macmillan, London, 2009

Yapko. M., "The Effects of Matching Primary Representational System Predicates on Hypnotic Relaxation." in the American Journal of Clinical Hypnosis, 23, p169-175, 1981

Zeig, J. ed. Ericksonian Methods: The Essence Of The Story, Brunner/Mazel, New York, 1994

Zeigarnik, A.V. *"Über das behalten von erledigten und unerledigten Handlu*ngen" (*The retention of completed and uncompleted actions*) p 1-85 in *Psychologische Forschung*, No. 9, 1927

Richard Bolstad and Julia Kurusheva

Culture, Gender and Relationships in NLP Coaching

A. Culture and Gender in NLP Based Coaching

Culture and Belief Systems

Over the last decades I have taught NLP in a number of cultural settings in Europe, America, Australasia and Asia. I am an NLP trainer and I am deeply committed to promoting the tools, methodology and deeper values of NLP as I understand it. It is quite clear to me also that NLP emerged from a particular cultural background in the United States of America. It also has gender biases built into it, and it deals inadequately with the issues of relationships and cooperation (as a glance at the personal history of the co-developers of NLP shows, including their many years in litigation as they argued about the ownership of "NLP"). In this chapter I want to encourage us to develop a more inclusive and co-operative NLP.

Chicago Professor of Geography James Blaut has been interested in the way that our "science" is shaped by our culture and history. He points out that much of North American and European writing presents "western" ideas as rational and not needing explanation. Meanwhile, "eastern" ideas can be dismissed as if they are merely superstitions adopted in response to the social climate of "oriental despotism". Blaut continues "Interestingly, we experience no discomfort and sense no threat when we read an account written by some anthropologist or cultural geographer about the beliefs, values, myths and so on, of some small and obscure society in some far corner of the earth. Indeed we expect an anthropologist to tell us more about the social or cultural reason why the "natives" hold to these ideas than about the validity of the ideas…. But when this ethnographic approach is applied to what are called "Western" ideas, in the realms of science, history and the like, the results are disturbing and the enterprise itself seems somehow improper. Ideas are, so to speak, surrounded by culture, and we can examine the surroundings and the ways ideas are imbedded in their surroundings." (Blaut, 1993, p 31-32)

Anthropologically then, we would expect that even a radical reframing of science such as NLP will retain certain characteristics from its source culture. I believe that the understandable reluctance to examine our own cultural context (referred to by James Blaut above) is present in the NLP community as well. There are a number of subtle cultural assumptions in the way NLP is usually taught. Here I will simply give a few examples from my own teaching experience. Japan is a country I have taught in most summers over the last ten years and provides some clear instances of cultural difference from New Zealand where I teach most of the year.

Goalsetting: Collective and Individual

On the first day I taught NLP in Japan, I introduced the notion of goalsetting. As people wrote out "wellformed" goals, I went around to check that they had understood the process. "What goal are you working on?" I asked one man. "I'm setting the goal to live by myself." He explained. "I'm in my forties now, and my mother has lived with me for a long time. I think I'd like to live alone.

Immediately, I realised that there could be some cultural ecology questions here. "Have you checked the ecology of this goal?" I asked. "Will it be okay to have the other consequences of making this change?"

"Oh sure," he explained. "It's what I really want…. It just has never occurred to me to ask the question you got us to ask. I always asked myself 'What *should* I do?'. Never 'What do I *want* to do?!' It's a whole new approach." The next person whose goal I checked was a woman who was setting the goal of leaving her husband…. Suddenly, to quote Steve and Connirae Andreas in Change Your Mind and Keep The Change (1987, p 188), it occurred to me that "Toto, I don't think we're in Kansas anymore!"

Goalsetting as such was not a new concept to these people. But what I had done was to (inadvertently) redefine goalsetting as an individualised process of asking what I want to do, separated from the social network in which I live. Previously these people had mostly set goals for themselves as subsystems imbedded within wider social systems.

An annual survey of secondary school students from a school in the city of Nagoya asks them "What are your goals for the future?" In 1960, five times as many replied "To become a person useful to society" (24%) as replied "To make money" (5%). But by 1976, this statistic had almost reversed, representing a huge values shift in Japan (Horio, 1994, p 308). None-the-less, the goal of "fitting in" still takes priority in many situations. Kate Elwood notes (2001, p 12) that when employees are asked their goal within a large Japanese company, they often say they want *teki o tsukuranai* (not to make enemies). One can see here that while Japanese society has certainly nurtured goalsetting, the goals involved have been very different to those we "expect" in western cultures. This subtle difference, I believe, makes NLP part of a huge cultural time bomb currently being positioned in Japan.

The president of Sophia University in Tokyo, Joseph Pittau, suggests out that the key career goal of most Japanese teenagers has previously been to get into a good university. This is the socially approved aim of childhood. The rest of one's life, it is believed, will fall into place once one has achieved this goal. "What one should do after entering one of these famous schools, or what one wants to do with one's life, are questions the Japanese do not think about very much." (from an article in the Asahi Shimbun newspaper, quoted in Horio, 1994, p 304). Japanese professor Teruhisa Horio frustratedly describes the resulting Japanese university study as "a four year moratorium on living and thinking" (Horio, 1994, p 308). Many Japanese students who come to our NLP trainings have already rejected this moratorium, and they choose to come to a western-run training for what they call the "free-thinking" approach. They say they find the very use of English language opens up a sense of freedom of thought, which they value. They realise already that westerners use goalsetting in a slightly different way, and they are interested to experience that way.

The choice whether to value independent goalsetting or directing one's life in a more socially approved way is a choice for each person and group to make. For us as NLP trainers, the point is to notice that the way we present NLP often assumes the western style of goalsetting behaviour, the western values. We teach people how to reach goals, and assume that the goals they will want are highly individualised.

Identity: Co-operation And Self-direction

Our students in Japan sometimes say they equate the English language with individualistic thinking. Of course, it's no surprise to NLP Practitioners that language shapes our expectations. Peter Farb studied Japanese American women, who spoke both English and Japanese. At some interviews he asked the questions in Japanese, at other interviews he asked the same questions in English. He found that a woman asked "What do real friends do?" in Japanese might say "Help each other" while the <u>same</u> woman, when asked in English, would say "be very frank." A woman asked "What happens when your wishes conflict with your family's?" would respond in Japanese "It is a time of great unhappiness" but in English "I do what I want." Different language filters actually create different human beings! (De Vito, p 440).

It would be tempting to make the western assumption that these women are denying their "real" feelings when they answer in Japanese. The Japanese way of experiencing this is a little more subtle. Tatemae and honne are two Japanese words "used to describe a situation in which a person's stated reason (*tatemae*) differs from his real personal intention or motive (*honne*)." explains the bilingual "Japan An Illustrated Encyclopaedia" (Andrews, Befu et alia, 1996, p 91) "Traditional Japanese social norms have greatly emphasised harmonious interpersonal relations and group solidarity. Self-assertion is strongly discouraged, and the individual often finds that he must sacrifice personal needs and emotions so as to avoid confrontation in the group. Social norms are considered indispensable: Japanese people are taught early to follow their personal aims but not to defy *tatemae* openly. The result is that in certain social situations it becomes difficult to discern the person's real intentions." However, as Kate Elwood suggests "Japanese people do not think of *tatemae* as a lie. They see it as something vital to the smooth functioning of human relationships." (2001, p 14) From a Japanese perspective, westerners frequently value honesty higher than good relationships. If your friend asks you if you like their new haircut, and you find it repulsive, would you tell them the absolute "truth"? Possibly not. You understand that part of your choice of response is to care for their need to be supported - a need which is called *amae* in Japanese (Andrews, Befu et alia, 1996, p 93).

The people on our Japanese trainings often report frustration with the *tatemae-honne* distinction, just as westerners get frustrated with social "niceties" in our own culture. Many Japanese people seize eagerly on communication skills which enable them to make the distinction more clearly (for example, Effectiveness Training, a model of clear communication which I have taught is the west and in Japan, is prospering in Japan more than in any western country, according to internal Gordon Training International memos). But wanting skills to deal more effectively with a culturally created "grey area" is not the same as wanting to reject that culture. The same Japanese person who expresses frustration with *tatemae* in a work conflict situation may be shocked at the insensitivity of a westerner who pours their own drink at the dinner that evening (Pouring one's own drink just because one is thirsty sends a message that one's host has not looked after one well enough. Waiting for the host to notice allows the host to save face and pour the drink for you. Waiting does not express one's *honne* fully, but it *is* socially caring behaviour. Put simply, it is "polite" in that context).

Another aspect of this cultural difference about social cohesion is the valuing of what is usually translated as "resignation" and "obedience". In the past, many Japanese have viewed endurance (even resignation; *akirame*) in the face of difficulty as a virtue. "Like all of nature, human life, with its pain and hardships, was accepted as transient. Because of this almost stoic resignation, many Japanese endured hardships without protest and accepted their place in a rigidly hierarchical society with a sense of *akirame*." (Andrews, Befu et alia, 1996, p 91). Does this mean that NLP would offer a new sense of choice to Japanese resigned to their fate and obedient to a brutal social code? For some participants it would. Merry White argues for others, the opposite might be true. White re-interprets the word *sunao*, usually translated as obedient. In the English notion of an obedient child is the implication that "natural" childhood behaviour will often tend to be anti-social or "disobedient". If the child co-operates with all requests, they are being "obedient" in the sense of submissive and self-controlling. The traditional Japanese assumption is more that co-operative behaviour will be the child's normal choice and will make the child more happy (because it will bring them so much social approval and closeness). White argues "Thus when we translate *sunao* as "obedient", we project our notions of authority and our idea of an innate capacity for evil onto the Japanese child. A more accurate translation of the term is "cooperative as an act of confirmation of the self". Hence a *sunao* child is a good participant in group activities, a good listener to adults, a good replicator of society's norms and standards. Being all these things makes him feel accomplished and enhances his identity -his most profoundly personal "self"."

Recommendations about Culture

As I said initially, my aim is not to define one cultural reality as more true than another, or to say what "all Japanese" or "all westerners" are like or should be like. Instead, my aim is to call for the attention of NLP trainers and other NLP practitioners who work in a cross-cultural setting. Understanding something of the cultures we are working in enables us to more fully identify the kind of differences in values and metaprograms which I give examples of here. We can thus present NLP in a more ecological way.

Merely to dismiss *tatemae* as lying may not respect the importance of sensitivity to others' feelings in Japanese society. To translate *sunao* as blind obedience may fail to understand the personal power engaged in choosing to co-operate with others in the context of Japanese culture.

In the same way, when giving examples of goals in a Japanese context, it becomes increasingly clear to me that co-operative and socially motivated goals are important to mention. The goal of creating a cooperative work team can be as empowering as the goal of earning more money.

Even where I deliberately offer culturally foreign experiences (such as using group games which involve more body contact than is normal in Japan) I can do so more effectively once I understand the cultural norms. NLP gives me tools useful for this task: tools for identifying verbal and nonverbal distinctions, for eliciting values hierarchies and metaprogram differences, and for pacing and leading from these to new places. Understanding all this also enriches my sense of what NLP is and where it comes from.

The Cultural Basis Of Our Metaphors For NLP

My own country, New Zealand, also provides me with examples of cultural difference. NLP Master Practitioner Hirini Reedy is a teacher of New Zealand Maori traditional skills such as Maori martial arts and traditional storytelling. While enthusiastic about NLP's contribution to Maori cultural studies, he is alert to the reframing of culture which the NLP models produces. He cautions, "As we enter the 3rd Millennium, the digitisation of information and the acceleration of change is seeing a greater need for NLP skills worldwide. This digitisation is even implicit in the name, Neuro Linguistic Programming (NLP) as coined by the founders of NLP. The name, NLP, suggests to me that we can encode and decode our internal thinking systems very much like programming a computer if you understand the necessary programming code. The use of the words such as auditory digital and now visual digital continues the influence of digital age terminology. The danger is that this digitisation of the human mind and body into its constituent modalities can sometimes take away the mystery and magic that has always been part of the human experience, part of our cultural makeup. Ancient cultures have always had an understanding of NLP processes as expressed through their mythologies, songs and dance, rituals, ceremonies and knowledge systems. We are now seeing many NLP leaders from around the world starting to integrate ancient teachings with NLP. Examples of recent discoveries include Tad James and his exploration into the teachings of Huna, the Hawaiian esoteric system of knowledge which led to the creation of his Time-Line Therapy. Dr Richard Bolstad and Margot Hamblett have been instrumental with integrating Chi Kung energy practices into their teachings of NLP here in Aotearoa [New Zealand]. In my opinion the use of metaphor and associated terms in NLP is perhaps creating new terminology for the ancient art of storytelling. Storytelling reflects the power of the spoken word, the oral tradition which preceded the advent of the written word and print media which has revolutionised the transmission of knowledge ever since." (Reedy 2000, p 2)

Reedy urges a mythological framing of NLP for Maori practitioners. He points out that in the traditional Maori worldview, genealogy (called *whakapapa* in Maori) linked each individual human being to their tribe and to all of nature (describing them as the descendents of the creator her/himself). "This whakapapa or kinship meant that the Maori saw the human form as a child of the universe, a microcosm of nature, subject to the same forces and energies that affect the seasons, the tides and the planets. Therefore many Maori rituals, beliefs and ceremonies focussed and honoured this universal kinship with Nature. The whakapapa concept can be used to explain the workings of the human mindscape where the neural pathways of thought can be navigated back to their parent source. This intimacy with nature meant that the many wananga (learning) systems of the Maori were attuned to the seasonal and daily cycles that affect the human mind and body. Essentially to the Maori, the classroom was nature, the sky the roof, the earth the floor. In this classroom there are many teachers of both human and non-human form. Before we can begin to gain insight into Maori concepts, protocols and language we must have this understanding of the Maori world view." (Reedy 2000, p. 3).

This call parallels a concern expressed by Robert Dilts in relation to all modelling. Dilts quotes Gregory Bateson saying "If you want to think about something, it is best to think about that thing the same way in which that thing thunk." (in Dilts, 1998, p 118). Dilts calls this code-congruence. Using the neurological levels model, he notes that when we model human skills without this "code-congruence", we may get capability level information and miss identity level information. Hirini Reedy is saying similarly that to think of Maori skills (for example martial arts skills or therapeutic storytelling skills) as being computer-like misses the whole sense of identity that the Maori user of those skills has; an identity linked with the natural world rather than the world of human constructions.

Maori psychiatrist Mason Durie points out that western psychology in general is analytical, looking for meanings in the smaller details. "Maori thinking goes in quite the opposite direction. You don't obtain knowledge by looking for the details, or dissecting, or uncovering, or going deeper and deeper. You go upwards. Knowledge is obtained from the relationship that a person has with Maori systems, not the relationship he has with his own feelings, nor his own thinking, nor his own intelligence, but the relationship that he has with the stars, with his land, with his family, and the things that are much bigger than him as an individual." (Durie, 1985). This is a profound difference in metaprograms.

Culture and Emotion

This is not merely a cognitive concern. Different cultural experiences produce different emotional states. Remember that an emotion is not merely a physiological or kinaesthetic response. It involves the attribution of meaning to physiological response. In experiments, we can inject people with noradrenalin and their kinaesthetic sensations will become aroused (their heart will beat faster etc). However, the emotional state they enter will vary depending on a number of other internal factors. They may, for example, become "angry", "frightened" or "euphoric". It depends on their other sensory representations and on their meta-representations -what they tell themselves is happening, for example (Schachter and Singer, 1962). The same kinesthetics do not always result in the same state!

In Japanese culture, there is an emotional state known as "*amae*". Japanese psychiatrist Takeo Doi says that this emotion could be described in English as a feeling of dependence or yearning to be looked after by another. He says that all people can feel this emotion, but that Japanese society has evolved to encourage and deepen its expression. "The Japanese, in short, idealised *amae* and considered a world dominated by *amae* as a truly human world; and the emperor system might be seen as an institution of this idea." (Doi, 1981, p. 60). This, he points out, also explains the origins of some distinctly Japanese psychiatric disorders such as *shinkeishitsu* (characterised by attention-seeking psychosomatic problems and fear or shame in front of other people - Doi, 1981, p. 101-102). Allowing this emotion of *amae* to flower requires a Japanese understanding of the positive value of mutual support. The emotion is simply unlikely to evolve in this form in a more individualistic culture.

In Aotearoa (New Zealand), Dr Joan Metge has studied an emotion known to New Zealand Maori as *whakamaa* (Metge, 1985). The literal translation of *whakamaa* is to make white, and the emotion refers to a kind of shame or severe withdrawal which occurs when a person feels that they have lost their spiritual power or *mana*. This mana comes largely from connection to (or respect from) others and from connection to the world. Without a sense of connection to nature and to the dignity of one's *whakapapa* (kinship networks) it is possible for a Maori person to physically sicken or even to die of whakamaa. Maori consultant Puti

Turner gives an example: "You work, you sit exams, and suddenly the results come out and you have not got through. Now that sort of experience on a Maori lad is whakamaa, because he has not achieved. All the people at home who know that he is going through secondary school are going to look at his parents and say, "Ha! See, your child has missed out!" He carries this tremendous responsibility." (in Metge, 1985, p. 41).

When we teach NLP in a different culture, then, we are confronted by different values and beliefs, different metaprograms and even different emotional states. In a western culture, *amae* may be considered intrinsically negative, but in Japanese terms it may be an appropriate and resourceful emotion which needs to be utilised correctly. In a western culture, the solution to *whakamaa* may seem to be to get one's sense of identity from one's own self. But as Maori psychiatrist Mason Durie explains, "Maori people would regard someone who is independent, who is directed by his own thoughts and feelings as a disturbed person and in a very bad way. He should see a counsellor! Because the antithesis of health is independent living, independent feeling and regarding yourself as sufficient as an individual; all very unhealthy thinking (in Maori terms). He has failed completely to acknowledge where he has come from, what his strength is, and probably where he is going." In Maori terms, the solution to *whakamaa* is to re-establish ones *mana*, not to smash it further by becoming even more isolated.

When A Culture Is Denied Expression

Such culturally unique emotional responses, values and metaprograms are transmitted to children very early in life, by both verbal and non-verbal methods. The responses are largely unconscious. However, when one culture becomes dominant in a community, it may become increasingly difficult for members of other cultures to manage with the cultural responses they have taken in at this deep level. Let me give you an example.

One day, a New Zealand man came to see me because of increasing arguments with the woman he lived with. He sat by me, looking down at the floor and explaining that one of his biggest failings was his inability to make eye contact with people. Also, when he and his partner argued, he somehow was unable to get across to her that he wanted to apologise. No matter how he demonstrated his sadness, sitting close to her and trying to do things for her, she didn't get the message. And the things they argued about really puzzled him. For example, when they went to her parents' place for the weekend, she wanted to ring up beforehand and sort out what food they would bring. He felt humiliated by this—it seemed rather petty and rude. Surely they should just take whatever they could, and things would work out.

Was this man a poor communicator? No, he was an excellent communicator. Then why was he having so much trouble? And why did he believe he was no good at communicating? Because he was playing football with the basketball rulebook. His way of communicating worked perfectly in the family he grew up in, because that family was Maori. It did not work with his partner because she was from a European-based culture: a culture where people value 'looking you in the eye' rather than looking down to indicate politeness; where people talk about their feelings rather than expressing them (at a funeral, for example, she might say, 'I'm so sorry' rather than simply weep and hold someone); where people negotiate the arrangements for hospitality rather than giving a *koha* (gift). Both ways of life work perfectly. And it's quite possible for people to live together even when they grew up in different cultures ... providing they understand the difference and know who they are. Problems begin when we pretend that cultures don't exist, and everyone is 'the same'.

This man didn't even think of himself as "Maori". He grew up in a Maori *marae* (community), but had consciously rejected that background and considered himself a "New Zealander" rather than a "Maori". In New Zealand, as in most colonised countries, it was for a long time the government policy to encourage such rejection of indigenous culture. Maori collective ownership of land was declared void, and Maori were required to get individual titles to land under the 1862 Native Lands Act. Maori children were punished for speaking Maori at school, under the 1867 Native Schools Act, and required to adopt English. Maori traditional religion and health care was illegal from 1907 under the Suppression of Tohunga Act. These laws remained in force until the end of the 1960s (Bolstad ed, 2001, p 21-26). It's as if someone said, "There's no difference between basketball and football. The reason why you're losing the game is because you're no good at sports (or too lazy to try). You'll have to learn *our* rules better." The fact is that there *are* differences. As I listened to this man describing each of his communication 'failures', I affirmed for him that his responses sounded perfectly sane and skilled *and* that they were very much as I understood Maori responses to be. After half an hour or so he was glowing with a new sense of understanding, and working out how he could contact a Maori NLP Practitioner to explore this further. We spent the last quarter of an hour rehearsing his process of explaining this to his partner in a way that would be respectful of her.

If we truly believe that NLP belongs to the whole world, then it is useful for us to passionately move beyond the ways in which our practice may have limited NLP to a small subsection of the available cultures on the planet. The ability to move between different cultural settings is an excellent example of the flexibility we pride ourselves in as NLP Practitioners. The Maori King Potatau Te Wherowhero said about education "*Kotahi ano te kohao o te ngira, e kuhuna ai te miro pango, te miro whero, te miro ma.*" (There is but one eye of the needle whereby the black thread, the red thread and the white thread must pass). His meaning was that the thread does not have to change colour to get through the needle. While the needle remains the same needle, it permits each thread to pass through in its uniqueness. In the same way, it is in our interests to have NLP available for people from many different cultural threads to pass through.

Is NLP More Effective With Men?

Gender provides us with a second perspective on the cognitive bias in the NLP. An interesting controlled study of NLP use in Psychotherapy was organised by Martina Genser-Medlitsch and Peter Schütz in Vienna, Austria in 1996 (Schütz et alia 2001, p 232-233). The test group were seen by members of a group of 37 NLP Master Practitioners (22 men and 15 women) who used a full range of NLP techniques with great success. In the assessment after NLP therapy and at 6 month follow-up, there was an interesting gender difference. Men improved more than women on 40% of the symptom dimensions as identified by the study. This difference was especially marked in the assessment of how fully clients felt in control of their life, and in reduction of paranoid thoughts, aggression, depression and anxiety.

This result suggests that NLP is more effective with men. The question is, is it the gender bias of the subject that determines the NLP results, or is it the gender bias of NLP that determines the subject's results?

Gender Differences In Communication And Metaprograms

Do men and women have different ways of experiencing life and of understanding NLP? If so, NLP models and theories may contain presuppositions that match men's ways of sorting experience better than they match women's. Do such different ways of sorting experience exist?

The answer is that there are some well researched differences between men's and women's *metaprograms* (to use an NLP term for personality traits). In general research into personality traits, the difference does not seem marked. In the world's most commonly used personality profiling system (Myers-Briggs personality profiling system, see Wiggins, 1989), research suggests that about 55% of women make decisions based on feelings and values, and 45% based on logical reasoning. The statistic is reversed for men. This 5% difference each way is statistically significant, but it still means that it would be naïve to try and predict decision-making style from gender alone. There is similarly a statistical difference in men's and women's ability to decode non-verbal signals in a conversation. Women score higher than men in the ability to decode emotional responses from voice tone and from facial expression, for all emotions except anger (where men score higher). But as with the Feeler-Thinker difference, the variation is small (Matlin, 2000, p 206-208). Out of six possible correct scores, men average around 4 and women around 4.5. Such differences are significant, but not significant enough to claim that men and women "come from different planets", as some authors have done.

One place where we can notice larger gender differences is in the type of psychiatric disorders which men and women suffer from when under pressure. While the *overall* rate of psychiatric disorders (including drug and alcohol abuse and personality disorders) is similar for men and women, there are certain psychiatric disorders which are more common for women and certain disorders which are more common for men. Adult women are twice as likely to present with depression as are adult men (though there is no difference in the rate amongst children). They are three times as likely as men to present with phobias, including agoraphobia, and about ten times as likely to present with eating disorders (Matlin, 2000, p 432-465).

However, the most dramatic differences are found when we check expectations and perception of events. Dale Spender conducted research where she had a man and a woman in a conversation together. In each case the man spoke for more minutes than the woman. The participants were then asked whether they felt that they had a fair share of the conversation. Most of the men felt that they had not had a fair share of time, even when they actually spoke for 75% of the time (Spender, 1989). It would not be surprising to find, after this, that many men in the NLP community doubt our claim that two thirds of NLP publications are by men.

Differences in expectation even alter the results of research. For example, there is much research showing that women have more difficulty than men performing a visualization task where they mentally rotate a geometric figure (this is actually the largest difference found in any spacial skill). However the difference disappears if the subjects are told that the skill being tested is one useful for interior decorating –a traditionally female area of skill in western society (Matlin, 2000, p 176). The research certainly reveals a gender difference, but perhaps not quite the one that the researchers expected. It seems that much of the result is based on women's expectations as to their ability.

Gender Differences In Responsiveness To Others

Even more significant in the application of NLP, is research suggesting that women are more responsive to expectations and feedback from others generally. In one study, participants perform a cognitive task, and then rate their level of self-confidence. A few minutes later, they receive a comment from the researcher, either telling them they did well or they did poorly (the comments are assigned randomly and are unrelated to their actual success). The participants are then asked to rate their self-confidence again. Female self confidence surges up an average of 40 points with positive feedback, and drops an average of 60 points with the negative feedback. Male self confidence shifts one point up with positive feedback and six points down with the negative (Matlin, 2000, p 186-188). Such comments affect women more both emotionally and cognitively. Further research shows that women not only feel more affected by such evaluations, but are more willing to *believe* the opinions expressed in others' evaluations of them (Roberts and Nolen-Hoeksema, 1994). They are more likely to have, in NLP terms, an External Motivation Source (Charvet, 1995, p 45-58).

This difference in "motivation source" certainly goes some way to explaining the disparity in the results found in the Austrian study of NLP therapy, mentioned above (Schütz et alia 2001, p 232-233). Here, one important difference in results involved whether the person felt in charge of their life. Women did not "improve" in this symptom area as well as men. Being in charge of one's own life, or "at cause", is an important notion in NLP. It is useful to consider that truly being in charge of one's life and "at cause" may have quite different meanings to men and to women. It may be that our framing of this notion in NLP presupposes a view of mental health that is more in keeping with the way men have already learned to behave. Men have learned to consider their own opinions as more important than others' opinions, as a measure of their own success. In that sense, they are "in charge of their own lives". By contrast, women, it seems, may consider others' opinions more fully.

The Presuppositions of NLP imply that life is "systemic" (Dilts 1998, p 7-10). This means that an individual person's results cannot be considered separate from the systems they interact in. In this model, no human being is ever totally autonomous, and a healthy response requires both identifying one's own causality and noticing the feedback loops in which one participates with others. This is the key foundation for *Transforming Communication*, an NLP course on co-operative relationships which is explained later in this chapter. In this course we emphasize the importance of hearing other's opinions and responding to their concerns, as *well* as the value of stating one's own concerns and opinions. Despite its recognition of the systemic nature of life, most NLP theory seems to us to have downplayed the first of these sets of skills (responding to others). Not only have women developed this first set of skills far more fully than men, but also the response they get from these skills provides their criteria for success. Training in *Transforming Communication* values the skills and criteria significant to both genders, balancing autonomy and systemic interaction.

The Feminist Critique In Psychotherapy And Media

In the field of Psychotherapy, women's views are more fully articulated than in NLP. One explanation is that in the field of psychotherapy, gender differences were recognized in the 1970s and 1980s and a "Feminist critique" of psychotherapy evolved to respond to them. The result of this critique has been an increasing satisfaction with psychotherapy amongst women, and an increasingly large contribution by women to psychotherapeutic literature. Thus Phyllis Chesler, author of a severe critique of therapy called *Women and Madness* (1972) later wrote (1990) "Despite my early critique of institutional psychiatry and of private patriarchal therapy geared to high income clients, I have come to believe that women can and do benefit from feminist therapy." NLP as a discipline had already radicalized and broken out of the psychotherapy mould before this new understanding of women's issues occurred in the therapy field. We may have missed something of value.

One of the key changes in attitude that this rethinking of psychotherapy led to was a reframing of the notion of "being in charge of one's life". Feminist therapist Miriam Greenspan refers to the standard joke in which men are considered to be incapable of asking for directions when lost. She points out that it is a strength to be able to ask for directions when one is lost. A man who cannot ask for street directions is not actually more "at cause" or "in charge of his life" than a woman who asks. Greenspan notes, "Women who fail to recognize their strength in being able to depend on others or who fail to recognize the ways that men depend on women, end up thinking of women as "dependent" and men as "independent". Such women often feel they've failed when they don't adopt a male style of autonomy – both in relationships and at work. But in many cases this "failure" is due to the fact that women do not really *want* to become autonomous in the way that men have been. They do not wish to become competitively embattled against others, or to see their own individuality as contingent upon the renunciation of their needs for intimacy or family." (Greenspan, 1983, p 298-299). This lack of recognition of men's dependence and the resulting sense of failure women sometimes feel in not being autonomous is explained clearly in Shelle Rose Charvet's article "The Purpose of Womanhood?" in Anchor Point (Charvet, 2003)

Shelia Ernst and Lucy Goodison urge that therapy support women in this useful human skill of inter-dependence. "Part of our therapy must emphasize our need to nourish ourselves and to seek nurturance from others." (Ernst and Goodison, 1981, p 315). Greenspan urges that, for the woman caught in male presuppositions about independence, "…to overcome her first type of dependence (the impossible feminine demand that a man can make her feel good about herself) she had to reclaim her right to the second type of dependence: her authentic need for intimate connection." (Greenspan, 1983, p 292).

Some men have argued that the traditional notion of the independent male does not actually serve their own sex well. "It can be hard for men to accept that 'real strength is recognizing your own weakness' since this threatens our very sense of masculinity." says men's movement activist Vic Seidler "This makes it difficult to realize that it is just this kind of sharing that others are demanding of us. It is this which promises to give relationships greater depth. It is also difficult for our partners when we swing between denying that we have emotional needs at all to feeling totally overwhelmed by our needs." (Seidler, 1985, p 156 and 174) The particular dilemmas faced by men in their attempts to be "autonomous" may well contribute to the psychiatric problems which are more prevalent for men (problems such as denying pain by alcohol abuse).

Individual And Social Change

A key change that the Feminist critique brought to psychotherapy was the understanding that the changing of society and the changing of individuals go hand in hand. The systemic nature of change is acknowledged in NLP (i.e. real change requires changes in the systems in which we are embedded). The NLP term "ecology" usually assumes the importance of examining how a client's relationships and social systems affect their symptoms. Women's critiques of psychotherapy expanded this idea of ecology to include all of society.

One place in NLP where many NLP trainers already recognize the importance of social realities is in the experience of children labelled by the school system. Richard Bandler says, for example, "When I was asked to work for a school district, I had a few things I wanted to go after. One of them is the whole notion of "learning disabilities", "minimal brain dysfunction", "dyslexia", or "educational handicaps". Those are very important sounding words, but what they all describe is that *the teaching isn't working*." Why is this reframe useful? Because, as Bandler notes, "I'd rather not explain failure that way. I'd rather think about it as a "*teaching* dysfunction", and at least leave open the possibility that we can learn to change it." (Bandler, 1985, p 125). This is the advantage of widening the frame to include the whole school system. By enhancing the collective power of children as a group, we may be able to truly change things for individual students. If we work individually with each "dyslexic" child, we are only dealing with the symptoms.

The need for collective solutions is also evident in terms of gender. We noted earlier that more women than men are depressed. The following are some more specific factors which research has shown to be correlated with depression in women (Matlin, 2000, p 436):

- several young children living with the woman
- low income
- unhappy marriage
- low self esteem
- low sense of personal accomplishment
- the woman follows traditional feminine gender stereotyping
- little sense of control over her own life

It is clear that, for many of these factors, each individual woman's experience is affected by the general social situation of women. Confirming for a woman client that it is realistically challenging to live with several young children means empowering her to identify actual changes in her lifestyle which may make life more fun (rather than just changing the submodalities in which she thinks of her life). And supporting her to act with other women to change this lifestyle opens up the possibility for her to feel in charge of her life in a way that is interdependent rather than "autonomous" in a traditional male sense. Indeed, in the social context in which women find themselves, their ability to be interdependent has been an important learned skill which successful therapy can help develop, rather than deny.

Interdependence: Virginia Satir's Example

Returning to the roots of NLP, we have an excellent model of interdependent work in the practice of Virginia Satir. The first NLP model (the metamodel) provides a series of questions, and was modelled from Satir (Grinder and Bandler, 1975). Research suggests that women ask more questions than men in conversations (Baird, 1976), a feature of their interest in and attention to other's opinions. A change process based on the metaphor of questioning may make more sense to women practitioners, inviting their clients into an interdependent communication structure. It may also give more control to the client than one based on the metaphor of verbal directions (including "embedded commands", see Bandler and Grinder, 1975, p 239).

But the metamodel is only one of the things we could learn from Satir's work in relation to interdependence. Satir gives another great example of working in a way consistent with this principle. "Some years ago I took on an assignment in a southern county to work with people on public welfare." She explains (Satir, 1993, p 204-206). "What I wanted to do was show that everybody has the capacity to be self-sufficient and all we have to do is to activate them. I asked the county to pick a group of people who were on public welfare, people from different racial groups and different family constellations. I would then see them as a group for three hours every Friday." Satir asked each person what their dreams were and what stood in the way of their reaching them. "One woman shared that she always wanted to be a secretary…. She said "I have six kids, and I don't have anyone to take care of them while I'm away." "Let's find out," I said. "Is there anybody in this group who would take care of six kids for a day or two a week while this woman gets some training here at the community college?"

The results were dramatic. Satir reports "Everyone found something…. The woman who took in the children became a licensed foster care person. In 12 weeks I had all these people off public welfare. I've not only done that once. I've done it many times." By accepting their need for mutual support, Satir demonstrated their ability to change the social context in which their problems occurred, and hence solve their problems. Her intervention with this one woman, for example, changed almost all the factors listed as correlating with depression in women (above). Satir explains about gender issues in particular, "I regard the emerging balance between women and men as being as earthshaking as the discovery that the world is round instead of flat." (Satir, 1988, p 379).

Note that Satir's aim was to demonstrate that people could be self-sufficient. However, for her, this self-sufficiency, this being "at cause", included their acting socially and asking for assistance from each other. She is encouraging interdependence rather than isolated independence. While not all NLP practitioners will be able to work in community groups as Satir did, all of us could benefit from modelling this attitude and supporting our clients to empower themselves interdependently.

Recognizing the power of interdependence would be one step towards creating an NLP that shares men's and women's wisdom more equally.

B. Couples Coaching

The Crisis Of Couples Counselling

It's no secret that one to one intimate relationships (such as marriage) are more challenging to maintain in the world today. In the United States, for example, between 50% and 67% of first marriages end in divorce, and the percentage is higher for each subsequent marriage and higher for non-marital intimate partnerships. One sad result of this is increased illness. Those of us who are able to stay in an intimate couple (whether we are male or female) will live approximately 4 years longer, making the couples lifestyle one of the most significant life extension interventions known (Gottman and Silver, 1999, p 4). The cost of separation in economic terms is the source of many jokes, but it is also a realistic fact that people who separate, after living together for any length of time, considerably affect their financial future.

Is there help for those whose relationships do not seem to be built to last? Of those couples who attempt to heal the rift by going to a couple's counsellor, 43.6% will separate within five years of their "therapy" and less than 18% will get any prolonged measurable benefit from their counselling. Most of these couples say that the therapy "helped", but from the research the result of that help is usually a continuation of destructive patterns of interaction, followed in half of all cases by divorce. (Gottman, 1999, p 3-6).

How NLP Emerged From And Transcends Traditional Couples Counselling

NLP, the field I teach in, emerged out of the work of one extraordinary couples counsellor. Often called the grandmother of Family Therapy, Virginia Satir assisted thousands of married couples and families to resolve old conflicts and create a more enjoyable life together. One day Satir was demonstrating couples counselling in front of a group of student psychotherapists. She stopped talking to the couple she was working with, and asked if any of her students could carry on, using her methods. On by one, students tried to help the couple, but none of them seemed to know how Virginia chose what to say. Virginia seemed to have some magic way of knowing just which question or comment would reveal and alter the complex dynamic of the couple's relationship.

At the back of the room, a young man was tape recording the training session. He was Richard Bandler, a computer programmer and a graduate student of linguistics at the University of California, and he had no training in psychology or couples dynamics. Finally, after Satir's students had failed, Bandler came to the front of the room and offered to talk to the couple. Amazingly, he seemed to know exactly how Virginia was constructing her questions and suggestions to the couple. In 1976 Richard Bandler and his Professor of Linguistics John Grinder wrote the first of several books explaining their discoveries about communication, human change, and teaching. Their first book, called "The Structure of Magic" (Bandler and Grinder, 1975) explained that by understanding how to utilise the inner "languages" of the brain (a methodology they later called neuro-linguistic programming or NLP) anyone could learn to achieve the excellent results of the most expert communicators, teachers and therapists.

Virginia Satir said in her foreword to this book (Bandler and Grinder, 1975): "It would be hard for me to write this Foreword without my own feeling of excitement, amazement and thrill coming through. I have been a teacher of family therapy for a long time .... I have a theory about how I make change occur. The knowledge of the process is now considerably advanced by Richard Bandler and John Grinder, who can talk in a way that can be concretised and measured about the ingredients of the what that goes into making the how possible." (Satir, in Bandler and Grinder, 1975, p. Viii).

Amazingly, forty years on, the one type of therapy that the students of Bandler and Grinder's method are usually least trained in is couples counselling! This section of the chapter launches itself from the couples counselling roots of NLP, explores the research based leading edge of twenty-first century couples coaching, and presents an NLP-based model of couples coaching. Using it fully presupposes some basic knowledge of NLP, for which I recommend my book Transforming Communication

2004).

When I talk to new coaches and NLP Master Practitioners, I frequently find that they have bought the idea that those original students of Satir had; the idea that there is some complex, pathological and hidden dynamic going on between the two people in a couple… some dynamic that the coach or counsellor needs years of experience with to successfully trick the couple out of.

Dan Wile (1992, p 29) shows how this theory has shaped traditional couples counselling. Discussing the foremost theorists in the field, he says "Thus Ackerman (1966) deliberately charms, ridicules, and bullies family members; Haley (1963b) and Watzlawick, Weakland, and Fisch (1974) strategically manipulate them with paradoxical instructions; Jackson and Weakland (1961) tactically place them in therapeutic double binds; Haley (1977) systematically browbeats certain partners who fail to do the tasks he assigns them; Minuchin and his colleagues (1967) "frontally silence" overbearing wives to "rock the system" and show their passive husbands how to stand up to them; Speck (1965) openly engages in "power struggles" with families . . . It is perhaps surprising, considering the dramatic nature of these methods, that they have been incorporated into the couples and family therapy traditions with so little discussion and debate."

This adversarial and analytical approach turns out to be as unnecessary in the case of couples counselling as it is in the case of individual therapy or coaching. Richard Bandler was able to replicate what Satir did, not because he understood some hidden dynamics that she was using, but because he was willing to treat the work as a simple task of linguistic analysis. In the last decade, couples therapists themselves have adopted Bandler's willingness to study what actually happens linguistically when a couple are in conflict, and what actually happens when a couple's relationship is successful.

The Gottman Revolution In Couples Counselling

Seattle's Washington University researchers and marital therapists John and Julie Gottman have been in the forefront of this revolution in couples work. Their in depth research on more than a thousand couples over the last thirty years has debunked many cherished theories about what makes intimate relationships work. It has shown, for example, that in general the personality characteristics and even the objective degree of similarity between the couple's personality types is irrelevant to marital happiness. Even the number of arguments between the couple does not determine a couple's sense of satisfaction and likelihood of separation. However, in happy couples, each person perceives the other as being basically a functional person (with certain quirks) and basically similar to them. In happy couples, each perceives arguments as useful and manageable expressions of differences. In unhappy relationships, each partner perceives the other as basically flawed and unlike them, and conflicts are experienced as emotionally traumatic (Gottman, 1999, p 19-21).

When couples are videotaped 24 hours a day, the difference between happy couples and unhappy couples is very small – for example it includes happy couples saying approximately 100 more words of positive comment per day (a mere 30 seconds more of positive talking) compared to unhappy couples. But those 30 seconds are crucial (Gottman, 1999, p 59). Furthermore there are subtle differences in the linguistic patterns that successful couples use before, during and after an argument. These differences in linguistic patterns pervade the whole relationship though, not just the arguments. Gottman's researchers have shown that they can accurately predict whether a couple will divorce just by listening to a five minute conversation between the couple, by identifying the specific language patterns used and seeing the specific non-verbal responses they make to each other (Gottman and Silver, 1999, p 3). But these detailed differences are not merely present in arguments. As Gottman says, his research has shown that "successful conflict resolution isn't what makes marriages succeed." (Gottman and Silver, 1999, p 11). The formation of an intimate relationship, Gottman's research shows, is the formation of a whole new culture. It is the quality of the friendship between the couple, as evidenced in their exact verbal and non-verbal communication, which counts, for both men and women.

What solution focused therapy did for individual coaching is similar to what Gottman's research has contributed to couples coaching. He says "In my therapy the entire problem-solving process is recast as one of identifying and harmonizing people's basic life dreams. Much of the process of conflict resolution is an exploration in using the marital friendship to help make one another's life dreams come true." (Gottman, 1999, p 184). NLP Practitioners and Solution Focused coaches will recognize this approach as the analogue of their own work with individuals. Gottman's research has added considerably to our knowledge of the specific patterns that work in relationships, and the specific coaching interventions that will enhance those patterns. Even where I may disagree with his conclusions (see next section), it is Gottman who has, for the first time, provided the research data to form realistic conclusions rather than psychobabble hypotheses. Next,

Gottman has demonstrated that by shifting from analysis and manipulation to coaching the couple to respond in the way that more successful couples do, he can double the success of couples counselling .

Some Confusion In Gottman's Conclusions

Before we go any further, it is fair to say that there is one core conclusion drawn by John Gottman which I (like many other solution focused coaches or therapists) would not agree with. It appears immediately below. In one and the same book, Gottman says:

A) "Active listening asks couples to perform Olympic-level emotional gymnastics when their relationship can barely work… One of the most startling findings of our research is that most couples who have maintained happy marriages rarely do anything that even partly resembles active listening **when they're upset**." (Gottman and Silver, 1999, p 11)

B) "The bottom-line rule is that, before you ask your partner to change the way he or she drives, eats or makes love, you must make your partner feel that you are understanding. If either (or both) of you feels judged, misunderstood, or rejected by the other, you will not be able to manage the problems in your marriage. This holds for big problems and small ones…There's a big difference between "You are such a lousy driver. Would you please slow down before you kill us?" and "I know how much you enjoy driving fast. But it makes me really nervous when you go over the speed limit. Could you please slow down?" Maybe that second approach takes a bit longer. But that extra time is worth it since it is the only approach that works.

The contradiction between these two statements is so clear to me that it needs little comment. Suffice it to say that I agree entirely with Gottman's comments in the second quote, from page 149 of his book, and I agree with Robert Scuka (2005, p 56) who critiques the comment above that in much more detail and summarizes "In conclusion, despite the creativity and usefulness of much of the empirical research conducted by Gottman, his interpretation of the results of that research and its meaning with regard to empathy is seriously flawed. More to the point, Gottman's inference and claim, that marital therapy should "abandon" teaching distressed couples how to empathize for the purpose of improving their relationship, is in no way legitimated by the research itself. It is also contradicted by some of Gottman's own assumptions, as well as the results of his own research." Reflective listening is indeed challenging to apply, especially in a conflict-ridden relationship, AND it is an essential skill for finding a way out of conflict; a skill which has not been taught to us and which couples benefit enormously by learning.

Repeatedly, as I read Gottman's research, I regret that he did not study a linguistics based model such as NLP before analyzing the language structures of the couples he studied. I find his references to language patterns are often confusing and unclear. For example, he quotes Dan Wile's critique of I messages (a skill which Gottman goes on to advocate) as if that critique is a critique of reflective listening (a skill which Gottman suggests is only useful outside of conflict situations - Gottman, 1999, p 9). He confuses "I messages" and "you messages", for example suggesting that "I think you are selfish" is an I message (Gottman and Silver, 1999, p 165). He does not define clearly how the core patterns he found to be harmful such as "defensiveness" differ from normal and healthy responses. For example he says about healthy relationships "When people feel attacked they tend to respond negatively; usually in stable, happy marriages they respond in kind, while in unstable and unhappy marriages they escalate the negativity." (Gottman, 1999, p 10). And yet he says about defensiveness that it is one of the four most serious problems in relationship and its most common form is "counter-complaining, or counterattacking when attacked." – i.e. responding in kind when feeling attacked as he previously said healthy couples do (Gottman, 1999, p 45).

However, in general, Gottman's research adds data which affirms and extends my own Transforming Communication approach to relationships. It further suggests that couples counselling is actually coaching the couple to communicate using these skills. In the field of parenting coaching, John Gottman says he admires the approach of Dr Haim Ginott, who teaches I messages, Reflective Listening and Win-Win Conflict Resolution in the same structure as we use in Transforming Communication. In discussing parenting relationships, Gottman again emphasizes the importance of "Communicating empathy and understanding of the emotions, even if these emotions underlie misbehaviour." (Gottman, 1999, p 330).

C. Transforming Communication For Couples

Clear Problem Ownership

Before discussing what a couples coach does, I want to review the Transforming Communication skills and emphasize what Gottman's research adds to these. To begin using the methodology of Transforming Communication in any relationship situation, one simply checks whether at this moment one's own present internal state is desired or not (a "problem", as Dilts notes in Dilts, 1993, p193, is any distance between present state and desired state). One then steps into what NLP calls "second position" and checks whether the other person's internal state is desired by them or not. There are four possible results to these checks (Gordon, 1974, p38-39):

1) Neither of us owns a Problem. If both states are desired, then no problem exists, and the focus of communication can be towards individual and mutual enjoyment. In the situation where neither of us owns a problem, a larger range of language patterns will be safe to use (safe in the sense of preserving both of our self esteem, and preserving the relationship). This area offers the most potential for us to grow personally, as each of us has energy free from problem-solving to focus on our goals and on discovery. It is the area where a couple build their "positive emotional bank account" that they may need to draw on in conflict resolution. Gottman's research shows that successful couples devote approximately 20 minutes a day to non-problem activities such as:

- Simply responding to each comment or nonverbal communication by their partner. Such communications are called "bids" (for attention or caring) by John Gottman and in a healthy relationship most bids are responded to. Either cooperation or disagreement are indications of a successful bid, but in unhappy couples over 50% of bids are not even detected by the partner (Gottman, 1999, p 201)
- Reviewing the history of their relationship and reframing it as a positive story of friendship.
- Making positive and appreciative comments about the relationship. The ratio of positive comments to negative comments in successful relationships is approximately 5 to 1, whereas in unsuccessful relationships it is less than 1 to 1. This is true both in conflict and in everyday interaction (Gottman, 1999, p 59-61). Indeed, Gottman found that in successful relationships, participants (women in particular) tended to monitor and limit the quantity of negative comments by their partners about anything at all. In unsuccessful relationships, they accepted that their partner had a right to be continuously and unproductively angry, unhappy and blaming of both them and others (Gottman, 1999, p 73-74) .
- Learning what creates sexual attraction for each of them, what creates the feeling of being loved and of loving for each of them, and what confirms their mutual commitment to the relationship. Robert Sternberg proposed, from his research, that intimate relationships

involve three variables: passion, intimacy and commitment (Sternberg, 1986). Successful couples learn the "strategies" each partner uses to create and confirm the existence of these three variables.

- Discussing each person's values and dreams, and finding shared values and creating shared meanings.
- Sharing meals together, and sharing housework together
- Checking in after time apart and each listening to how the other's day has been.
- Going out together, both for practical purposes such as shopping, and for entertainment
- Making love and intimate touching/holding. Effective couples accept that people have different levels of need for these behaviours, and that as a partner they will support their loved one in meeting those needs. University of Oregon researchers John Howard and Robyn Dawes (1976) found that while rate of sexual intercourse and rate of arguing varied from couple to couple, any couple who argue more frequently than they have sex are likely to divorce in the near future.

If one of the people is in an undesired state, then they "own a problem" in the terms first used by Dr Thomas Gordon (1955). This does not mean that they are "at fault" or "should" change something. It simply means that they are not in their desired state. Possible results 2), 3), and 4) relate to this situation.

2) The other person owns a problem. If I am in a relationship where at this moment I feel okay, and the other person does not (i.e. they are in an undesired or "problem" state), it can be useful to focus my attention on assisting them to reach their desired state. This process, called Helping, is of course a common one when you are assisting a client to change. It also occurs when you are listening to your spouse talking about a difficult day, or when you offer to assist your co-worker to learn how to perform a new work task. The most effective skills for Helping will be ones that linguistically identify the problem space and the desired state as existing inside the other person's experience (I will say, for example, "So what you want to change is..." rather than "So what I think you should change is..."). These skills avoid patronising the person by suggesting what they "should" aim for, "should" feel and "should" be able to cope with. These skills include:

- Non-verbal rapport. Gottman's research demonstrates the power of what NLP calls matching and mirroring. Couples who can understand each other actually adjust their bodies to experience what the other person is experiencing. They breathe in time with each other, sit in similar positions, use similar voice tonality, and even their heart rates match (Gottman, 1999, p 27).

- Open questions that invite the other person to talk. These usually begin with the words "How...?" and "What...?" rather than the more intrusive "Why...?" or the more leading "Did you...?", "Didn't you...?" and "Don't you...?"

- Reflective listening. This involves restating the person's own experience, opinions and feelings, in words which are similar to theirs e.g. "That was an unpleasant experience then." "You wanted to get a different perspective." In this situation in particular (where the other partner owns a problem), Gottman's research identified that reflective listening was the most powerful response offered by members of successful relationships (Gottman and Silver, 1999, p 87-89.

3) I own a problem. If I am in a relationship where at this moment the other person feels okay, and I do not (i.e. I am in an undesired or "problem" state), it can be useful to focus my attention on finding a way for me to reach my desired state. This process could be called Problem Solving. As we know in NLP, people own a problem in response to particular internal representations. If the representations related to my problem state are about the other person (if I'm upset or angry or hurt "about something they did", for example) then this process of problem solving is called Assertion. For example, I own a problem where I'm frustrated about my spouse's failure to wash the dishes, or where I'm resentful that I ended up doing extra work when my partner didn't arrive home on time. The most effective skill for Assertion will be one that linguistically identifies the problem and the desired state as existing inside my own experience ("What I want to change is..." rather than "So what you might want to do is..."). This skill is called an "I message" (Gordon, 1974, 139-145). In a conflict, a clear I message identifies:

- the sensory specific behaviour that is the subject of the concern,
- the internal state (emotion) which I have generated in response to this behaviour,
- any sensory specific effects on me of that behaviour.

An example of the format for an I message would be "When...[sensory specific behaviour], I feel...[congruent description of my internal state] and the effect on me is... [sensory specific effects of the behaviour]". This structure avoids insulting or blaming the other person, and avoids patronising them by telling them what they "should" do. By not suggesting one specific solution, it leaves the process of generating solutions until the other person's situation has been heard and can be taken into account (as in examples below). Helping skills by themselves will be ineffective in the area where I own a problem, suggesting to the other person that it's up to them what solution is reached.

4) We both own a problem. This situation implies that some combination of linguistic skills will be useful (So what you want is... and what I want is...). Where we both own a problem in response to related internal representations, then this situation is a "Conflict". This doesn't mean that we are necessarily opposed to each other, or that one of us must win and one lose. It simply means that we both are upset, angry, hurt etc about related issues (e.g. I think we should spend more time together and the other person wants more space. I want to use the family car tomorrow and so does my partner) Such situations benefit from a combination of the helping and assertive skills, as well as from specific conflict resolution skills (including win-win conflict resolution, consulting and modelling).

John Gottman's research reveals that successful couples differ not merely in their handling of conflicts, but in their handling of each of these four Problem Ownership areas. That means that effective coaching of couples needs to teach the couple to respond differently in each of the four areas also (Gottman, 1999, p 59-61).

Effectively Raising A Concern

The situation would be very easy if problem ownership stayed constant throughout any conversation. If this was the case, in the "no-problem" situation, a conversation would involve simply exploring positive states and outcomes together. In the "other owns a problem" situation, a conversation would involve simply pacing the other person's dilemma, assisting the other person to clarify what their outcome is, and guiding them through processes to assist change towards that. In the "I own a problem" situation, a conversation would involve simply asserting my position and identifying the changes I want.

In real life, it is more useful if I continuously monitor the changing internal states of myself and the other person, and adjust my language use to best represent the shifts of problem ownership, many of which are of course a result of my own previous communications. For example, in the midst of helping my partner solve her or his problem, I may discover that I myself am uncomfortable with the way my partner insists that I listen to complaints about what goes wrong, and does not shift to an outcome (solution focused) frame. From using Helping skills ("So for you the problem is..." and "So what you want is...") I would then shift to using Assertive skills ("One thing I'm finding frustrating about the way you're talking is..." and "I'd find it easier to help if...").

Most particularly, once I have used an Assertive skill, a common outcome is for my partner to shift into the problem state themselves (to feel uncomfortable in response to my communication). When a person hears my I message "I resented the way you didn't get that report to me on time as we'd arranged. It involved me in a lot of extra work" it is rare for them to respond with congruent joy and enthusiasm to improve next time. If you think of times when someone has, however skilfully, asserted themselves with you in this way, you'll notice that you're more likely to experience feelings of embarrassment, discomfort, hurt, annoyance, and mismatching responses. That is to say, you're more likely to own a problem about the message, and possibly about the issue.

If I've used an I message (Assertion skill) and the other person owns a problem about that, the next step to getting my problem solved will be to shift back from Assertion, and help them solve their own problem. To do this, I simply use reflective listening (a Helping language pattern), to pace their concern (e.g. "You think I'm over-reacting..."). As NLP points out, there is no resistance, only a lack of rapport. Once the other person feels fully heard in their own problem state (evidenced usually by a nod of the head), then it becomes possible to restate my I message taking into account their comment. As they have now been heard, their "emotional temperature" is reduced, and they are more able to hear my concern and respond positively to it.

The process of resolving such a situation by alternating between I messages and reflective listening is called the two step" in Transforming Communication because it is like a dance. Here's how it might sound in practice, in a discussion where Joan is using the model in a concern with her work colleague, Frank (notice that if Frank knew the model, the process would be even more fluent, but Joan can use the model regardless of this):

Joan: Frank, I have a problem I'd like to discuss. You arrived home an hour later than expected a couple of times last week and I didn't get the time to myself in the evening that I was hoping for, and I guess I feel a bit resentful about spending that much of my day child-minding. [Joan "owns" a problem: she is the one who is concerned about what has happened, so she uses an I message.

Frank is feeling Okay, so initially he doesn't own a problem.]
Frank: [sighs] Lighten up Joan. I had a busy day; that's all.
Joan: You think I'm over-reacting, and you had a lot of extra stuff to do. [Frank responds indicating that he owns a problem, so Joan does the Two Step and reflective listens him.]
Frank: [nods] Sure. And it's no big deal.
Joan: Well, I still want to know that I have time to myself to do the things that I really want to do. My day is long too. [Frank's nod indicates he feels paced/understood, so Joan Two Steps and restates her I message.]
Frank: Look, I guess I just forgot how important this can be to you. I'll be more careful. How about, if I do arrive late in future, I could adjust later and give you extra time on the weekend.
Joan: Thanks. I would appreciate your help with that.
Frank: Okay. I just wasn't thinking. Sorry. [Frank is now apologising. As he's still not feeling totally comfortable, Joan again acknowledges his comments before thanking him for changing his approach.]
Joan: Well I'd appreciate sort of knowing that the time for myself is there. Thanks.

This, of course, is a "best case" scenario. There are two other possible outcomes of this discussion, described below. Both are "conflicts".

John Gottman found that such discussions and conflicts occurred in even the best relationships, and that effective couples might get very emotional (even angry) as they talked about such issues, but they avoided certain key destructive behaviours. Those seven core behaviours to avoid (listed by Gottman and Silver, 1999, p 25-46) include:

- Harsh Start-up of the discussion with an angrily stated "You message"
- Criticism of the person as a person rather than complaint about their behaviour.
- Contempt of the other person, conveyed nonverbally by raised eyebrows and a sneering facial expression, or verbally by mockery of the person's position, sarcasm and hostile humour. This is the most serious of the seven behaviours, it is the fastest way to predict separation, and it is virtually unseen in successful relationships (Gottman, 1999, p 128)
- Defensiveness, expressed by arguing/blaming back while refusing to acknowledge the other's concern or accept that they have a problem.

- Stonewalling, expressed by simply stopping talking without negotiating, or leaving the room.
- Becoming Emotionally Flooded, as a result of these behaviours, as evidenced by the person being physically over-aroused, with a pulse above 95 beats per minute.
- Failure of Repair Attempts and Self-nurturing behaviours, e.g. to call a halt for time to calm down, or to apologise and ask to start again, as these last patterns occur.

Three Types Of Conflict

The Two Step process will lead to one of three outcomes. Depending on which outcome occurs, you can easily identify which steps to take next to most effectively resolve the conflict.

Outcome 1) Misunderstanding. The Two Step process itself resolves the conflict (as above). Such conflict could be considered a simple miscommunication. In the example above, for instance, once Frank has clearly heard what Joan's problem is (which is assisted by her use of I messages and reflective listening -both her use of clear first position and clear second position) the problem is solved. Conflicts of the type described as Closed Calibration Loops by Bandler and Grinder in the book Changing With Families (see Transforming Communication p 160-162) are of this type. No further action may be needed.

Outcome 2) Conflict of Needs. As a result of the Two Step process, it becomes clear that both people have a concrete problem. Both people can understand that the other person has a problem, though they are reluctant to solve the other person's problem as this would leave them with their own difficulty. Thomas Gordon calls this a Conflict of Needs. In NLP terms it is a conflict which both parties have agreed to keep at the neurological level of environment, behaviour or capability (their values and sense of identity are not a subject of discussion, only how and where they do what). John Gottman calls this a "Solvable Conflict" and recommends developing solutions which honour both parties "dreams" in the conflict. In such a situation, Gordon recommends the skilled use of his 6 step win-win conflict resolution model (Gordon, 1974, p217-234), which is an analogue of NLP's 6 step Reframing. Gordon's six steps are:

1. Identify the problem in terms of two sets of needs, rather than two conflicting solutions. Needs are more chunked up descriptions than solutions, and are comparable to evidence procedures in NLP ("How will you know that this problem is solved?" rather than "What specific way would you suggest to solve this problem right now?")

or even to Positive Intentions ("If you get this solution, what do you get through that, that is even more important?) . Gottman describes this as discovering what the "dreams" behind the stated solution are.

2. Brainstorm potential solutions which could meet both sets of needs/outcomes/dreams.
3. Evaluate the ability of these proposed solutions to meet both sets of needs.
4. Choose a solution or more than one solutions to put into action.
5. Act
6. Evaluate the results.

An example would be if the conversation between Frank and Joan went like this:

Joan: Frank, I have a problem I'd like to discuss. You arrived home an hour later than expected a couple of times last week and I didn't get the time to myself in the evening that I was hoping for, and I guess I feel a bit resentful about spending that much of my day child-minding. [Joan "owns" a problem: she is the one who is concerned about what has happened, so she uses an I message. Frank is feeling Okay, so initially he doesn't own a problem.]

Frank: [sighs] Lighten up Joan. I had a busy day; that's all.

Joan: You think I'm over-reacting, and you had a lot of extra stuff to do. [Frank responds indicating that he owns a problem, so Joan does the Two Step and reflective listens him.]

Frank: [nods] Sure. And if I come home without completing that stuff, I'll end up in rouble at work.

Joan: So you want to make sure you get the things done at work that are your responsibility. Well, I still want to know that I have time to myself to do the things that I really want to do. My day is long too. Maybe we can find a way to meet both those concerns. [Frank now understands that Joan has a concrete problem, as his nod indicates, but if he agreed to help her, he'd have a problem of his own (trying to guess what issues were serious enough for her). This is what Thomas Gordon calls a Conflict of Needs and John Gottman calls a solvable problem. Joan sums up the two sets of needs/outcomes, and invites Frank to begin win-win conflict resolution to identify a solution which will meet both sets of needs/outcomes.]

Frank. [nods] Yeah. I guess I could adjust later and give you extra time on the weekend if I get home late in the week.

Joan: Thanks. That would work for me too. I would appreciate your help with that.

Frank: Okay. Let's do that.

Outcome 3) Conflict of Values. As a result of the Two Step process, it becomes clear that at least one person believes that the conflict involves their deeper beliefs, values or sense of identity. In Robert Dilts' NLP model these are disagreements at a higher neurological level (Dilts, 1993, p 55-56). Such a person will be reluctant to engage in the sort of conflict resolution demonstrated above because their values are "non-negotiable". Put another way, Person A believes that Person B is trying to change Person A's values/identity, which Person A considers is really "none of Person B's business". This is what Thomas Gordon calls a "Values Collision" (Gordon, 1974, p283-306). Note that in this situation it is less likely that a satisfactory solution will be reached in one session.

John Gottman found that 69% of all relationship conflicts were in this category, in both successful and unsuccessful relationships (Gottman and Silver, 1999, p 130). Gottman calls these conflicts "unsolvable problems", where the partners' basic dreams are in conflict. He doesn't mean that nothing can be done about such conflicts; simply that they cannot be resolved in a session of "problem-solving" talk. In fact, he notes that successful couples learn to respect and honour each other's differing values, and accept that the difference will continue for some time.

Thomas Gordon also recommends that many values conflicts are best dealt with by learning to live with the difference, or to altering the relationship so that the other person's values do not clash so frequently with theirs. Skills that are recommended by Thomas Gordon for actually influencing others values include values consulting, and modelling. Modelling involves demonstrating, in one's own behaviour, the effectiveness of one's values. Values consulting is a skilled linguistic influencing process which requires (Gordon, 1974, p294-297):

1. Ensuring you have been "hired" as a consultant (that the other person agrees to listen).
2. Preparing your case, especially any relevant information.
3. Sharing your expertise and opinions in simple I message form ("I believe...") and shifting gears to active listen the other's opinion.
4. Leaving the other to make up their own mind, rather than attempting to force a new value. People rarely change values in direct interaction with someone who shares the opposing value. It is more common for them to change at a later time, having been left in a positive state, to choose.

If you attempted to resolve Conflicts of Values as if they were Conflicts of Needs, it could well lead to disillusionment with the conflict resolution process, and the belief that "some people just cannot be engaged in a win-win conflict resolution way". Here's how the conversation between Frank and Joan might go if it was a Conflict of Values:

Joan: Frank, I have a problem I'd like to discuss. You arrived home an hour later than expected a couple of times last week and I didn't get the time to myself in the evening that I was hoping for, and I guess I feel a bit resentful about spending that much of my day child-minding. [Joan "owns" a problem: she is the one who is concerned about what has happened, so she uses an I message. Frank is feeling Okay, so initially he doesn't own a problem.]

Frank: [sighs] Lighten up Joan. I had a busy day; that's all.

Joan: You think I'm over-reacting, and you had a lot of extra stuff to do. [Frank responds indicating that he owns a problem, so Joan does the Two Step and reflective listens him.]

Frank: [nods] Sure. I mean, that's my life. My work is also important to me. I don't really feel comfortable negotiating that with you. [Frank identifies a difference in values about the issue]

Joan: So you see that as your life to decide about. Well, I have a different way of thinking about that particular part of it – the timing piece. I'd like to discuss it some more some time. Would you be willing to hear my thoughts about that? [Joan reflective listens Frank's value and identifies the difference.]

Frank: [sighs] Maybe.... Yeah, I guess so. I don't want to get into a heavy discussion about it now though.

Joan: Great. How about the kids are out on Saturday: maybe we could put aside half an hour to clarify our approaches with each other. [Joan arranges to meet with Frank at a time that is easier for him to discuss their values difference. There, she will continue to use reflective listening and I messages to advocate her value, acting as what Thomas Gordon calls a "Values Consultant", and modelling her values.]

Frank: Okay; that'll work.

D. Coaching Couples To Transform Their Communication

I enjoy working with couples, especially when we can share a model of relationship such as Transforming Communication. Assisting couples to change successfully involves a strategy; an organised sequence of internal representations and external actions performed by the person assisting. I have described this helping sequence in terms of a simple 7 stage model, using the acronym RESOLVE (Bolstad, 2004). The 7 stages of this model are:

Resourceful state for the Practitioner
Establish rapport
Specify outcome
Open up model of world
Leading to desired state
Verify change
Ecological exit

Resourceful State

The first task of a coach working with a couple is to get into a resourceful state to help. This involves understanding what kind of things go wrong in relationships, and what kind of things can be done to support things going well. Generally, when couples come for counselling or coaching, they are either experiencing serious, unpleasant, unresolved conflict or at least one partner feels lonely and has major unmet needs for love and closeness. More often than not, at least one person is not hopeful about the chances of creating what they want within this relationship. In the largest survey ever done on reasons for divorce, 80% of divorced men and women said their relationship broke up because they gradually grew apart and lost a sense of closeness, or because they did not feel loved and appreciated. John Gottman's research shows that this is the core issue which (in only 20-27% of cases of divorce studied) led to an extramarital affair, and not the other way around. Affairs do not generally cause couples to move apart; being apart makes affairs possible. Furthermore, the loss of friendship and love is the core issue for both men and women, so, as Gottman says, maybe they do come from the same planet (Gottman and Silver, 1999, p 16).

In using the coaching metaphor to discuss what you do with a couple, I am recommending that you see yourself as someone hired by the couple to improve their performance, like a sports coach. This coaching metaphor, as used by John Gottman, implies certain things about your intervention:

- The couples coach knows something about what makes relationships work. Like a sports coach, he or she has some skills to share. For me, those skills include most of all the ones I summarised in the last section on Transforming Communication.
- Couples coaching is an emotionally positive experience, where the coach is an ally who helps identify and extend existing relationship

strengths and support clients in reaching for their own best dreams. The coach is not trying to manipulate the clients towards her/his own ideal marriage. Gottman says "My views on what works well in marriages are based solely on what "real people" do to have stable and satisfying marriages, whatever their socioeconomic, ethnic, and racial attributes…. I have often described my goal as fostering the "good enough marriage." I am likely to think a marriage is good enough if the two spouses choose to have coffee and pastries together on a Saturday afternoon and really enjoy the conversation, even if they don't heal one another's childhood wounds or don't always have wall-socket, mind-blowing, skyrocket sex—or even if they aren't very individuated and even appear to some to be "symbiotic." It works for them." (Gottman, 1999, p 185)

- Couples coaching is aimed at empowering the clients themselves to use tools to validate each other, to calm themselves down when they are emotionally flooded, and to communicate in the way that the most successful relaters do. Gottman asks the client to act more positively, rather than providing the positive input himself as one might at times with an individual client. For example, he says: "Let me just stop you here, Mike. Research has shown that there are some patterns of interaction in marriages that are very destructive of love. These are being contemptuous and insulting, and being threatening. I cannot let you interact like that here. I suggest that you don't at home either…. So please rephrase your complaints…." (Gottman, 1999, p 190).

- Couples coaching provides a graduated series of attainable steps – a training in relationship skills from the easiest to the most challenging. John Gottman explains his role metaphorically by saying: "I think of the model of a boxing coach, who, after the bell signals the end of a round, gives the boxer one very simple suggestion that can be used in the next round." (Gottman, 1999, p 190).

Establish Rapport

When you work with a couple, two people are going to walk into the session, not one. You will want to build rapport with both people, and of course one (often the person who arranged the session) may feel more in rapport with you already. While it is tempting to pay most of your attention to that person, it is the other person whose rapport you need most of all, to have permission to help with this relationship. In successful couples coaching, there are, in a sense, three clients: each of the two people, and their relationship itself. The relationship is like a business partnership – it acts as an entity itself.

If only one person wants to preserve the relationship, you have not been hired by the relationship at all, but by one individual. In that case, what you are doing is much more like individual therapy with two people, each of whom has their own agenda. It helps to get clear about this at the start. I begin a couples session by asking what each person expects and wants from our time together.

Virginia Satir, for example, would often start by saying "I'm wondering what, as you're all sitting here, as you're thinking about it, what is it that you expect." (from the transcript of a first session by Virginia Satir, recorded in Haley and Hoffman, 1967, p 99). Satir's question is addressed to all those present. Her reflective listening will also be often addressed to all those present. For example, she summarises their response to this initial question by saying "You obviously are coming here to get all the help I can offer… it was hard for you to figure out why Gary was saying what he was saying. Just as hard as it was for him to figure out why you were saying and doing what you were doing."

Gottman explains "In the initial assessment the spouses need to tell their own stories of their marital dilemma, and its history, and they need to present their theories of what the problems are in their marriage. This seems to be an essential need of all couples coming for therapy. During this process it is important that the therapist listen fairly and nonjudgmentally to both spouses, periodically summarize what is heard (and ask if there is anything else still missing from this summary), and form therapeutic alliances with both people." (Gottman, 1999, p 194)

Gottman suggests that there are two situations in which he refuses to engage clients in couples coaching: cases where a partner is physically violent, and cases where there is an ongoing extramarital affair. Physical violence requires the building into the system of safety structures and it is unreasonable to expect that a person whose life is in danger will participate honestly in creating a new relationship. Gottman's research showed that in such situations, shame results in the abused partner covering up their actual feelings in conjoint sessions (Gottman, 1999, p 118). Where there is an additional (extramarital) relationship, the coaching session is unable to include all the relevant people, and hence shares the fate of trying to counsel half a relationship by discussing relationship dynamics with only one partner. Partially to determine whether either of these conditions exist, Gottman recommends arranging brief individual sessions with each member after the first coaching session, to elicit a genuine sense of how committed each person is to the relationship – whether they really want to stay.

SPECIFY Outcomes

Usually the couples' initial outcomes are described in "away from" terms. They tell you what they want to avoid, to move away from. John Gottman's research shows that merely avoiding or "resolving" individual conflicts will not ensure that a relationship survives. He recommends beginning couples work with much more general tasks, designed to create positive experiences as quickly as possible, and to help him understand what outcomes he will be working towards. These tasks involve a number of questionnaires designed to have each member of the couple describe the quality of their friendship and the level of their conflict resolution skills, both now and when they first were attracted to each other.

When Gottman asks the couple to describe the story of their dilemma, he also directs their focus towards positive strengths by saying "I guess we'll just start by telling me how you met." (Gottman, 1999, p 134). Virginia Satir also asked couples to describe the story of their relationship, in particular to reassociate the couple back into the experience they had when they fell in love and when their relationship was going well. She says, for example "So now let's see how it was, as you think about it, when the family was all happy together." (in Haley and Hoffman, 1967, p 112). In NLP terms this experience re-anchors the couple back into the feelings of love and attraction. It also goes some way towards deconstructing the significant reframes of the relationship history that a quarrelling couple develop, Gottman explains "I have found over and over that couples who are deeply entrenched in a negative view of their spouse and their marriage often rewrite their past." (Gottman and Silver, 1999, p 42).

From collecting this story, Gottman is able to shift to the most significant outcome setting that he does, which is to ask the couple to tell him what their dreams of life together at its best would be. He encourages couples to rediscover these dreams within the very conflicts that they have been having, using the process NLP calls identifying positive outcomes. While he will later coach the couple in doing this themselves, at first it is Gottman who restates the complaints as dreams of how the relationship could be, for example (Gottman, 1999, p 138):

Emma: I want more of that. I now know in my life for the first time what it's like to be in love with someone And being in love, you crave, you want. There are things that have to be done, but I miss that lengthy courtship. I thought it would continue once we were

married. And it really hasn't. We have just not had the time. So…
Gottman: So that's a potential issue – how to build more time together
    into your marriage.

It is quite a moving experience for a couple to hear their worst frustrations reframed as dreams. As examples, Gottman suggests (1999, p 238) that by exploring you may discover that a client shifts from saying:

* "My partner is careless with money" → "I want to have the independence at the end of life that my parents don't have, so I can relax about growing old."
* "My partner is tight with money" → "I want to lead a moral and generous life within a world that is often very unfair to others. I want to carry on my parents' tradition of giving money to charity."

Gottman's idea is that people stay in relationships when those relationships nourish or at least respect the existence of their dreams. The goal to "resolve our conflicts" just isn't big enough to make a relationship work!

Insoo Kim Berg and the other Solution Focused therapists (Berg, 1994)have emphasised that setting outcomes with a member of a couple involves asking for specific, positive descriptions of both what they will do different and what their partner will do different in response. It also involves checking for times when the problem has not occurred (both real or imagined) to check what skills the person has available already. Examples of solution focused questions could include:

a. Asking for a description of the person's outcome. For example:

* "What has to be different as a result of you talking to me?"
* "What do you want to achieve?"
* "What would need to happen for you to feel that this problem was solved?"
* "How will you know that this problem is solved?"
* "When this problem is solved, what will you be doing and feeling instead of what you used to do and feel?"
* "What would your partner need to know was different so that they realise that this problem is solved?"
* b. Asking about when the problem doesn't occur (the exceptions). For example:
* "When is a time that you noticed this problem wasn't quite as bad?"

* "What was happening at that time? What were you doing different? What was your partner doing different"

c. If there are no exceptions, asking about hypothetical exceptions using the "Miracle" question: "Suppose one night there is a miracle while you are sleeping, and this problem is solved. Since you are sleeping, you don't know that a miracle has happened or that your problem is solved. What do you suppose you will notice that's different in the morning, that will let you know the problem is solved?" After the miracle question, you can ask other follow-up questions such as:

* "What would your partner notice was different about you?"
* "What would your partner do differently then?"
* "What would it take to pretend that this miracle had happened?"

Open Up The Partners' Models Of The World

Creating successful relationships involves reframing what is happening in the relationship. The research on successful partnerships shows that happy partners adopt an "optimistic explanatory style" to account for their partner's behaviour. They assume that all the things they approve of in their partner are a result of the positive qualities that they so love. All the things that they don't approve of are simply a result of circumstances such as their partner's childhood, stressful events in their immediate life situation, or misunderstandings. These are the same rose tinted glasses which people who enjoy life use to look at their own situation through (Seligman, 1997).

Leslie Cameron-Bandler suggests that to assist a couple who want to develop a more tolerant attitude to their partner's behaviour you can use a technique based on this type of optimistic explanatory style (1985, p 210). She suggests that you identify the behaviour the person objects to in their partner. Then tell them:

* Imagine yourself doing that behaviour in your relationship, and ask "What circumstances would cause me to behave in this way?" and "What understandable goal might I be trying to reach by doing this behaviour?"
* Ask yourself "How could I behave differently towards my partner, knowing the possible circumstances or goals that might cause that behaviour?"

- Ask yourself "In what way is this behaviour that I object to actually a manifestation of some quality that, at other times, I admire in my partner?"
- Ask yourself "What are the qualities I most want from my partner in this relationship?" and then "How could I more fully live and express those qualities myself, in this situation where my partner behaves in this way that I object to?"

In order to have this optimistic explanatory style, it helps for clients to understand that they and their partners may have different personality traits (what NLP calls metaprograms), different values, and different beliefs. In general, just knowing this will be enough to enable a shift towards a positive relationship. At times, these differences will be the basis of ongoing conflicts of values. Most of these, Gottman's research shows, can be easily incorporated into a successful relationship. One of the most challenging differences is in opinions about the appropriate way of handling emotion. Some successful couples shout and "let off steam" a lot, while other equally successful couples avoid such expression of strong negative emotions altogether, and others express emotions verbally and acknowledge the emotions verbally. All three styles work. Where the two people in a relationship have different emotional styles, the challenge of relationship is greatly increased though (Gottman, 1999, p 95)

Questionnaires such as the Myers Briggs or Kiersey Bates personality questionnaires, or in NLP the LAB Profile questionnaire, elicit metaprogram differences that will be important for a couple to understand. For a trained NLP Practitioner, such differences may be obvious in their first interaction with a couple. An example I teach about early on n NLP training is the difference in sensory preference (visual, auditory, kinaesthetic, auditory digital) as demonstrated in the following conflict:

Brent: [glancing up right repeatedly, and talking in higher, faster voice] Well my first concern is that I can't see how we're supposed to get things done when Jill leaves the house in such chaos. It doesn't look to me like she's at all committed to the relationship.

Jill: [looking down right fairly constantly, and talking in a slower, deeper voice] I can't understand why Brent gets so gripped up about this. He charges in and out of the house a couple of times every day. And even though we're doing things together, we never get much time to touch base. Feels to me like that's where the lack of commitment is!

Brent: Now see, this is the problem. When we do meet, it's as if Jill has a very black and white picture of my part of the relationship. I try to give her a sense of vision about where I see us going with this, and she's kind of got her eyes fixed on the desk in front of her, you know. So our discussions are me trying to get the bigger picture, and her focused on what needs doing today.

Jill: It's not so easy to feel motivated by the grand scheme when you don't feel comfortable with the situation at hand. If we had more time to work through things on a daily basis, I'd feel more like we had somewhere to launch things from.

Another part of opening up a couple's models of the world involves teaching them to understand what happens between them as a system, rather than as a direct one way influencing process. Clients frequently come in believing that their partner (who has personal problems) initiates the conflict between them. I want the couple to understand that both people could begin from very understandable positions and yet end up, by a sequence of interactions, in conflict.

For example, Gottman describes a common systemic male-female conflict pattern that results from the different ways men's and women's bodies respond to stress. Under stress, men secrete more noradrenalin, making them more prone to fear and anger. This makes stressful emotional situations more challenging for men to "pull out" from. Women under stress secrete more oestrogen, a hormone which encourages bonding. To a woman's body, emotional stress is a signal to move closer to others; to a man's body, it is a signal to attack or flee. Consequently, men avoid raising issues that may lead to emotional stress.

By the time women raise an issue, their frustration level is already high, and they are more likely to use criticism and blaming in their start-up (the first of Gottman's "four horsemen of the apocalypse" that indicate divorce risk). Men then tend to respond with defensiveness (the second horseman). Since their attempt to resolve the conflict has been rejected, women then often express contempt (the third horseman) and this is damaging enough to result in the man avoiding any further discussion, thus "stonewalling" (the fourth horseman). (Gottman, 1999, p 41-47).

None of the steps in this sequence can be understood without knowing what precipitated it, and the whole system is a cycle which plays over and over until separation occurs. I reflective listen whole sequences such as this, once I have heard them from the couple (e.g. "So it's a little scary for you to bring up issues John, and that gets you frustrated and means you start off with fairly strong statements sometimes Joan, and then when you defend yourself John, it gives you the sense that nothing is possible here Joan, so that after a while John you get the sense that there's so much hostility here that it makes sense just to check out of the whole conflict. Is that right?") In such a sequence, to blame one partner for the conflict is irrelevant. The only relevant response is to change both people's responses. That is my next task with a couple.

Leading to New Ways of Relating

The central task of my session with a couple involves exploring the actual structure of their communication with each other in the session, and literally coaching them in how to engage in such discussions. The structure of this communication is more important than the theoretical content (which may be any of the above issues, or some issue that the couple have been disagreeing about previously). I use the Transforming Communication model as a basis for our discussing what is happening between the couple, and for selecting which skills will be most useful to use at a particular time.

This is where couples work becomes fundamentally different to individual work. The metamodel is an NLP tool for getting people to send sensory specific I messages, and to initiate sensory specific feedback in the communication process (see Transforming Communication p 122-123). It was developed by classifying linguistically all the questions that Virginia Satir asked as a family therapist. Once we have identified the outcomes for our work together, most of my interaction with the clients is done using questioning tools such as the metamodel, to reframe experiences in sensory specific terms, and using reflective listening tools to validate their expanding learnings, as in the following example from early in a coaching process:

Person A: "You're being incredibly insensitive; that's what's wrong here!"
Coach: "So that's what really upsets you. Can I just check, how, specifically, is he/she being insensitive?"
Person A: "Well, the way she/he wasn't listening when I said all that."
Coach: "Oh; so you had the impression he/she wasn't listening. [to Person B] Were you?"
Person B: "Of course I was. I heard every word. That's so insulting."
Coach: "So as far as you were concerned you were listening. [to Person A] And as far as you were concerned, she/he wasn't. What would let you know she/he actually was listening?"
Person A: "Well, if he/she looked in my direction of course."
Coach: [to Person B] "Did you know that was what she needed to see to

feel listened to?"

Person B: "No. "

Coach: "So this may have happened several times, and when she/he complained, you would have felt insulted; is that right?"

Person B: "Yes. And I suppose that once I feel that way, I actually do listen less."

Person A: "Exactly. So how am I supposed to know if you're listening, if you don't even look at me?"

Coach: "That's what we're after isn't it. A way you can know that he/she's really hearing you. And one solution is for him/her to look at you. Another thing I might add is...Do you feel listened to by me?"

Person A: "Sure."

Coach: "Because I'm aware that one thing I'm doing is checking whether I've understood what you say before I reply each time. Sort of restating it to find out if I got it right. And that gives us both feedback about whether I understand you."

In this sequence, the coach uses the metamodel questions, combined with reflective listening. She/he also models and teaches this feedback process. It would have been so easy for the therapist to have assumed (with person A) that they both knew what "not listening" or even "being insensitive" meant to each of them. In couples therapy the secret is to internally question every definition and every presupposition! Just because one person refers to something and the other person nods doesn't mean they both know what they're talking about.

If a client says "You always sound so angry. Can't you just be friendly?" a coach could intervene and ask the person to rephrase their comment as an I message. They might also respond using reflective listening: " She sounded angry when she said that. Do you mean she always sounds that way to you?" or "You'd like her to be more friendly. What specifically would she do that would be "being friendly"?" These questions are metamodel questions. More examples of this process are given in Satir, Bandler and Grinder's book Changing with Families. The metamodel, again, encourages the other person to send clear "I messages". Notice, however, that I do not recommend initially that you teach the metamodel to the couple. The metamodel is a mismatching skill; it chunks down and disagrees with the other person, and requires a high level of rapport to be used successfully.

My focus in coaching is to help the couple learn a new process of relating, not to solve particular content issues. As in all communication, the content is seductive; by which I mean that it's tempting to get involved in the issues, in finding a solution, in who said what when, in who really has what values, metaprograms or negative anchors. The key to successful couples work is to pay attention most of the time to the process. Sorting out a particular conflict is a great experience, but without understanding the structure of effective communication, the couple are likely to return again and again to get help with future conflicts. Knowing this means I'm willing for us not to complete discussing a particular content in the session, if we can use the time to install a more successful communication process.

Once I have shared the full Transforming Communication model with clients, I can coach them to run through it with specific conflicts which have puzzled them. For example;

Person A: "For example, we had a conflict yesterday about which shirt he should wear to the restaurant."

Coach: "OK, great. Can I just check who owned a problem at that time, when you started talking about that?"

Person A: "Well I think he has a problem letting go of old shirts that are no longer wearable."

Coach: [to Person B] "Did you have a problem, in the terms we mean – were you upset about that?"

Person B: "Not until she hassled me about it."

Coach: [to Person A] "OK. So you had a problem?"

Person A: "I guess. I think he needs to throw out some of those old shirts."

Coach: "Great. Let's replay that. How would you start, knowing that you have a problem?"

Person A; [to Person B] "I'd like you to let go of some of those old shirts."

Coach: "Can I check; what is the sensory specific behaviour, how do you feel about it, and are there any concrete effects on you."

Person A: "OK. When you wear one of those old shirts with a hole in it, I feel embarrassed, and the effect is that I don't want to go out with you."

Coach: "I get the behaviour and the feeling in there. Can I just check; the concrete effect. Is that something that you think he would agree is an actual result that has to happen when he does that, or is it something he thinks is in your control."

Person A: "Hmmm. In my control. So what's the concrete effect?"

Coach: "Doesn't look to me like there is one. That's still fine. If you send the I message, let's find out what happens."

Person A: "I'll see. [to Person B] When you wear one of those old shirts with a hole in it, I feel embarrassed."

Person B: "Well I'm very fond of that shirt. It has special meaning to me."

Person A: [to Coach] "I'm so tempted to get back into this.... But I know the next step is to reflect what he said..." [to Person B] "So you like it."

Person B; "Sure. It's my shirt, my choice. I don't tell you what shirts to wear."

Coach: "If I can pause you at that point" [to Person B] "It's not necessary to raise the issue of what other conflicts you have or don't have. You could even reflect her concern."

Person B: [to Person A] "So you don't like that shirt because it looks scruffy?"

Person A: "Right. I guess this is a values difference. I enjoy looking at you much more when you're wearing something tidier."

Person B: "Well, that's useful to know. I like when you enjoy looking at me… and I also want to choose my own shirts."

Person A: "Fair enough."

Coach: [to both] "How was that?"

Person A: "More successful than what I did last night, but still not resolved.

Person B: "Yeah"

Coach "And that may be the way it is – unresolved. Because this is a values conflict with no concrete effect. It's still really important, and over time this may change."

Because my aim is to have the couple self monitor and use the skills of effective relating themselves, I can also coach them nonverbally by asking them to discuss their issue standing up, and to shift one step forward each time their partner's communication leads them to feel closer, one step back each time it leads them to feel more distant. In teaching Transforming communication, we use a very sophisticated version of this "sociometric" process" to demonstrate the "Two Step", and with newer clients the simple "distance-closeness" version gives valuable feedback. This only needs to be done for a few sentences to give clear feedback to all of us, not only about the effect of such unhelpful strategies as criticism, but also about whether one or both partners have anchored themselves into such a negative state that any comment at all comes across as an attack and creates distance.

When the anchoring is that destructive, I would usually recommend individual sessions. Extramarital affairs and major arguments frequently create emotionally traumatic responses which benefit from the NLP Trauma cure or Time Line Therapy™. I strongly recommend arranging such session for both partners, in that case, because there is a risk of labelling one person as the "sick" partner otherwise. One person's session may of course involve primarily trauma cure work while the other person's involves values clarification or even coaching in how to respond to conflicts.

Verify Change

The time that the clients are with me is certainly only a small fraction of the time they have available for enhancing their relationship. Setting them tasks to do in their own time greatly increases the value of their coaching. Even more interestingly, clients can be asked to design their own task based on their own assessment of their current situation. This, of course, is a behaviour that would be useful for them to continue after the coaching has officially finished. As they report back the next session on the tasks they have attempted, tasking also gives me valuable feedback about how fully they are now able to put into practice what they have learned in our sessions. Tasking, rather than mere verbal reporting, forms the most effective feedback, because as mentioned earlier in this article, most couples counselling clients report very favourably on their counselling sessions even when the result of those sessions is the dissolution of their relationship. Here are some examples of the type of tasks couples may assign themselves:

- To spend 10 minutes each day checking in and reporting on what is happening in each person's life.
- To spend 10 minutes each listening to the other person talking about their dreams of what this relationship could offer.
- To spend 15 minutes with one person listening to the other, using reflective listening about an issue outside the conflict between the two people; then reversing the roles and repeating.
- To have a 30 minute discussion about a values conflict, not aiming to reach an agreement but to understand the dreams behind the values being expressed.
- To resolve a minor conflict of needs using the win-win process.
- To have each person design an evening which meets some need, value or dream of theirs that they feel is not fully met in the relationship usually, and have the couple experience these evenings over the next fortnight.
- To experiment with some small behaviour that each person would like to do but has felt unable to so far in the relationship.
- To work together on some small one hour joint project of mutual benefit.

It is useful to comment here on what other therapists would describe as provocative or paradoxical interventions. Usually these are interventions that set the couple the task of doing what they thought was the problem. They are very useful when the couple have been "trying unsuccessfully" to do what they think is right, and have built up a kind of "internal resistance" to success. These tasks are "paradoxical" only in a "logical" sense, and do not require the coach to "trick" or manipulate the couple. They can be explained quite openly to the couple. Perhaps the most well known example of such a task is in sexual therapy where a couple who have been attempting unsuccessfully to have sexual intercourse will be given the task of mutual pleasuring without any actual intercourse. Freed from the "requirement" to try and "consummate" their sexual contact, they can then relax and enjoy lovemaking. The effect of "not having full sexual contact" is now reversed. Instead of being a problem, it becomes a solution. This experience of just pleasuring is itself often all the couple need in order to make sexual intercourse possible (Kaplan, 1974, p 232-236).

As another example, I had a couple come to see me when one partner had very little sexual response within the relationship but had good sexual response to a fantasy situation (a fantasy which he felt uncomfortable about discussing). As we talked it became clear that his struggle not to think about the fantasy situation meant that he was shutting down his sexual responsiveness with his partner. I gave this couple the task of "taking the energy from the fantasy into their relationship" – not actually acting out the fantasy (which is frequently not what a person with such a fantasy congruently "wants" anyway) but requiring him to fantasise while making love. This is the very thing they both feared, of course, and prescribing it seems paradoxical. However since they were now doing this in the service of their relationship, the task actually reversed the effect of the fantasy. This prescription is also used by sex therapist Helen Singer Kaplan (1974, p249-251).

John Gottman, like most couples coaches, will often give a couple the task of having a conflict happen, while they are on their own, at a prescribed time. This is exactly what the couple has feared, but since they are now choosing consciously to have the conflict, the experience is fundamentally different. That in itself changes the nature of not only this conflict but all subsequent conflicts. From being things that happen uncontrollably, conflicts become events that the two people can choose to have. Conflicts become planned explorations of their dreams and needs. Gottman will often require the couple not to reach any conclusion at all, once again freeing them to listen to each other and share their actual responses, without feeling that they need to "convince" the other or to find and commit themselves to a perfect solution (Gottman, 1999, p 247-251).

Ecological Exit

It would be a dangerous illusion to suggest to a couple that after couples coaching their problems are "solved". They will still want to monitor their own emotional state, checking that their friendship feels strong, and monitor their conversations, checking that they use their new skills. Gottman suggests that couples coaching is complete as soon as a couple demonstrate their ability to have a conflict, make mistakes, and self correct afterwards. He also recommends that couples build into their life some ongoing rituals of positive emotional connection - such as times they go out for a meal, ten minute check in times after their day apart, ways of celebrating their successes both individual and as a couple (Gottman, 1999, p 288-291).

Summarising The Chapter

A. Culture, Gender and NLP

NLP emerged from a particular cultural background, and it maintains the biases of that background. NLP as it is usually taught promotes goalsetting as an independent and self-assessed activity, in contrast to goalsetting in Japan, where fitting into the group context is considered far more significant. In a more cooperative culture like Japan, a sense of identity is more often gained by cooperation and monitoring ones communication so as to protect others from distress. Mutual dependence, or Amae is an essential part of the Japanese conception of emotional health and social adjustment. Similarly in New Zealand Maori culture, it is important to understand the significance of emotions such as whakamaa, which arises when the person senses that their spiritual power has been harmed in the social setting. The solution to this challenge, in a Maori context, is to re-establish one's connection with others, and with the spiritual sources of energy and "self-esteem".

Even the metaphors that we use to explain NLP, such as the "programming" metaphor, reveal the cultural origin of the field. In Maori terms, for example, metaphors that connect people with the wider picture of life on the planet are more valued, and the whole process of analyzing human activity into specific "programs" is culturally foreign. When a culture is submerged in a post-colonial situation, then the members of that culture often find it incomprehensibly difficult to achieve success in the dominant culture. They are playing the game with an unaccepted rulebook. Redesigning NLP so that it makes as much sense in more cooperative cultures as it does in more individualistic cultures is an important way of ensuring that all our clients can benefit from these extraordinary skills.

For similar reasons, there is also some evidence that NLP processes as they are presently applied are more effective with men than with women. Research shows that there are male/female differences in the preference for certain metaprograms. There are several statistical differences including a tendency for men to be less successful at decoding body language and to make decisions more by thinking. More markedly, women tend to have an external motivation source and men an internal motivation source. While these differences seem to be learned and are not universal, a lack of understanding of them may well account for differences in NLP results.

The Feminist critique of psychotherapy has interesting implications for us in the field of NLP. Women writers in the psychotherapy field have suggested that the traditional view of individual autonomy as a criterion of "mental health" may presuppose a way of behaving that is more comfortable for many men than it is for many women. A more balanced view, these women writers say, would allow for the *interdependence* of human beings, valuing the human skills of being able to ask for and give help. It would also recognize that social and personal change are interlinked, and that empowering individuals often includes supporting them to discover collective solutions. This more balanced approach is foreshadowed in the work of Virginia Satir, one of the original models for NLP. Weaving the value of interdependence more fully into our work in NLP must be an important step towards delivering an NLP which meets both men's and women's needs.

B. The Revolution In Couples Therapy

Not only do over half of all couples in western relationships find maintaining their relationship difficult, but traditional couples counselling offers little help. John Gottman's research on the specific language patterns of successful couples's meshes well with NLP's modelling of language patterns to provide an alternative approach. This approach is a solution focused skills coaching approach.

C. Transforming Communication For Couples

The Transforming Communication model of relationships is based on clear problem ownership, which enables each person to monitor whether anyone is not happy with the situation they are in (whether anyone "owns a problem" to use the jargon) and respond with appropriate skills for the four very different situations that occur. When neither person owns a problem, then relationship enhancing processes such as appreciation, shared pleasure and shared activities can be used. When the other owns a problem, rapport skills, open questions and reflective listening assist them to feel understood and find their own solutions. When I own a problem, I send an I message describing the behaviour I'm not happy with, the way I feel about that, and any concrete effects on me. In response to the person's reaction to this, I use reflective listening to help them hear my message. In this way I avoid Gottman's high risk behaviours – harsh start-up, criticism, contempt, defensiveness, stonewalling, emotional flooding and failed repair attempts.

In a simple misunderstanding, this will solve the problem. In a conflict of needs, we will identify each of our basic needs/outcomes and find win-win solutions to meet both sets of needs/outcomes. In a conflict of values, we will model our own values and share them as values consultants with each other, accepting that there may be no immediate solution.

D. Coaching Couples To Transform Their Communication

The coaching model has seven key steps to it:

Resourceful state for the Practitioner. This includes getting your role clear as an ally who will coach the couple in the use of new skills.

Establish rapport. In this case you want to check your level of rapport with each person and check whether you are hired to support the relationship as an entity.

Specify outcomes. Invite the couple to recontact their highest outcomes for the relationship – their dreams of what this could provide them and ask solution focused questions to help get specific examples of both what they want and what skills they already have.

Open up model of world. Reframe the relationship as a system where each person's responses are involved in generating the others'. Have them identify how different values, beliefs and metaprograms (personality styles) shape their responses. Have them step into each other's shoes and experience how they could generate the kind of response they have seen in their partner.

Leading to desired state. Coach the couple to change their communication both in conflict situations and in everyday positive situations, so that they create a relationship that honours their dreams. Coaching involves the use of reflective listening, metamodel questioning, and direct instruction in application of the Transforming Communication skills.

Verify change. Give the couple tasks to complete at home to enhance both the positive experiences in their relationship and the conflict experiences. At times tasks will prescribe actions which seem to contradict the clients' aims, in order that they have space to present themselves as they are rather than as they are trying to be. Once they are self correcting in the completion of tasks such as conflict resolution, coaching is successful.

Ecological exit. Encourage clients to build in ongoing monitoring systems to check both their emotional state and their use of the Transforming Communication skills.

Bibliography:

Abramovitz, J.N. et alia, <u>Vital Signs 2002</u> W.W. Norton & Company, New York, 2002

Andreas, S. and Andreas, C. <u>Change Your Mind And Keep The Change</u> Real People Press, Moab, Utah, 1987

Andreas, S. Virginia Satir: The Patterns of her Magic Science and Behaviour Books, Palo Alto, California, 1991

Andrews, A.A., Befu H. et alia <u>Japan: An Illustrated Encyclopaedia 197 Keys To The Japanese Heart and Soul</u> Kodansha Bilingual Books, Tokyo, 1996

Baird, J.E. 'Sex Differences in Group Communication: A Review of Relevant Research', page 179-192 in *Quarterly Journal of Speech* 62, no.1, (April), 1976

Bandler, R. <u>Using Your Brain - For A Change</u> Real People Press, Moab, Utah, 1985

Bandler, R., Grinder, J. and Satir, V. Changing With Families, Science and Behaviour Books, Palo Alto, California, 1976

Bandler, Richard and Grinder, John, The Structure of Magic, Meta Publications, Cupertino, California, 1975.

Berg, I. K. Family Based Services W.W. Norton & Co., New York, 1994

Blaut, J.M. <u>The Colonizer's Model Of the </u> World Guilford, New York, 1993

Bobes, T. and Bobes, N.S., The Couple Is Telling You What You Need To Know Norton, New York, 2005

Bolstad, R. ed <u>New Zealand Treaty Education Kit For NLP Master Practitioners</u> Transformations, Christchurch, 2001

Bolstad, R., M. Transforming Communication Pearsons, Auckland, 2004

Bubenzer, D.L. and West, J.D. Counselling Couples Sage Publications, London, 1993

Cameron-Bandler, L. Solutions Real People Press, Moab, Utah, 1985

Charvet S.R. "The Purpose of Womanhood" p 42-43 in Anchor Point magazine, Volume 17, Number 2, February, 2003

Charvet, S.R. Words That Change Minds Kendall/Hunt, Dubuque, Iowa, 1995

Chesler, P. "Twenty years since "Women and Madness": Towards a Feminist Institute of Mental Health and Healing" page 313-322 in Journal of Mind and Behaviour 11 (3 and 4), 1990

Chesler, P. Women and Madness Allen Lane, Harmondsworth, England, 1972

Chia, M. and Arava, D.A. The Multi-orgasmic Man Harper Collins, San Francisco, 1996

Chia, M. and Chia, M. Healing Love Through The Tao: Cultivating Female Sexual Energy Healing Tao, Huntington, New York, 1986

Chopra, D. The Path To Love Harmony, New York, 1997

Chu, V. The Yin-Yang Butterfly Simon & Schuster, London, 1997

Colgan, Dr A. and McGregor, J. Sexual Secrets Alister Taylor Publishers, Martinborough, New Zealand, 1981

De Vito, J. A. Human Communication: The Basic Course, Harper and Row, New York, 4th Edition

Delis, D.C. and Phillips, C. The Passion Paradox Piatkus, London, 1990

DeLozier, J. and Grinder, J. Turtles All The Way Down Grinder, DeLozier and Associates, Bonny Doon, California, 1987

Dilts, R. Modelling With NLP Meta Publications, Capitola, California, 1998

Dilts, R. with Bonissone, G. Skills For The Future, Meta Publications, Cupertino, California, 1993

Doi, T. The Anatomy of Dependence Kodansha, Tokyo, 1981

Duncan, R.C., Konefal, J. and Spechler, M.M. "Effect of Neurolinguistic Programming training on self-actualization as measured by the personal orientation inventory." P 1323-1330 in Psychological Reports, No. 66, 1990

Durie, M. "Counselling Maori Clients" Video of an address by Dr. Mason Durie to the N.Z.C.G.A. Annual Conference, Palmerston North, May 1985

Elwood, K. Getting Along With The Japanese Ask Co., Tokyo, 2001

Ernst, S. and Goodison, L. In Our Own Hands J.P. Tarcher, Los Angeles, 1981

Ferguson, M Forever Feminine: Women's Magazines and the Cult of Femininity, Heinemann Educational Books, London, 1985

Franzoi, S.L. Social Psychology Brown & Benchmark, Madison, 1996

Gilligan, C. Rogers, A.G. and Tolman, D.L. Women, Girls & Psychotherapy: Reframing Resistance Haworth Press, New York,

1991

Gordon, T. "Teaching People To Create Therapeutic Environments" in Suhd, M. M. ed Positive Regard, Science and Behaviour Books, Palo Alto California, 1995, pp 301-336

Gordon, T. Group Centered Leadership: A Way of Releasing The Creative Potential In Groups, Houghton-Mifflin, Boston, 1955

Gordon, T. Leader Effectiveness Training, Peter H. Wyden, New York, 1978

Gordon, T. Parent Effectiveness Training, Peter H. Wyden, New York, 1970

Gordon, T. Teacher Effectiveness Training, Peter H. Wyden, New York, 1974

Gottman, J.M. and Silver, N. The Seven Principles For Making Marriage Work Three Rivers Press, New York, 1999

Gottman, J.M. The Marriage Clinic W.W. Norton and Co., New York, 1999

Greenspan, M. A New Approach to Women & Therapy McGraw-Hill, New York, 1983

Grinder, J. and Bandler, R. The Structure of Magic Science and Behaviour, Palo Alto, California, 1975

Haley, J. and Hoffman, L. Techniques of Family Therapy basic Books, New York, 1967

Haynes, J.M., The Fundamentals of Family Mediation State University of New York, Albany, 1994

Horio, T (Translated by Platzer, S.) Educational Thought and Ideology in Modern Japan University of Tokyo, Tokyo, 1994

Howard, J.W. and Dawes, R.M. "Linear prediction of marital happiness" p 478-480 of Personality and Social Psychology Bulletin, No 2, 1976

Kaplan, H. Singer The New Sex Therapy Penguin, Harmondsworth, England, 1974

Matlin, M.W. The Psychology Of Women Harcourt College, Fort Worth, Fourth Edition 2000

Metge, J. In And Out of Touch: Whakamaa In Cross Cultural Context Victoria University Press, Wellington, 1985

Perls, F.S. Gestalt Therapy Verbatim Real People Press, Moab, Utah, 1969

Phillips, R. Divorce In New Zealand Oxford, Auckland, 1981

Prather, H. and Prather, G. I Will Never Leave You Bantam, New York, 1995

Prior, R. and O'Connor, J. NLP & Relationships Thorsons, London, 2000-06-28

Reedy, H. "NLP Within The Maori World" p 2-3 in Trancescript Number 19, February 2000

Roberts, T. and Nolen-Hoeksema, S. "Gender comparisons in responsiveness to others' evaluations in achievement settings, p 221-240 in Psychology of Women Quarterly, No. 18, 1994

Satir, V. "Everybody Has A Dream" p 204-206 in Canfield, J. and Hansen, M.V. Chicken Soup For The Soul Health Communications Inc, Deerfield Beach, Florida, 1993

Satir, V. Conjoint Family Therapy Science and Behaviour Books, Palo Alto, California, 1967

Satir, V. The New Peoplemaking Science and Behaviour Books, Mountain View, California, 1988

Schachter, S. and Singer, J.E. "Cognitive, social and physiological determinants of emotional state" in Psychological Review, 69 (12) p 379-399, 1962

Schütz, P., Schneider-Sommer, S., Gross, B., Jelem, H. and Brandstetter-Halberstadt, Y. Theorie und Praxis der Neuro-Linguistischen Psychotherapie Junfermann Verlag, Paderborn, 2001

Scuka, R.F., Relationship Enhancement Therapy Routledge, New York, 2005

Seligman, M.E.P. Learned Optimism Random House, Milsons Point, Sydney, 1997

Spender, D. The Writing Or The Sex Pergammon, New York, 1989

Statistics New Zealand New Zealand Official Yearbook, 2002 New Zealand Government Printers, Wellington, 2002

Sternberg, R.J. "A Triangular Theory of Love" in Psychological Review, 93, p 119-135, 1986

Symons, D. The Evolution of Human Sexuality Oxford University, Oxford, 1981

Wegner, D. "Transactive Memory In Close Relationships" in Journal of Personality and Social Psychology, Vol 61, No. 6, p 923-929, 1991

White, M. The Japanese Educational Challenge Kodansha, Tokyo, 1987

Wiggins, J. S. "Review of the Myers-Briggs Type Indicator" page 537-538 in Conoley, J.C. & Kramer, J.J. (Eds.) The Tenth Mental Measurements Yearbook, University of Nebraska Press, Lincoln, Nebraska, 1989

Wile, D.B. Couples Therapy: A Non-Traditional Approach Wiley, New York, 1992

Wilson, G.D., and McLaughlin, C. The Science of Love Fusion Press, London, 2001

Undoing Life to Living

A) The Boxes

Getting Out Of The Box

What if all the things that upset people could be shown not to exist? What if they could realize that the changes that they so desperately want are easy and even inevitable? Imagine if all of human suffering had involved people putting themselves and their experiences into imaginary boxes and then throwing away the mental keys? And what if this chapter could give you a mental key to unlock every problem that ever was? What we will show you in this section will give you a totally new way of looking at your life.

First, let us invite you to repeat an exercise we demonstrate on every NLP Training we do. Stand up with your feet slightly apart, and with space around you in front and behind. Bring your left arm straight up in front so it's horizontal and pointing to the front. Now, keeping your feet still, turn your body to the left, pointing with the finger as far as you can comfortably turn. Be careful only to go as far as you can before it gets tight. Notice, by the point on the wall, how far round you are pointing when it's tight. Next, turn back to the front keeping your feet still. Now, close your eyes and make a picture of what you would see if you turned again, but this time with your hand going 40 centimetres further round. Imagine where on the wall or window that would mean your hand is pointing. Sense what it would feel like to be that much more supple, so that your body just flowed around. Imagine what you would say to yourself if you could go that much further. Now open your eyes and physically turn again to the left. See how much further you have turned. Imagining yourself going further causes your brain to make the adjustments to create that in reality.

But here's the most important learning of all from that exercise. When people hear about NLP, and its ability to heal psychological and physical problems seemingly instantly, and without any "deep trauma release", they tend to assume that this must mean that the "real" problems are being suppressed, or even avoided. Think back to the pointing exercise. The second time, you went right past where your arm got tight the first time. You didn't need to force yourself further round. So what happened to the *tightness* that was there the first time? Did you suppress it? Is it still really there, waiting to be "healed" at some deeper level? No, the tightness doesn't need to be acknowledged, healed, released, analyzed, understood or "dealt with" in any way at all. The tightness never existed. There was only the process of tightening. And if you don't tighten, then there is no tightness. There never was a "thing" called tightness. "Tightness" is just a word created out of the verb "to tighten". It's much easier to change what you're doing than to change "what is" or "what you have".

Six Years Of Tightening Ended In One Sentence

At one of our free talks in 2007, a woman came up to Richard afterwards and told him an extraordinary story. For six years she had suffered severe back pain and restricted movement. She had been treated by medical doctors and alternative therapists but the pain had continued, and indeed she was only able to slowly shuffle into the lecture theatre. At the end of the two hour presentation, she was able to move freely and without any pain. She said she remembered the precise words that Richard had been saying when her pain disappeared. It was when he mentioned that people who have "pain" often say to themselves things like "I don't want this pain to be here for the rest of my life; I can't cope with this pain; I don't want to wake up tomorrow with this pain." In NLP, we understand that when I say "I don't want something." it involves me thinking about that thing. The example I usually use to explain this is an imaginary "blue tree". If I say I don't want to think about a blue tree, then in order to understand what I am saying to myself, I create an image of a blue tree. In this case, the woman realized that her words were giving an instruction to her body to feel the pain every day. The words even suggested that the pain had an "objective" existence. Each sentence she said to herself made "the pain" seem more real. But there is no pain; there is only the process of hurting. This process involves certain actions in the brain. If other actions occur, then the hurting will stop. The task of someone who wants to be comfortable is not to "get rid of the pain", but simply to do something different. There is no "thing" which needs to be taken away, and that is true even when the hurting is in response to a "real" event such as an injury.

Nothing Matters

This means that our language, when we refer to "the pain" or "the tightness", does not accurately describe what we know to be the facts. Alfred Korzybski first recognized this in 1931 and wrote a book called "Science and Sanity" to discuss the implications. The whole idea of Neuro Linguistic Programming (NLP) emerged from his work. Korzybski said in 1941 "Modern scientific developments show that what we label "objects" or "objective" are mere nervous constructs inside of our skulls." Korzybski said we needed to understand how our brain uses language to construct "objects" from the flow of experience. He explains "We have not only to *"know"* elementary facts of modern science, including neuro-linguistic [science], but also to *apply* them." (Korzybski, 1994, p liii, lviii)

The modern scientific developments that Korzybski referred to in 1941 are collectively called Quantum Physics. Quantum Physics is a new way of understanding physics which emerged over the last century and produced practical results (such as the laser and the computer micro-chip) which are the basis of most modern technology. Originally, quantum physics developed from the study of the smallest subatomic particles and units of energy. Max Planck first showed that energy given off by an atom came in tiny packages or "quanta", and Niels Bohr demonstrated that when a subatomic particle absorbs a number of these quanta it instantly changes place and movement pattern - it disappears from one place and instantly appears somewhere else! (a "quantum leap"). Although, overall, we can predict how many particles will leap one way and how many another way, we cannot tell where a particular particle will go. Even weirder, the particle acts as if it has gone every possible way at once, and *then* decided which one to stick with, once the observer (scientist) checks where it is.

Heisenberg's Experiment

A famous experiment used by Werner Heisenberg demonstrates this. In this experiment, particles of light (photons) are "shining" out from a light source onto a screen which has two slits cut in it. Behind the screen is a piece of photographic film (like in a camera), on which any light particle will leave a dot. You would expect that the result will be two sets of dots as shown in diagram A.

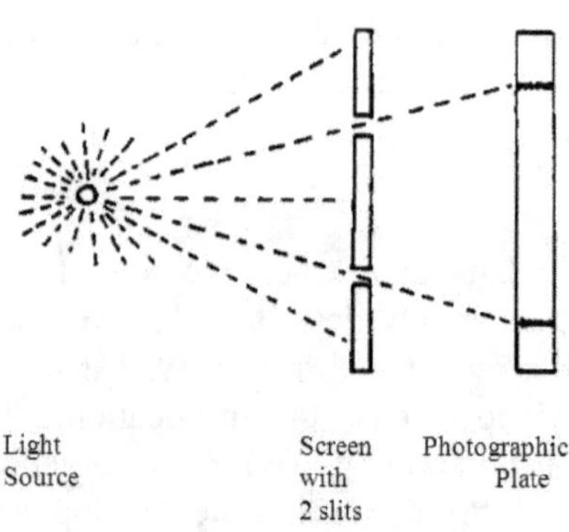

Actually, though, the photons behave as if they were both particles <u>and</u> waves or ripples of energy in space, and they interfere with each other's path, causing over time a ripple pattern like that in Diagram B.

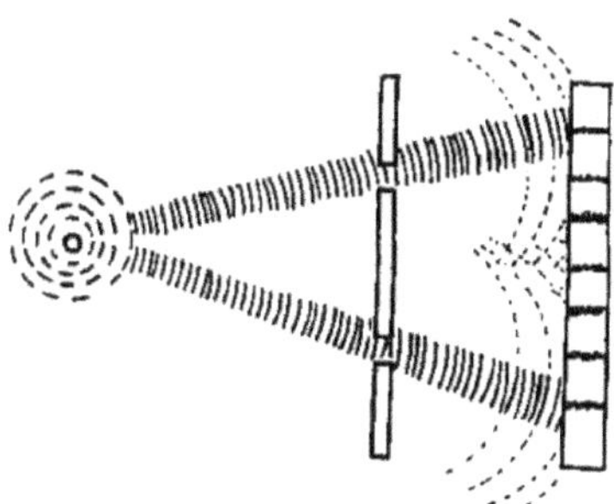

A <u>really</u> strange thing happens though, when we send *one* single photon at a time. Now there cannot be any interference. And yet the same pattern appears on the photographic plate (diagram B). It is as if each photon checks all possible paths and gets interfered with by its own possible paths. If we cover one slit, the interference pattern disappears (Diagram C). How does each photon "know" whether the other slit is open or not?

It seems that, at the quantum level, everything happening at a particular time is related to all the other conditions present at that time. Changing one element changes everything else, even those elements not "logically" related. (Peat 1991, p.58).

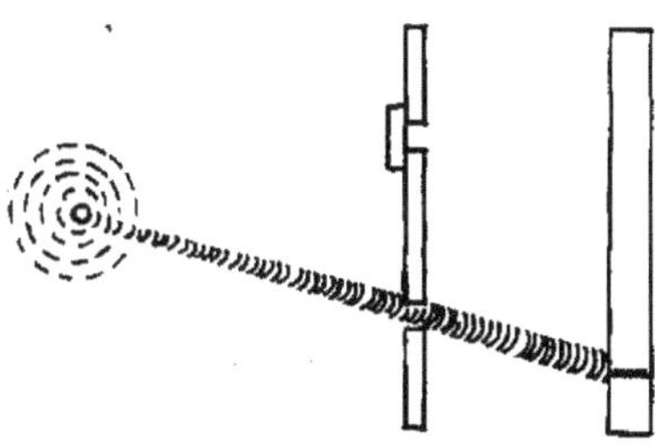

So, when a photon is half way from the light source to the photographic plate, where exactly is it? The answer, it turns out, is that it is everywhere it could possibly be. Once we find it, by checking, it appears to be in a set place (observation *brings it into existence!*). But up till that moment, it was potentially in a range of places. Quantum physics co-developer Erwin Schrodinger (Peat, 1991, p.69) described an imaginary experiment which makes metaphorical sense of this. The original experiment involves a cat. Let's use a light switch for our example. A light bulb is placed in a closed box, with a container switch. In the box also is a device which measures and amplifies a random event: such as measuring whether a radioactive atom has randomly released a particle of radiation. If the particle *is* released, the switch turns the light on. After a half an hour, the question is asked: Is the light on or off? The way quantum physics works, the light is both on and off. It is all possible states *until* the box is opened. Then it becomes one or the other! Observing it causes it to "collapse" (to use the jargon) from being in all possible states into being in one specific state!

So, some fairly weird things are happening with tiny particles. At first, quantum physicists themselves found these experiments confusing. Werner Heisenberg wrote (Capra, 1989, p.31): "I remember discussions with Bohr which went through many hours till very late at night and ended almost in despair; and when at the end of the discussion I went alone for a walk in the neighbouring park I repeated to myself again and again the question: Can nature possibly be so absurd as it seemed to us in these atomic experiments?" Heisenberg finally found a model that made sense of his research when he spoke to the Indian poet and teacher Rabindranath Tagore, in 1929. "After these conversations with Tagore ... some of the ideas that had seemed so crazy suddenly made much more sense." (Capra, 1989, p.43). The eastern Hindu and Buddhist models of the universe as a constant flow of energy had long been teaching the same truths Quantum Physics was discovering.

Quantum Physics and the Human Neurology

But even if small particles do behave in strange ways, what does that have to do with human beings? Well, it turns out that our brain is designed to receive quantum level information and convert it to ordinary mechanical action, and vice versa. The human eye, for example, receives and responds to single photons (Peat 1991, p.83). The human nose responds to single molecules of substances. David Bohm and other physicists such as Karl Pribram (see Bohm, 1980, p.198) have noted that human thought behaves like the photons in the above experiment. When we check where in the brain a memory <u>is</u>, it seems to be stored everywhere, until we actually measure it. We can, by measuring, identify specific areas in the brain related to specific tasks (a visual area, a kinaesthetic area etc). However, if these areas are removed, visual memory seems still to operate.

In 1992 a team of physicists at Southampton University in England designed an experiment like the above photon one, but using human brains. EEG electrodes (which measure brain waves) were attached to the right and left side of several dozen people's heads. The people then performed a complex "left brain" task (identifying numbers flashed on a screen). In the next room, the physicists every so often measured or checked the EEG pattern from one side or other of each person's head. When they simply looked at the results on the left side, the person's performance in the next room was improved. When they scanned the right side, performance dropped. This study indicates that during thinking, the brain is in a quantum mechanical state: it is in all possible states. Simply measuring what state it's in (like checking, with photographic film, *where* the photon is, in the previous experiment) causes the brain to "end up" in a definite place. But until that moment it is responding to (or interfered with by) all potential choices. (Zohar and Marshall, 1994, p.57).

Nominalization

Quantum physics demonstrates that the states in our brain – states such as happiness, depression, anxiety, decision, belief, and indecision – are "condensed out of the quantum field of all possibilities" by our observation of them, by our thinking about them. Our thinking makes "solid objects" out of the quantum flow of energy. In linguistics this has long been understood, and the process of creating solid objects in language is called nominalization. Some languages have separate structures for nouns (names of "things") and for verbs (actions), but in English as well as most European and Asian languages, it is possible to convert a verb, adverb or even an adjective into a noun. For example, the verb *investigate* can be converted into the noun *investigation*, the adjective *slowly* can be converted into the noun *slowness*, and the adjective *intense* can be converted into the noun *intensity*. As nouns, *investigation*, *slowness* and *intensity* sound like things. In reality they are descriptions of actions (investiga*ting*, act*ing* slowly, and act*ing* intensely). These actions have been "nominalised" (turned into nouns).

Notice how it changes my experience to say I have an intensity, instead of just saying that I performed a certain action intensely. If I say I spoke intensely, it sounds like something I did, which could change a moment later. If I say I have an intensity, it suggests that there is a (possibly permanent) object called "intensity" inside me. It condenses my way of acting out into a "particle" called intensity. In reality, life is ever changing, and I can change the way I act from one moment to another. The nominalization "intensity" makes it seem like my action exists as a separate "thing", in a box. Depression, anxiety and insanity are boxes in exactly the same way, but believing in them has serious consequences.

In this article we want to show you the implications of letting the light out of the box.

Richard Bandler and John Grinder, the co-developers of NLP, found that it was sometimes challenging for students to identify nominalizations. They suggest the following exercise (Bandler and Grinder 1975).

"Form a visual image from the following sentences. In each case, see if you can imagine placing each of the non-process or non-verb words in a wheelbarrow.
> *I* want to make a *chair*.
> *I* want to make a *decision*.

Notice that all the non-verb words in the first sentence (*I, chair*) can be placed in your mental wheelbarrow. This is not the case with the second sentence (*I, decision*). I can be placed in a wheelbarrow, but a decision cannot. In the following sets of sentences, use this same visual test to train yourself in recognizing nominalizations:

> *I* have a lot of *frustration*.
> *I* have a lot of *green marbles*.

> *I* expect a *letter*.
> *I* expect *help*."

B) Letting The Light Out Of Boxes

"Anxiety" and other "Clinical Psychiatric Problems"

"Anxiety" is the condition which will bring more human beings into psychiatric treatment than any other (Beletsis, 1989, p264). 33% of all people visiting their family medical practitioner have it as a key complaint, and Psychiatrists say that a similar percentage of the general population will develop a "clinically significant anxiety disorder" at some time in their life (Barlow, Esler and Vitali, 1998, p 312). Understandably, a plethora of medications such as Valium (diazepam) have been used to treat anxiety. The users of these drugs have been shown to exhibit the same level of fear and avoidance behaviour after the drug treatment as before (Franklin, 1996, p7). Unfortunately, the craving for a quick-fix (such as pills seem to offer) is implicit in the very nature of anxiety. The anxious person wants their "anxiety" to stop as soon as possible, and a drug seems to offer an instant way out. Again and again though, cognitive NLP-style change processes have been compared to diazepam and related drugs and shown far more successful (Barlow, Ester and Vitali, 1998, p 310). How do such cognitive treatments work so much better than drugs?

Here is a simple experiment which explains the NLP model of how people create "anxiety"....

Think of a fresh lemon. Imagine one in front of you now, and feel what it feels like as you pick it up. Take a knife and cut a slice off the lemon, and hear the slight sound as the juice squirts out. Smell the lemon as you lift the slice to your mouth and take a bite of the slice. Taste the sharp taste of the fruit.

If you actually imagined doing that, you mouth is now salivating. Why? Because your brain followed your instructions and thought about, saw, heard, felt, smelled and tasted the lemon. Your brain treated the imaginary lemon as if it was real, and prepared saliva to digest it. Now, let's talk about this the way Psychiatrists sometimes talk about "anxiety".

The medical condition you are experiencing in your mouth right now is known as Ptyalism. This is a chemical imbalance where the salivary glands overproduce the chemicals commonly called saliva. In some cases there is a genetic predisposition to Ptyalism. Luckily there are drugs that offer effective treatments for this imbalance and such drugs are called antisialogogues. Some of the most effective antisialogogues are the anticholinergic drugs such as Sal-Tropine, a form of atropine sulphate specifically marketed for this condition. Unfortunately, research shows that the users of these drugs exhibit the same level of salivation after the drug treatment as before, so if you really want to solve the problem, this may need to be a lifelong treatment.

Of course, there is another way to solve the problem. Think about something else instead of lemons!

Actually, Ptyalism is a nominalization for the process, the action, of salivating, and salivating is a healthy response to certain other processes such as thinking about lemons. In the same way, anxiety is actually a process, or an action, which involves specific body processes such as feeling restless, sweating, shaking, tightening the chest muscles creating discomfort while breathing etc. And this in turn is a healthy response to certain other processes such as thinking about what it would be like if the plane the person was on crashed in flames. In short, there is no "anxiety disorder" – just the process of **worrying**. If a person thinks about lemons all day, their mouth waters. If they think about airplanes crashing all day, their heart pounds.

The person who is worrying may have eagerly accepted a Psychiatrist's diagnosis of "clinical anxiety condition" though, because it comes with an implied promise of a cure – anti-anxiety medications. As they accept it, they condense the wave-form of all possible mental-bodily events out into the "particle" of "anxiety condition". It now seems increasingly real, and they talk about it as if it was a solid thing inside them. Now, it seems almost immovable. Actually, relief is literally just a thought away, because anxiety is not a thing; it is an action.

In the same way, "Depression", "Mania", "Psychosis" and "Addiction" are processes that a person does, not objects that they have. The approach of NLP and cognitive therapy in general has been to discover how a person creates each of these "conditions" and how they would create a different "result".

"Disturbing Memories", "Childhood Traumas" and "Limiting Beliefs"

Many of us in the field of "alternative psychology", including NLP Practitioners, have understood that anxiety and depression are nominalizations, but have simply traded them in for "new, improved" nominalizations, which we "install" in our clients as eagerly as Psychiatrists previously installed their diagnoses. Amongst these are "memories", "values" and "beliefs", all of which involve thinking.

A twentieth century psychiatrist named Martin Orne demonstrated the real nature of "memories" in an experiment in front of BBC television (Barnes, 1982). He interviewed a woman, asking her a number of questions, including how she slept the night before. She said she had, as usual, slept an excellent night's sleep. Orne then invited her to relax, essentially producing what hypnotherapists would call a light trance or relaxed state, and he then "reminded her" that she had been awakened during the night by what sounded like gunshots. He then brought her attention back from trance to the room, and asked her again how she slept. She described the disturbing noises that she now believed had awoken her. Orne then replayed a tape of her pre-relaxation statement saying that she had slept excellently. Far from realising that the gunshots were a "false memory", the woman was now very puzzled as to how she could have forgotten those disturbing sounds at the start of the interview. She was so convinced of her "memory" that she was willing to argue with the evidence of the audiotape. Of course, most people have had the experience of discussing a past event with a friend, and finding that the friend has incorrectly remembered the details. Many close relationships have come to grief over such disagreements. We know that what Orne was able to do with a light form of relaxation can also occur in everyday life.

It's not just our memory of sensory experiences that are fragile in this way. NBC television captured an excellent demonstration of brief hypnosis being used to alter "beliefs" and even "values". Dr Herbert Spiegel (1980) worked with a successful businessman with left wing political views. Spiegel relaxed the man, and told him that communists were planning to take over radio and television stations in America. Spiegel suggested that the man would be able to remember details of this conspiracy. When the man was then awakened, he did indeed have an elaborate story about the plot and how he had first heard of it. He expressed grave concerns about the left wing, saying that he had changed his opinion recently about their approach. Spiegel then removed the hypnotic suggestion and showed the man the videotape of this entire sequence. The businessman was extremely disturbed to witness himself talking "like an ultraconservative".

In everyday life, such shifts in valuing and believing are more common than we would like to think. The easiest way to notice them is to realise how inconsistent *other* people's "values" can be; for example how a person who "falls in love" can suddenly find that they share the "values" of their beloved, even where these values contradict previous "values of their own". "Values" and "Beliefs" are not fixed things which need to be "cleared" from the system if they are not working. Valuing and Believing are active processes and if you value or believe differently the "content" of your "beliefs" and "values" changes (instantly). Memories are not real things like "DVD" movie recordings stored in the brain. There is only the process of remembering, and each time we re-member an "event" we do it differently. Dr Elisabeth Loftus has conducted over 200 research experiments demonstrating that remembering can be altered, without hypnosis, by simple suggestion. Loftus' research demonstrates, unfortunately, that we simply cannot tell whether a "memory" is real or not. In one of her studies, she selected subjects who (according to their own and their family's reports) had never been hospitalised for an ear infection as a child. She then had a relative tell each subject that when they were a child they were hospitalised overnight with an ear infection. After this 20% of subjects claimed to remember the hospitalisation, even when they were advised of the research occurring. Subjects even "remembered" details such as who had visited them in the hospital. Dr Loftus' research has been most of all designed to demonstrate the lack of correlation between "memories of childhood trauma" and actual events then or actual consequences now.

As early as 1932, researcher F. C. Bartlett wrote "Remembering is not the re-excitation of innumerable fixed, lifeless, and fragmentary traces. It is an imaginative reconstruction, or construction, built out of the relation of our attitude towards a whole active mass of organised past reactions or experience, and to a little outstanding detail which commonly appears in image or in language form. It is thus hardly ever really exact, even in the most rudimentary cases of rote recapitulation, and it is not at all important that it should be so." (Bartlett, 1932, p 213). To put this in ordinary English, Bartlett is pointing out that even when we are remembering basic facts, memory is not an exact replay. It is an imaginative reconstruction based on our attitudes about the events and what they meant to us, more than on what actually happened. How we remember depends on how we feel right now at the moment of remembering. This could be said even more strongly for belief, because in order to maintain the process of believing, a person needs to continuously create internal "experiences" or "memories" that confirm the reality of their "belief". Dr Herbert Spiegel's demonstration of shifting a person's politics by suggesting new "memories" demonstrates how dependent the process of believing is on the process of remembering. We collapse "memories" and "beliefs" out of the wave-form of our internal experience in order to make sense of what we are doing in the world around us. But we only limit ourselves when we assume that they are real things.

Freedom involves the ability to re-member at any moment in ways that are more useful, and to adjust our believing to align with what works for us.

"The Internal Critic", "The Wounded Child" and other "Parts"

Speaking of "re-membering", another set of nominalizations which have become popular over the last decades in western society are parts of the mind. Beginning with Freud's "discovery" of the "Id", "Ego", "Superego" and "Unconscious mind", we have had a dazzling selection of inner beings discussed in the psychology texts over the last century.

John Grinder and Richard Bandler understood the risk of this very clearly at the start of their development of what is now called "NLP". They said in the second book that they published "Don't get caught by the words "conscious" and "unconscious." They are not real. They are just a way of describing events that is useful in the context called therapeutic change. "Conscious" is defined as whatever you are aware of at a moment in time. "Unconscious" is everything else." (Bandler and

Grinder, 1979, p 37). Later in that book they talk amusedly about other models of therapy such as Transactional Analysis (TA) where people do get caught by the words and actually "believe" in their "parts". They say "All TA people have ... a "critical parent," saying "Am I doing this right?" No one else does, though—until they go to a TA therapist, and then they have a critical parent. That's what TA does for you." (Bandler and Grinder, 1979, p 179).

Notice how much more challenging it seems when I say I have an internal critical parent, as opposed to merely saying that sometimes I have talked critically to myself. Imagine how much more work I will end up doing if I have an internal child who needs nurturing, as opposed to merely saying that sometimes I have wanted to act in ways that care for myself more. Of course, I may decide to pretend that I have internal "parts" or "roles" that persist over time, and Bandler and Grinder use the example of suggesting that people use their "creative part" to find new solutions. They are not condemning the notion of parts as a useful fiction; simply urging us to think carefully about which "parts" we wish to condense out of the quantum wave-form of all possible actions. For example, if I believe that I have a "wounded child" inside me, then by definition I will always be at risk of behaving in ways that are "wounded" whatever I imagine that to mean. The tendency, even within NLP, to refer to responses as "parts" may also simply be a result of NLP's heritage from within psychotherapy. Often when a person comes to an NLP Practitioner with a dilemma about how to act, the person describes each of their responses in moving form, and then the NLP Practitioner (unnecessarily) condenses these active processes into the "solid result" of static "parts" of the person. NLP "parts integration" processes could just as easily be done as "action integrating" processes.

So far, no-one has claimed to find any specific area of the brain where an "inner child" or a "critical parent" lives. But what about psychiatric conditions where a person really seems to have more than one "personality"? Psychiatrist Don Condie and neurobiologist Guochuan Tsai used a fMRI scanner to study the brain patterns of a woman diagnosed with "multiple personality disorder". In this disorder, the woman experienced herself as switching regularly between her normal personality and an alternative personality called "Guardian". The two personalities had different "memories", held separate "beliefs" and "values", and behaved quite differently. The fMRI brain scan showed that her experiences of these two personalities were associated with the use of different neural networks (different areas of the brain lit up when each personality emerged). If the woman only pretended to be a separate person, her brain continued to use her usual neural networks, but as she felt "the Guardian taking over her consciousness", precise, different areas of the hippocampus and surrounding temporal cortex (brain areas associated with memory and emotion) were activated.(Adler, 1999, p 29-30). Is this evidence that, at least in such extreme cases, "parts" of the brain actually exist?

A study by Dr Lewis Baxter (1994) suggests not. Baxter showed that clients with obsessive compulsive disorder (OCD) have raised activity in certain specific neural networks in the caudate nucleus of the brain. As this brain activity increases, the person experiences themselves as being "taken over" by uncontrollable thoughts, for example about the need to wash their hands. Baxter could identify these networks on PET scan, and show how, once the OCD was treated, these networks ceased to be active. The person with OCD is in a very similar situation to the person with the multiple personality disorder, except that they are aware as the other "part" takes control. Interestingly, Dr Baxter found that activity in these "OCD" neural networks could be shut down either by treatment with the antidepressant Prozac, or by asking the person to talk to themselves using what NLP would call a "reframe" (saying a statement that puts their experience in another frame, such as "When my hands feel itchy it doesn't mean I need to wash them; it just means they are healthy"). The fact that a person's brain is more active in a certain place at the time when they behave in a certain way is obvious. But it does not prove that some "part" of their personality is "possessing" that area of the brain. It merely means that when they use those neural networks, they are less able to use other neural networks. Another example makes this clearer. It's not so easy for a person to do data entry on a computer at the same time as singing a song, but that doesn't prove that there is a "song singing sub-personality" in the brain.

"Relationships" and "Interpersonal Dynamics"

In a relationship between people, our society encourages us to pay attention to three "things" – the two people and the "relationship". In a very real sense, there is only relating.

Gregory Bateson, whose work inspired much of NLP, explained our interaction with the world using the analogy of a man cutting down a tree with an axe (Bateson, 1991, p 164). He points out that in order to swing the axe, the man needs to pay attention to where the last cut was. The cut, it could be said, causes him to swing in a certain place. And each cut could also be said to result from the specific properties of the axe; how heavy it feels, and how well balanced. So the axe, it might be claimed, controls the cut, which controls the man. Actually, of course, Bateson is explaining that tree-cutting is a system, and that a description of the actions of the man separate from the rest of the system he is interacting in, may be useful for communication, but have little use scientifically. John Grinder explains that all interaction between *people* needs to be understood similarly. He says "If we are dancing together there is a loop. You may, because of cultural tradition, say that John is leading and Pauline is following. I doubt that you would say that if you saw the two of us dancing very long, but nevertheless you can punctuate this circuit so that I'm leading or she's leading." (DeLozier and Grinder, 1987, p 59).

An important implication of this is that I am "a different person" in each of my relationships, in the sense that I respond differently to each set of interactions. As a result, it is not possible to find "Mr Right" or "Ms Right" by observing how a person behaves before beginning to relate with them, because all your observations will be of a different person or different people (the people they "are" when interacting with others). As a consequence, when I change the way I interact, I can change the "personality" of the person I interact with. "Personality" exists only as an abstraction of a particular sequence of relating. Relationship researcher John Gottman has shown that the way individuals in a distressed relationship interact with each other has very little correlation with the way they interact with other people (Gottman, 1999, p 20). There is, in his research, only one exception: men who demonstrate physical violence with one person tend to do so with other people.

The variation in "personality" between different relationships also explains something else. Extensive research by John Gottman has shown that the personality characteristics of each individual and even the objective degree of similarity between the personality characteristics of the two are almost irrelevant to their happiness as a couple. However, in happy couples, each person *perceives* the other as being basically a functional person (with certain quirks) and basically similar to them. In unhappy relationships, each partner *perceives* the other as basically flawed and unlike them (Gottman, 1999, p 19-21). In a very real sense, subjective perceptions *are all there is to* "the relationship".

Traditionally, relationship theorists have understood something of this, but have then gone on to nominalise the interactions themselves and discuss the "relationship" between a couple as if those dynamics were a semi-fixed "entity". Even the couple in a troubled relationship tend to do this, finding "hidden patterns" in their previous interaction, and thinking of these as real and established "syndromes". Gottman explains "I have found over and over that couples who are deeply entrenched in a negative view of their spouse and their marriage often rewrite their past."

(Gottman and Silver, 1999, p 42). Ironically, if the couple go to a couples therapist, frequently that person will do exactly the same, suggesting that there is a set "pattern" that needs to be either "healed" or "broken".

"Life", "Death" and "Life Missions"

"Have you ever asked what the purpose of your life is?" and "Do you know what God wants you to do with this life?" were once amongst the favourite opening lines of Christian evangelists. The fact that new age and even NLP teachers now use these questions does nothing to eliminate the dramatic presupposition that the questions hide – the presupposition that there exist "a purpose" and that your life is an entity rather than the experience you have in living.

This is the presupposition now being directly challenged by people such as Neal Donald Walsch, who denies that we have some "mission" to discover and instead says (Walsch, 1996, p 51) "You do not live each day to discover what it holds for you, but to create it. You are creating your reality every minute, probably without knowing it." This was also the original teaching of such ancient religions as Hinduism. The Hindu texts are very specific about being in charge of one's own destiny. The Yoga Vasishtha emphasises "There is nothing like destiny other than the effect of our previous efforts" [II-6-4] and "Man determines his own destiny by his thought. He can make those things also happen which were not destined to happen." [V-24-28] (Sivananda, 1995, p 108). The notion that we are creating our "reality", including "missioning" ourselves, shifts our focus from "what is being discovered" to "how we are creating". Having watched hundreds of NLP Master Practitioners struggling with the process of "finding their mission", worrying if they have the correct "one", it seems much more useful to understand now that what is important about missioning is the attitude. Missioning is creating an overall movement in life, instead of a series of unrelated goals and responses. In this view, living is not something we do in order to "achieve" our mission; instead, living fully is missioning. This shifts our emphasis from *what* we do, to *how* we do it.

In the same sense that a mission is not an end result that we can try to reach, then death is not an end result that we can try to avoid. There is only the process of living. Most cell types in the human body have an average lifespan of a few years, and skin cells, in particular are constantly dying in order to be replaced by more resilient, younger cells (see, for example, Tunn et alia 1989). Our body depends on this ongoing process of dying. "Death" cannot be separated out from the rest of the process of living, and somehow avoided – the attempt to do so would not nourish living at all, but would interfere with life processes. Living includes dying, at every moment. A flower is very beautiful, but if it does not wither, there is no fruit and therefore no new life. This is not to say that death "should" be embraced, any more than it "should" be avoided. "Death" as a thing separate from life only has meaning in our thinking. It is humans who fear or avoid death as some ultimate state. Life itself does not make this distinction. To trim your fingernails does not mean somehow morbidly celebrating the death of those cells – it simply means knowing that this changing is part of the flow of living.

"The Self" or "The Ego"

When NLP co-developers Bandler and Grinder first proposed the idea of nominalisations to their mentor Gregory Bateson, he pointed out to them that the biggest nominalisation of all was the idea of a "self". William James, who wrote the first ever text of "Psychology", considered this a core concept in his new science.

James (Volume 1, p 291-401) put up an excellent case for the self being an illusory concept: "The consciousness of self involves a stream of thought, each part of which as "I" can 1) remember those which went before, and know the things they knew; and 2) emphasise and care paramountly for certain ones amongst them as *"me"* and *appropriate to these* the rest. The nucleus of the *"me"* is always the bodily existence felt to be present at the time. Whatever remembered-past-feelings *resemble* this present feeling are deemed to belong to the same *me* with it.... This me is an empirical aggregate of things objectively known. The *I* which knows them cannot itself be an aggregate, neither for psychological purposes need it be considered to be an unchanging metaphysical entity like the Soul, or a principle like the pure Ego, viewed as "out of time". It is a *Thought*, at each moment different from that of the last moment, but *appropriative* of the latter, together with all that the latter called its own.... *If the passing thought be the directly verifiable existent which no school has hitherto doubted it to be, then that thought is itself the thinker*, and psychology need not look beyond."

In NLP terms, James is explaining that the self is merely a nominalisation. It is a nominalisation for the process of "owning", of "identifying", or as James puts it, the process of "appropriating". As such "Self" is simply a word for a type of thinking where past experiences are appropriated or owned. This means that there is no "thinker" separate from the flow of thought. The existence of such an entity is purely illusory. There is just the process of thinking oneself the owner of previous experiences, goals and actions.

Information flows into our neurology via the five senses from outside, from other areas in the neurology, and possibly also as a result of other interactions between our body and the universe. There is a very simple mechanism by which, from moment to moment, our thinking then divides this information into two sets. I see the door and I think "not-me". I see my hand and I think "me" (I "appropriate" the hand to myself, or "own" it; I "identify" with it). Or, internally I see the craving for chocolate and I think "not-me". I see the ability to read this article and understand it and I think "me" (again, I appropriate or own it; I identify with it). Actually, all these pieces of information are in one mind! The notion of self and non-self is an arbitrary division; an internal sorting process. This division may be useful metaphorically, but it is a division which has "taken over" and now thinks it runs the neurology.

The owning of experiences as "me" and the disowning of experiences as "not me" occurs largely unconsciously, but is continuously active. A vast array of sensory experience is available at every moment, and the process of owning selects out one section at a time as "mine". It seems, for example, as if "I" am first holding a book, and then "I" am looking at the words, and then "I" am saying the words to myself, and then "I" am making pictures of the meaning. Actually, all of the senses are functioning all of the time, but conscious attention is shifting from one sense to another as the sense of "I" *appropriates* or identifies with each sense in turn.

This sense of self is very useful in being able to discuss actions and make decisions, and it is also the source of much of the distress we experience as humans. It is what allows a person to feel weak, alone and unsupported in the world (a situation which then artificially creates the need to be "protected", "taken care of", or "part of something greater" which is the source of the desire for authoritarian control in personal relationships, government and religion). This nominalization of the "self" ultimately separates one from immediate experience by suggesting that there is an "ideal" self to yearn and hunger for. If I have a self, then, even more than a mission, it suggests a goal that I am supposed to live up to. Once I believe that I have a concrete self, then I can worry about whether I am being true to myself, whether I am loving myself, whether my self is worthy or inadequate, good or evil and so on.

The Buddhist teacher Wei Wu Wei begins his book on Zen with this poem: (Wu Wei, p1)

"Why are you unhappy?
Because 99.9 per cent
Of everything you think,
And of everything you do,
Is for yourself -
And there isn't one."

How The Brain Creates The "Self"

We now know where this process begins in the brain. The posterior superior (back upper) parts of the brain's parietal cortex is called the Orientation Association Area or OAA (Newberg, D'Aquili and Vince, 2002, p 4). It analyses the entire visual image into two categories: self and other. When this area is damaged, the person has difficulty working out where they are in relation to what they see. Just trying to lie down on a bed becomes so complicated that the person will fall onto the floor. Like many brain structures, there is actually a left side OAA and a right side OAA. The left OAA creates the sensation of a physical body, and the right OAA creates a sense of an outside world in which that body moves.

Andrew Newberg and Gene D'Aquili have studied the OAA in both Tibetan Buddhist meditators and in Franciscan nuns (Newberg, D'Aquili and Vince, 2002, p 4-7). Newberg and D'Aquili used a SPECT (single photon emission computed tomography) camera to observe these people in normal awareness, and then at the times when they were at a peak of meditating or praying. At these peak moments, activity in the OAA ceased as the person's brain stopped separating out their "self" from the "outside world" and simply experienced life as it is: as one undivided experience.

The Buddhist meditators would report, at this time, that they had a sense of timelessness and infinity, of being one with everything that is. The nuns tended to use slightly different language, saying that they were experiencing a closeness and at-oneness with God and a sense of great peace and contentment. The stilling of the sense of separate self creates an emotional state which is described variously as bliss, peace, contentment or ecstasy. Newberg and D'Aquili speculate that the same stilling of the OAA occurs in peak sexual experiences, and that earlier in human history this may have been the main source of such states of oneness (and may be its evolutionary "purpose" in the brain – Newberg, D'Aquili and Rause, 2002, p 126).

What we can be sure of from this experiment is that the human brain is *designed* to experience the profound states of oneness and the resulting bliss that spiritual teachers have reported throughout history. In fact, in some senses, this way of experiencing life is more fundamental to our brain than the categorisation of the world into "me" and "not me" which is happens in our ordinary awareness. The experience of oneness is also truer to the nature of the universe as revealed by quantum physics. Spiritual experience is as natural to us humans as seeing or talking. When the categorisation of sensory experience by the VCA and the OAA is stilled, the oneness of the universe is blissfully revealed. Newberg, D'Aquili and Rause say, this is "why God will not go away" in our history.

Happold (1970) notes that such blissful self-free states are described in all spiritual traditions. In the Christian Bible, St Paul writes "I live, yet not I, but Christ liveth in me" The earliest Islamic poet of Iran, Baba Kuhi writes "I passed away into nothingness, I vanished; And lo, I am the All-living - only God I saw." The Hindu saint Paramahansa Yogananda explained "When one is illumined, he sees himself as the one Spirit throbbing beneath all minds and bodies." The Taoist teacher Huai Nan Tzu says "Those who follow the Natural order flow in the current of the Tao." The Buddhist teacher Dogen Zenji, in the GenjoKoan copy of his masterwork *Shobogenzo* (The Eye and Treasury of the True Law), makes the statement: "To study Buddhism is to study the self. To study the self is to forget the self. To forget the self is to be enlightened by all things."

Living Life As A Journey

Most of the religious texts in the world attempt to explain extraordinary experiences and understandings using languages which, as Alfred Korzybski notes, are inadequately designed for the purpose. Jewish rabbi David Cooper says that to understand what was meant we need to think of God as a verb. "The closest we can come to thinking about God is as a process rather than a being…. We can relate to God as an interactive verb. It is God-ing. Moreover from this perspective, creation should not be treated as a noun. It too is an interactive verb; it is constantly creation-ing. And dear reader you should not treat yourself as a noun – as Joan, or Bill, or Barbara, or John. With regard to God as an interactive verb, you are also verbs; you are Joan-ing, Bill-ing, Barbara-ing, or John-ing in relation to God-ing, just as I am David-ing." (Cooper, 1998, p 69-70)

What would life be like without the illusory nominalisations that we have been exploring in this chapter? A recurring metaphor for this state in spiritual teachings is the concept of life as a "way" or a "journey" rather than a destination. Jesus described himself as a "way" by which people could come to God" and the Chinese philosophical concept of the Tao simply means "the way". In the Taoist sense, there is no "way to happiness" because happiness is not in a box somewhere. Happiness is the way. Love is not an end result, it is the way of living.

Jill Bolte Taylor's story provides a non-religious neuroanatomical description of this sense of life as a path. On December 10th, 1996, 37 year old Indiana Neuroanatomist Jill Bolte Taylor suffered a massive stroke, the result of bleeding from a damaged blood vessel which destroyed most of the left side of her brain. Over the next weeks, she was in the unique position of knowing with a scientist's precision exactly what damage and repair was occurring in her brain. Her book, "My Stroke of Insight: A Brain Scientist's Journey" is a moving story identifying what works in recovery from brain injury, and also reporting what life without the controlling dominant left hemisphere (which creates nominalizations) is like. After her stroke, she was left with almost no functioning left brain. Her consciousness existed entirely in the non-verbal, creative, intuitive and holistic (denominalised) right brain. As a neuroscientist, she was aware of the actual process occurring and her report is an extraordinary bridge between the world of brain injury, the world of neuroscience and the world of mystical experience. What history has recorded as unusual and profound spiritual awareness was, she discovered, the basic functioning mode of her right brain.

She explains "In the absence of the normal functioning of my left orientation association area, my perception of my physical boundaries was no longer limited to where my skin met air. I felt like a genie liberated from its bottle. The energy of my spirit seemed to flow like a great whale gliding through a sea of silent euphoria…. Without a language centre telling me: "I am Dr. Jill Bolte Taylor. I am a neuroanatomist. I live at this address and can be reached at this phone number," I felt no obligation to being her anymore. It was truly a bizarre shift in perception, but without her emotional circuitry reminding me of her likes and dislikes, or her ego centre reminding me about her patterns of critical judgement, I didn't think like her anymore…. I had spent a lifetime of 37 years being enthusiastically committed to "do-do-doing" lots of stuff at a very fast pace. On this special day I learned the meaning of simply "being."…. All I could perceive was right here, right now, and it was beautiful." (Bolte Taylor, 2006, p 67-68). She adds "For many of us, thinking of ourselves as fluid, or with souls as big as the universe, connected to the energy flow of all that is, slips us out just beyond our comfort zone. But without the judgement of my left brain saying that I am a solid, my perception of myself returned to this natural state of fluidity." (Bolte Taylor, 2006, p 69). She later concluded "I loved knowing my spirit was at one with the universe and in the flow with everything around me. I found it fascinating to be so tuned in to energy dynamics and body language. But most of all, I loved the feeling of deep inner peace that flooded the core of my very being." (Bolte Taylor, 2006, p 82).

Summary

In this chapter we have looked at several illusory "things" (nominalisations) that obscure success in the coaching process and in life itself. They include:

- Anxiety and other clinical problems
- Disturbing memories, traumas and limiting beliefs
- Internal critics, inner children and other parts
- Life and life mission
- The self or ego

Jill Bolte-Taylor's story reminds us that our brain has another way of experiencing the world, rather than dividing it up into "things". This way is described in all the spiritual traditions of the world. Coaching is more than merely fixing problems. We can understand it as an ongoing process of inviting people to denominalise their life and experience the flow of existence. It is an invitation to the ultimate journey.

Bibliography:

Adler, R. "Crowded Minds" in New Scientist, Vol. 164, No. 2217, p 26-31, December 18, 1999

Bandler, R. and Grinder, J. <u>Frogs Into Princes</u>, Real People Press, Moab, Utah, 1979

Bandler, R. and Grinder, J. <u>Reframing: Neuro Linguistic Programming and the Transformation of Meaning</u>, Real People Press, Moab, Utah, 1982

Bandler, R. and Grinder, J. <u>The Structure of Magic (Volume 1)</u>, Science and Behaviour Books, Palo Alto, California, 1975

Barlow, D.H., Esler, J.L. and Vitali, A.E. "Psychosocial Treatments for Panic Disorders, Phobias and Generalised Anxiety Disorder" in Nathan, P.E. and Gorman, J.M. <u>A Guide To Treatments That Work</u>, Oxford University Press, New York, 1998

Barnes, M. Producer, "Hypnosis On Trial" (TV Program) BBC, London,

1982

Bartlett, F.C. <u>Remembering</u> Cambridge University, Cambridge, England, 1932

Bateson, G. <u>A Sacred Unity</u>, HarperCollins, New York, 1991

Baxter L. R. "Positron emission tomography studies of cerebral glucose metabolism in obsessive compulsive disorder." Journal of Clinical Psychiatry, 1994, 55 Supplement: p 54-9.

Beletsis, C.J. "Trance-Forming Anxiety: Hypnotic and Strategic Approaches to Treatment" p 264-280 in Yapko, M.D. ed <u>Brief Therapy Approaches to Treating Anxiety and Depression</u>, Brunner/Mazel, New York, 1989

Bohm, D. and Peat; D. <u>Science, Order and Creativity</u>, Bantam, Toronto, 1987.

Bolstad, R, "NLP: The Quantum Leap" in <u>NLP World</u>, Vol 3, No. 2, July 1996, p5-34

Bolstad, R. <u>Transforming Communication</u>
    Capra, F. <u>Uncommon Wisdom</u>, Flamingo, London, 1989.

Bolte Taylor, J. <u>My Stroke of Insight: A Brain Scientist's Journey</u>, published by Jill Bolte Taylor, Bloomington, Indiana, 2006

Cooper, D.A. <u>God Is A Verb: Kabbalah And The Practice Of Mystical Judaism</u> Riverhead Books, New York, 1998

DeLozier, J. and Grinder, J. <u>Turtles All The Way Down</u> Grinder, DeLozier and Associates, Bonny Doon, California, 1987

Dilts, R., Grinder, J., Bandler, R. and DeLozier, J. <u>Neuro-Linguistic Programming: Volume 1 The Study of the Structure of Subjective Experience</u>, Meta Publications, Cupertino, California, 1980

Franklin, J.A. <u>Overcoming Panic</u>, Australian Psychological Society, Carlton, Victoria

Gottman, J.M. and Silver, N. <u>The Seven Principles For Making Marriage Work</u> Three Rivers Press, New York, 1999

Gottman, J.M. <u>The Marriage Clinic</u> W.W. Norton and Co., New York, 1999

Happold, F.C. <u>Mysticism</u> Penguin, Harmondsworth, Middlesex, 1970
    James, W. <u>The Principles Of Psychology (Volume 1 and 2)</u>, Dover, New York, 1950.

Korzybski, A. <u>Science and Sanity</u>, Institute of General semantics, Englewood, New Jersey, 1994

Loftus, E. "Creating False Memories" p 70-75 in Scientific American, Volume 277, #3, September 1997
    Newberg, A., D'Aquili, E. and Rause, V. <u>Why God Won't Go Away</u> Ballantine, New York, 2002
    Peat, D. <u>The Philosopher's Stone</u>, Bantam, New York, 1991.

Sivananda, S. <u>Practice Of Karma Yoga</u> Divine Life Society,

Shivanandanagar, India, 1995

Spiegel, H. "Hypnosis and Evidence: Help of Hindrance?" p 73-85 in Annals of the New York Academy of Sciences, 347, 1980

Tunn, S., Nass, R., Ekernkamp, A., Schulze, H., and Kreig, M., "Evaluation of average life span of epithelial and stromal cells of human prostate by superoxide dismutase activity" in The Prostate, Vol 15, Issue 3, Pages 263-271, 1989

Walsch, N.D. Conversations With God; Volume 1, G P Putnam's Sons, New York, 1996

Watzlawick, P. How Real Is Real?, Vintage, New York, 1976

Wu Wei, W., Ask the Awakened, Routledge & Kegan Paul, London, 1963

Zohar, D. and Marshall, I. The Quantum Society, Flamingo, London, 1994.

Memory Reconsolidation

A New Metaphor For NLP Work
© Dr Richard Bolstad

Part A: What Memory Is And Is Not

Memory is a change in any system as a result of an experience. If you bend a piece of metal and then straighten it again, the metal is not the same - it carries the "memory" of the event. In a more complex way, our nervous system records changes as a result of the events we experience. For us as humans, memory is our delight and our terror, the source of our happiest reminiscences and our worst nightmares. To live without it (as in Alzheimers disease) is frequently viewed as a fate worse than death. And once we understand its original design, we can far more effectively use it to remember what we want to remember, and to forget what we want to forget. But memory was never designed to do what most of us try to use it for: to identify which things "really happened" at some time in the past.

In this chapter I will:
    A) explain in more detail what memory is and is not.
Then I will discuss four key ways to use this knowledge to create a more satisfactory life:
    B) Changing the emotional response we have to particular memories
    C) Remembering large amounts of new factual information reliably
    D) Planning for future events more effectively
    E) Recovering from physical health issues which are partially recreated by memory

What Memory Is, In The Human Brain

In an animal such as a human being, the brain and nervous system, made up of billions of nerve cells, glial cells and other specialised cells, coordinate actions across the organism. To do this, these cells need to show history-dependent behaviour by responding differently as a function of their previous input, and this "plasticity" (changeability) of nerve cells and their synapses especially is what we usually call memory. Memories, then, are changes in the nervous system's functioning which enable an animal to effectively respond to current events, based on what has been learned from past events. These changes in functioning (learnings) are only incidentally related to the structure of the real previous events which they were initiated in response to, and the idea that these changes somehow represent a faithful recording of those events is a human pretention.

So what actually changes when a memory is created? Well, firstly, there are simple changes at the synapses where nerve cells registering an event are activated, including increases in neurotransmitter release, and these changes may last for seconds or minutes. Secondly, long-lasting memory depends on wider scale changes such as the physical growth of new nerve cell connections (dendrites), and increases in the number of synaptic connections on those cells. These changes happen wherever the event was registered in the brain and body. In the outside areas of the brain (the cerebral cortex) the changes occur in the specialized areas where the sensory system data is processed (eg the visual area at the back of the brain, the somatosensory or kinesthetic area at the top of the brain, the auditory areas on the sides of the brain, and the specialized verbal or auditory digital areas mainly developed on the dominant side of the brain. These changes are all connected together based on the principle that "neurons which fire together, wire together". Otherwise there would be no memory, because each separate change would be encoded separately, so that, for example, a red square would trigger a bigger response when seen again, but there would be no way for the brain to know what the red square was related to and therefore what to do about it (Squire and Peller, 2000).

These sensory areas of the brain, altered by a memory event, are also connected to two other important areas where there are memory changes. Firstly, in certain types of memory, there are changes in the frontal areas of the brain, and when these frontal areas are changed as part of the memory, then conscious awareness of the memory tends to be reported (the links between the frontal cortex and the sensory cortex areas are especially damaged in Alzheimer's disease causing a loss in conscious memory). Secondly, and even more importantly, there are changes in the limbic system in the centre of the brain. This is an area associated with emotional responses and with identification of spatial and temporal coordinates (so it records the emotion associated with the memory, and the place and time of the memory event). To be exact, inside the limbic area, the amygdala records the emotional valence (how important it is either positively or negatively - so the amygdala responds especially to things that generate fear, anger, sexual desire, hunger etc), and the hippocampus records the spatio-temporal coordinates.

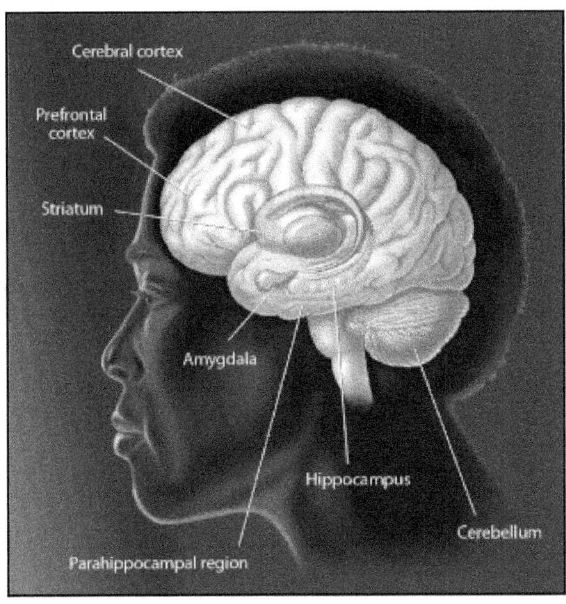

The hippocampus is so central to the initial structuring of each memory that if the hippocampus is damaged, new memories are unable to be laid down, even though memories in the distant past may well be intact (Squire and Paller, 2000). Initially, as a person stores a new memory, the hippocampus is the site at which many of the changes occur. It is a kind of a buffer zone where new memories can be temporarily stored until the brain transfers them safely to long term memory sites. Researchers Björn Rasch and Jan Born explain that the transfer of memories out of the Hippocampus serves an important function. The hippocampus operates as a short term buffer area and if memories were immediately transferred to other destinations new memories might run the risk of overwriting earlier memories (Rasch and Born, 2013). Over the first 7 or so days after the event, the memory is primarily stored in changes in the hippocampus, but over the next few weeks it is "consolidated", and "storage" of these changes is transferred more widely to other brain areas such as the sensory cortex and even to the cerebellum. the cerebellum is the lower brain, which eventually stores behavioural sequences such as walking and dancing, so that these remain intact even if the original sites of these memories in the sensory cortex are damaged by Alzheimers or another condition.

Sleep seems to be an important factor allowing for full consolidation of at least some memories. Björn Rasch and Jan Born say "Specifically, newer findings characterize sleep as a brain state optimizing memory consolidation, in opposition to the waking brain being optimized for encoding of memories. Consolidation originates from reactivation of recently encoded neuronal memory representations, which occur during SWS [Slow Wave Sleep] and transform respective representations for integration into long-term memory. Ensuing REM [Rapid Eye Movement - i.e. dreaming] sleep may stabilize transformed memories." (Rasch and Born, 2013).

It had always been known that eye movements to the sides occur during this sleep, and it was hypothesized that maybe sleepers are scanning things in their dream images. However even people blind from birth have these movements. The next part of the puzzle was that researchers noticed that these eye movements during sleep are similar to those that happen when awake people imagine a new image.

Finally, scanning people's brains while asleep, researchers from Tel Aviv University found that there was a burst in the activity of neurons that occurred just after the person's eyes flickered. This activity reflected a change of concept or scene (not image processing) during sleep. The scientists demonstrated that this was the same brain activity that occurred when awake patients were shown pictures, especially those related to their memories. "About a 0.3 seconds after the picture appears, these neurons burst -- they become vigorously active," Dr. Yuval Nir, who co-authored the study published in Nature Communications, explained to BBC News. "This also happens when people just close their eyes and imagine these pictures, or these concepts."

The new research was conducted over a period of four years, using data collected from 39 individuals who suffer from epilepsy. The patients already had electrodes implanted in their brains to try and help manage their seizures, and this allowed Dr. Nir the perfect chance to measure the activity of around 40 individual neurons -- mainly within the medial temporal lobe located towards the bottom of the brain -- while the volunteers slept. Dr. Nir told New Scientist magazine "Every time you move your eyes, a new image forms in the mind's eye." (Andrillon et alia, 2015). And this is exactly what NLP had been saying about eye movements.

The amygdala not only gives emotional significance to a memory, it also signals the brain about the required strength of the memory structure (telling the brain to store more important memories more vividly) and it determines whether an emotional response is strong enough to overide frontal (conscious) decisionmaking. With a damaged amygdala, a person tends to engage in more unsafe behaviour and to be unable to assess the seriousness of danger, hunger etc. Damage to the amygdala due to drugs such as alcohol leads to faulty decision-making by heavy users of those drugs, and, by contrast, the stress of PTSD and other over-activations of the panic system lead to physical hypertrophy (overdevelopment) of the amygdala, making the person overly cautious or "phobic" and "paranoid".

Reconsolidation of Memories

Each time you "think about" a memory, what you do is activate the same neural network as when you first experienced it, or the network of neurons to which that memory has been transferred in the process of consolidating it. That means that you "reconsolidate" it - i.e. by activating the memory, you bring it back into a state of activation, and so over the following 15 minutes or so, the memory has new changes added to it (after all, the principle that "neurons which fire together wire together" still operates, so if you remember an event, your current experiences and thoughts are now connected to the memory of the original event). As we will see, reconsolidation can significantly and permanently alter a "memory" changing the entire emotional valence of the memory (making a memory that was fear inducing become desire-inducing, for example). There is no "undo" function in the brain by which you can go back and reverse previous edits to get to the "original" memory. Memory, then is an active and synthetic process, and memories are changed irreversibly at every "re-membering" of them.

Reconsolidation of memories eventually organises them into very different places in the brain. At one time in my life, I needed to use my conscious mind to tie my shoelaces. Now days, my "unconscious mind" performs that function. What do I mean when I say that last sentence? I mean that another area of the brain now runs my shoelace tying strategy automatically when it is triggered by the sight of my shoes untied. Even a person severely affected by the memory loss of Alzheimer's disease may continue for some time to be able to tie their shoelaces, because such strategies are stored in areas of the brain less affected by that condition (Schacter, 1996, p 134-137). Such memories are called "procedural memories".

There is another type of memory which patients with Alzheimer's continue to have too. Memory researcher Daniel Schacter discusses the results of an experiment with words which reveals this other type of memory. First, he shows people a series of words, each of which is to be studied carefully for 5 seconds. The first set of words are: *assassin, octopus, avocado, mystery, sheriff, climate.* Next, he shows people a second set of words and asks if any of this second set were in the first set. The second set are: *twilight, assassin, dinosaur, mystery.* If your memory functions well, you recognised two of these from the first list. Next, Schacter asks people to complete the following English words by filling in the blanks. Third set: *ch----nk, o-t--us, -og-y---, -l-m-te.*

Most people who have seen the first set of words have difficulty coming up with two in this third set of words (chipmunk and bogeyman) but find octopus and climate rather obvious. That's because your memory has been "primed" by studying the first set. Now, here's the interesting thing. Priming memory also works for people with Alzheimer's disease, who cannot recall consciously whether any of the second set were in the first set. Priming even works for people who are exposed to spoken information when they are unconscious due to anaesthetic! (Schacter, 1996, p 170-172). Whereas conscious memory requires activation of the frontal cortex, the unconscious memories of priming and the unconscious memories of a procedure such as shoelace tying are stored deeper in the brain. These other types of memory/skill are unconscious, and they are very useful. We do not need to make such memory systems conscious. Unfortunately, these unconscious memories operate on automatic. They can be "primed" by irrelevant and even harmful stimuli which a person happens to come across.

Reconsolidation As An Observer

Another important memory distinction in memory is the difference between Observer memory (distanced memory where the rememberer sees themselves in the memory event - what NLP calls dissociated) and Field memory (where the rememberer re-experiences the memory from inside their body - what NLP calls associated). Field memory is closer to the original experience, of course. Observer memory is obviously well "reconsolidated", and the reorganisation of an entire memory from another perspective seems to require a mature nervous system (it is a skill that young children have difficulty with).

In his neurological research on observer memory and its effect, David Schachter noted that accessing a memory using observer memory removes emotional response bond consequently the person will claim that the original event must have had less emotional significance. He was able to point out that Sigmund Freud already commented on this benefit of observer memory 100 years ago. Freud noticed that his clients remembered their disturbing childhood memories this way and speculated that this may have had a protective effect (Searching for

Memory, Schachter, D.L., 1996, p 21-22). Freud called these observer memories "Screen memories" because they screen us from disturbing memories of our childhood. (Freud, 1899, p311). In NLP there are several processes which utilise this reconsolidation of memories as observed "movies".

Remember The Way Psychotherapy Was

Before discussing several methods of utilizing memory more effectively, I want to comment in more depth about the misunderstandings of memory that abounded in the twentieth century. What happens when we don't realise the truth of memory reconsolidation and brain plasticity? Early psychotherapy demonstrates several results of this error. In 1895, Sigmund Freud published the "founding document" of western psychotherapy; "Studies on Hysteria". In it he announces his discovery that childhood trauma causes psychiatric problems. He says "Quite frequently it is some event in childhood that sets up a more or less severe symptom which persists during the years that follow.... Not until they have been questioned under hypnosis do these memories emerge with the undiminished vividness of a recent event." (Freud and Breuer, 1974, p 60). This dramatic error has burdened over a century of attempts to help people. In fact, Hyppolyte Bernheim (1980) had demonstrated the fallacy of Freud's claim four years before the publication of "Studies on Hysteria". There is in fact, as readers will by now realise, no "undiminished vividness of a recent event."

To emphasise the falseness of Freud's early claims, a twentieth century hypnotist and psychiatrist named Martin Orne duplicated Bernheim's experiment in front of BBC television (1980). He interviewed a woman, asking her a number of questions, including how she slept the night before. She said she had, as usual, slept an excellent night's sleep. Orne then invited her to relax, and "reminded her" that she had been awakened during the night by what sounded like gunshots. He then woke her up fully and asked her again how she slept. She described the disturbing noises that she now believed had awoken her. Orne then replayed a tape of her pre-hypnosis statement saying that she had slept excellently. Far from realising that the gunshots were a "false memory", the woman was now very puzzled as to how she could have forgotten those disturbing sounds at the start of the interview. She was so convinced of her hypnotically induced memory that she was willing to argue with the evidence of the audiotape.

Of course, most people have had the experience of discussing a past event with a friend, and finding that the friend has incorrectly remembered the details. Many close relationships have come to grief over such disagreements. We know that what Orne was able to do with a light form of hypnosis can also occur in everyday life. Psychologists Daniel Simons and Daniel Levin conducted an extraordinary study in the 1990s to demonstrate how our "normal life" memory fools us. Imagine you are walking down the street and a stranger stops to ask directions. While you're talking to him, two men pass between you carrying a large wooden door. After they move on, you finish giving the directions, and the stranger advises you that you've just been the subject of a psychology experiment. He asks you if you noticed anything odd after the men with the door passed between you. He then explains that the original person who asked for directions actually walked off behind the door, and was replaced by your current interviewer. The original man now re-appears; he is a different height and build, has different clothes on, and has a different voice. But amazingly, 50% of people approached in this way do not notice the substitution occurring (Simons and Levin, 1998). The experiment demonstrates that much of what we "remember" is fabricated by our mind in order to fit with what we *think* must have happened.

Values And Belief Shifts in Memory

It's not just our memory of sensory experiences that are fragile in this way. NBC television captured an excellent demonstration of brief hypnosis being used to alter beliefs and even values. Dr Herbert Spiegel (1980) worked with a successful businessman with left wing political views. Spiegel relaxed the man, and told him that communists were planning to take over radio and television stations in America. Spiegel suggested that the man would be able to remember details of this conspiracy. When the man was then awakened, he did indeed have an elaborate story about the plot and how he had first heard of it. He expressed grave concerns about the left wing, saying that he had changed his opinion recently about their approach. Spiegel then removed the hypnotic suggestion and showed the man the videotape of this entire sequence. The businessman was extremely disturbed to witness himself talking "like an ultraconservative".

In everyday life, such shifts in values and beliefs are more common than we would like to think. The easiest way to notice them is to realise how inconsistent *other* people's values can be; for example how a person who "falls in love" can suddenly find that they share the values of their beloved, even where these contradict strongly held previous opinions of "their own". Dr Elisabeth Loftus has conducted over 200 research experiments demonstrating that memories can be implanted, without hypnosis, by simple suggestion. Does this happen in the therapeutic context, where real memories are also being explored? Certainly. Here is one small example given by Loftus: "In Missouri in 1992 a church counsellor helped Beth Rutherford to remember during therapy that her father, a clergyman, had regularly raped her between the ages of seven and 14 and that her mother sometimes helped him by holding her down. Under her therapist's guidance, Rutherford developed memories of her father twice impregnating her and forcing her to abort the foetus herself with a coat hanger. The father had to resign from his post as a clergyman when the allegations were made public. Later medical examination of the daughter revealed, however, that she was still a virgin at age 22 and had never been pregnant. The daughter sued the therapist and received a $1-million settlement in 1996." (Loftus, 1997, p 70).

This story presents an example of a person radically altering their beliefs and values as a result of a "therapeutic" conversation. Clearly, people do recall true information during therapy and hypnosis. Loftus' research demonstrates, unfortunately, that we simply cannot tell whether a new memory is real or not. In one of her studies, she selected subjects who (according to their own and their family's reports) had never been hospitalised for an ear infection as a child. She then had a relative tell each subject that when they were a child they were hospitalised overnight with an ear infection. After this 20% of subjects claimed to remember the hospitalisation, even when they were advised of the research occurring. Subjects remembered details such as who had visited them in the hospital. When people are likely to change their entire response to their family and community as a result of such a memory, this is a serious matter. To their credit, several people within the NLP/Ericksonian community have already expressed concern about this (eg Time Line Therapy Association, 1994; Yapko, 1994). They have pointed out that, as therapists, we need to caution clients very explicitly that any "memories" they recover during NLP work are unlikely to be acceptable as evidence in a court of law, and that there is a considerable chance that such memories could be contradicted by other evidence (ie that they will prove false to facts).

The Shifting Sands Of Memory

In fact, there are no memories that remain "intact" as if they were video-recorded. This was understood by researchers as early as 1932, when F. C. Bartlett wrote "Remembering is not the re-excitation of innumerable fixed, lifeless, and fragmentary traces. It is an imaginative reconstruction, or construction, built out of the relation of our attitude towards a whole active mass of organised past reactions or experience, and to a little outstanding detail which commonly appears in image or in language form. It is thus hardly ever really exact, even in the most rudimentary cases of rote recapitulation, and it is not at all important that it should be so." (Bartlett, 1932, p 213).

"Memories" are reconstructed in the present, out of a jumble of data stored at previous times. They are shaped by our present brain; by our mood, our present belief systems and so on. As an example of the way the present-day brain shaped our memories, consider the studies of what is called "inattentional blindness". When the posterior parietal cortex of the brain is damaged on one side, a very interesting result occurs. The person will fail to pay attention to objects seen on the affected side of their visual field. This becomes obvious if you ask them to describe all the objects in the room they are sitting in. If the affected side is the left, for example, when they look across the room, they will describe to you all objects on the right of the room, but ignore everything on the left. They will be able to confirm that those objects are there on the left, if asked about them, but will otherwise not report them (Kalat, 1988, p 197; Miller, 1995, p 33-34).

Edoardo Bisiach (1978) is an Italian researcher who studied people with such damage. He quickly discovered that this damage affected more than their current perception. For example, he asked one patient to imagine the view of the Piazza del Duomo in Milan, a sight this man had seen every day for some years *before* his illness. Bisiach had him imagine standing on the Cathedral steps and got him to describe everything that could be seen looking down from there. The man described only one half of what could be seen, while insisting that his recollection was complete. Bisiach then had him imagine the view from the opposite side of the piazza. He then fluently reported the other half of the details. The man's memories were being assembled by his present brain system, and his present brain system was "faulty" so his memories were all altered accordingly.

Such is precisely the problem we face in working with the person who is depressed. They may tell us that they have never been happy, because every memory they go to think of is processed by the same brain that is generating their depression. They can no longer easily attend to the happy experiences they once had. In the same way, the person who is angry may report that no-one has ever been kind to them, and the person who is sad may remember that they have never been loved. As psychotherapy evolved, therapists increasingly recognised this. Family therapy founder Virginia Satir considered that one of her main functions as a therapist was to help people reconstruct more useful memories, for example. In the transcript of her work called "Forgiving Parents"

(Andreas, 1991, p 104-107) Satir deals with a client, Linda, who claims that her mother never nurtured her, never tucked her in at night, and never bathed her. Virginia simply says "I don't believe it." and Linda eventually concedes that maybe her mother might have bathed her every so often.

In the work of psychotherapist and hypnotist Milton Erickson, we see the notion of re-developing memories taken to its ultimate conclusion, with the story of the February Man (Erickson and Rossi, 1989). In a series of sessions Erickson works with Jane, who says she had a childhood without loving parenting, and is afraid that now she herself will be unable to be a good mother. In trance, Erickson "journeys back" to her childhood, visiting her every February to provide loving support and reframes for her childhood experiences. For example he points out to her that although stubbing her toe is a painful experience "Maybe someday you will talk to a little girl about her stubbing her toe. You will really want to know what a stubbed toe felt like. Isn't that right?" (p 47). He explains to Ernest Rossi about this process, "You don't really alter the original experience, you alter the perception of it, and that becomes the memory of the perception." (p 77). Jane will now remember this moment of childhood "pain" as a moment of learning about how to be a good mother.

9/11 And "Flashbulb Memory"

One type of memory that there has been a great deal of objective research about is "Flashbulb memory" - the belief that memories of powerful and emotionally significant events such as the 9/11 attack in New York (September 11, 2001) persist without much "reconsolidation". In fact, the research shows that this is simply not true. Take 9/11. "Within about a week, memory scientists from New York to Michigan to California (now known as the 9/11 Memory Consortium) were querying people on what they remembered. The resulting set of data contained responses from more than 3,000 people in seven cities. Following up with those same people one year and three years later, the researchers found a decline in flashbulb memory accuracy that gradually levelled off after year one. In the first year, people's memories were consistent with the initial responses only 63 percent of the time. After that, however, they only lost 4.5 percent of their accuracy per year." (Pappas, 2011).

Firstly, the emotional experience associated with the memory changes. People assume that at the time they felt the same way they feel now about the events: in fact their current feelings are often based on knowledge which they could not even have at the time of the event.

Unfortunately, in their research, the Memory Consortium found that people's confidence that they were remembering accurately was increased by the level of amygdala activation occurring as they remembered, and not by the level of hippocampal activation (that is to say, the stronger the emotion, the more convinced the person was that their memory was accurate, but the actual strength of place memories did not increase their confidence). Secondly, in the process of reconsolidation, considerable editing of the sequence of events occurs. "In the case of 9/11, people will sometimes claim to have seen live video of the first plane hitting the North Tower of the World Trade Center, Talarico said, despite the fact that such video was not broadcast until days after the attack." Their memory has (completely unconsciously) spliced in images actually seen days later and resequenced them to make sense. These two changes also clearly occur in relation to people's reports of traumatic childhood memories, many of which contain emotional responses entirely dependent on their adult information about the events.

Event Memory Parcels

This sort of sequential change raises an interesting question about how the brain decides to "parcel" memory, which is, after all, potentially a fairly continuous sequence while we are awake, into discrete "events". (Brenner and Zacks, 2011). Charles B. Brenner and Jeffrey M. Zacks report on a 2011 research study by Gabriel Radvansky, Sabine Krawietz and Andrea Tamplin. In this the researchers "seated participants in front of a computer screen running a video game in which they could move around using the arrow keys. In the game, they would walk up to a table with a colored geometric solid sitting on it. Their task was to pick up the object and take it to another table, where they would put the object down and pick up a new one. Whichever object they were currently carrying was invisible to them, as if it were in a virtual backpack. Sometimes, to get to the next object the participant simply walked across the room. Other times, they had to walk the same distance, but through a door into a new room. From time to time, the researchers gave them a pop quiz, asking which object was currently in their backpack. The quiz was timed so that when they walked through a doorway, they were tested right afterwards. As the title said, walking through doorways caused forgetting: Their responses were both slower and less accurate when they'd walked through a doorway into a new room than when they'd walked the same distance within the same room." You may have had this experience yourself. You get up from an activity in one room and go into another room to get something you need ... only to find that your brain has closed the memory network you were operating with and you cannot recall what you came for!

Brenner and Zacks ask why the brain needs uses markers such as; passing through a door as opportunities to forget. They conclude that "some forms of memory seem to be optimized to keep information ready-to-hand until its shelf life expires, and then purge that information in favor of new stuff. Radvansky and colleagues call this sort of memory representation an "event model," and propose that walking through a doorway is a good time to purge your event models because whatever happened in the old room is likely to become less relevant now that you have changed venues." The event model gives your brain a series of algorithms for dividing up the endless flow of life into discrete "events" that can be stored in a separate neural network and transferred to other areas of the brain in reconsolidation.

Neural Networks and Strategies

Realising that the brain parcels our memories into discrete "events" raises once more the question: why does the brain want such detailed memories anyway? The answer is not to keep a photo album of our life: it is to help us decide quickly and efficiently what to do whenever a new situation occurs that may have antecedents in our prior experiences. Being able to respond in a more effective way to a repeated experience is called learning, and for the brain, memory is all about learning, and not about recording truth. The "TOTE" was developed by neurology researchers George Miller, Eugene Galanter and Karl Pribram (1960), as a model to explain how learning of complex behaviour occurred. Ivan Pavlov's original studies had shown that simple behaviours can be produced by the stimulus-response cycle. When Pavlov's dogs heard the tuning fork ring (a stimulus; or in NLP terms an "anchor"), they salivated (response). But there is more to dog behaviour than stimulus-response.

For example, if a dog sees an intruder at the gate of its section (stimulus/anchor), it may bark (response). However, it doesn't go on barking forever. It actually checks to see if the intruder has run away. If the intruder has run away, the dog stops performing the barking operation and goes back to its kennel. If the intruder is still there, the dog may continue with that strategy, or move on to another response, such as biting the intruder. Miller, Gallanter and Pribram felt that this type of sequencing was inadequately explained in Pavlov's simple stimulus-response model. In Miller and Pribram's model, the first stimulus, (seeing the intruder) is the Trigger (the first T in the "TOTE"; Pavlov called this the "stimulus", and in NLP we also call this an "anchor") for the dog's "scaring-intruders-away" strategy. Obviously, the intensity of the trigger is what actually activates the strategy (in this case the closeness of the intruder). This intensity is measured in each sensory system by smaller sections of the sensory cortex, called in NLP "submodalities". The barking itself is the Operation (O). Checking to see if the intruder is gone yet (checking that the submodalities are reduced) is the Test (second T). Going back to the kennel is the Exit from the strategy (E). This sequence of information flow through the cortex might be written as $V^e \rightarrow K^e \rightarrow V^e/V^c \rightarrow K^e$ (Visual external trigger $\rightarrow$ Kinesthetic external action $\rightarrow$ Compare Visual external situation now to constructed image of the desired visual situation $\rightarrow$ Kinesthetic external action). Notice that the checking stage (Test) is done by comparing the result of the operation (what the dog can see after barking) with the result that was desired (what the dog imagines seeing –a person running away). In the notation, comparison is written using the slash key "/".

Let's take another example. When I hear some music on the radio that I really like (trigger or anchor), I reach over and turn up the radio (operation). Once it sounds as loud as I enjoy it sounding (test), I sit back and listen. The strategy, including the end piece where I listen (another whole strategy really) is $A^e \rightarrow K^e \rightarrow A^e/A^r \rightarrow K^e \rightarrow A^e$. Once we understand that every result a person achieves is a result of a strategy which begins with some trigger and leads them to act and test that action, then we have a number of new choices for changing the way they run their strategy and the results they get.

Strategies are learned behaviours, triggered by some specific sensory representation (a stimulus). What does "learned" mean? The human brain itself is made up of about one hundred billion nerve cells or neurons. These cells organise themselves into networks to manage specific tasks. When any experience occurs in our life, new neural networks are laid down to record that event and its meaning. To create these networks, the neurons grow an array of new dendrites (connections to other neurons). Each neuron has up to 20,000 dendrites, connecting it simultaneously into perhaps hundreds of different neural networks.

Steven Rose, in some of the earliest work on the neurology of memory (1992) gives an example from his research with new-hatched chicks. After eating silver beads with a bitter coating, the chicks learn to avoid such beads. One peck is enough to cause the learning. Rose demonstrated that the chicks' brain cells change instantly, growing 60% more dendrites in the next 15 minutes. These new connections occur in very specific areas –what we might call the "bitter bead neural networks". These neural networks now store an important new strategy. The strategy is triggered each time the chick sees an object the right shape and size to peck at. This is a visual strategy of course. The trigger (seeing a small round object) is Visual external (V^e) and the operation (checking the colour) is also Visual external (V^e). The chick then compares the colour of the object it has found with the colour of the horrible bitter beads from its visual recall (V^e/V^r) and based on that test either pecks the object or moves away from it (K^e). We would diagram this strategy: $V^e \rightarrow V^e \rightarrow V^e/V^r K^e$.

Obviously, the more strategies we learn, the more neural networks will be set up in the brain. California researcher Dr Marion Diamond (1988) and her Illinois colleague Dr William Greenough (1992) have demonstrated that rats in "enriched" environments grow 25% more dendrite connections between neurons than usual, as they lay down hundreds of new strategies, reconsolidating them throughout the brain. Autopsy studies on humans confirm the process. Graduate students have 40% more dendrite connections than high school dropouts, and those students who challenged themselves more had even higher scores (Jacobs et alia, 1993).

How do messages get from one neuron to another in the brain? The transmission of impulses between neurons and dendrites occurs via hundreds of precise chemicals called "information substances"; substances such as dopamine, noradrenalin (norepinephrine), and acetylcholine. These chemical float from one cell to another, transmitting messages across the "synapse" or gap between them. Without these chemicals, the strategy stored in the neural network cannot run.

The particular mixture of chemicals present when a neural network is laid down must be recreated for the neural network to be fully re-activated and for the strategy it holds to run as it originally did. If someone is angry, for example, when a particular new event happens, they have higher noradrenalin levels. Future events which result in higher noradrenalin levels will re-activate this neural network and the strategy they used then. As a result, the new event will be connected by dendrites to the previous one, and there will even be a tendency to confuse the new event with the previous one. If my childhood caregiver yelled at me and told me that I was stupid, I may have entered a state of fear, and stored that memory in a very important neural network. When someone else yells at me as an adult, if I access the same state of fear, I may feel as if I am re-experiencing the original event, and may even hear a voice telling me I'm stupid.

This is called "state dependent memory and learning" or SDML. Our memories and learnings, our strategies, are *dependent* on the state they are created in. Since this is a system, what we see, hear, smell, taste or touch may also "trigger" or "anchor" a state of mind by activating a neural network that occurred when that sensory stimulus was present previously, as Pavlov discovered.

Submodalities

The triggering of a neural network, then, is dependent on the emotional valence of that network (i.e. it is "state dependent"). The brain has a very specific way of linking the information about your emotions (stored in places such as the amygdala) into the actual sensory experience you are having or remembering (eg into the picture you are seeing). The emotional information is "coded" visually (and in the other senses) as a result of some specific detailed distinctions made within the cortex. Inside the visual cortex, there are several areas which process "qualities" such as colour, brightness and distance. When you are hungry, food often looks bigger and brighter (television advertisers know this – they makes the food on their adverts bigger and brighter too). In NLP these qualities are known as visual "submodalities" (because they are produced in small sub-sections of the visual modality). The first fourteen visual submodalities listed by Richard Bandler (1985, p 24) were colour, distance, depth, duration, clarity, contrast, scope, movement, speed, hue, transparency, aspect ratio, orientation, and foreground/background.

To give a sense of how these submodalities "code" emotional information, consider the following study. In research by Emily Balcetis, an assistant professor in NYU's Department of Psychology, and David Dunning, a Cornell professor of psychology, volunteers tossed a beanbag towards a gift card (worth either $25 or $0) on the floor. They were told that if the beanbag landed on the card, they would be given the card. Interestingly, the volunteers threw the beanbag much farther if the gift card was worth $0 than if it was worth $25 — that is, they underthrew the beanbag when attempting to win a $25 gift card, because they viewed that gift card as being closer to them. These findings indicate that when we want something, we actually view it as being physically close to us. Moving an object, in our imagination, closer to us makes us see it as more significant and triggers the neural network with memorised instructions about how to respond to it. This is then the basis for several

NLP processes such as the "visual swish", in which an image of a desired future self is moved quickly closer and becomes brighter.

How The Memory System Can Be Utilized

Clearly, there are times when it is useful to be able to remember events and information vividly, and times when it is useful not to be uncontrollably triggered into the activation of memories of events. Understanding how the memory process works in the brain helps us do both these things more effectively.

Understanding the neurophysiology of memory also prevents us being caught in mistaken ideas about memory - ideas that then limit our choices needlessly. These include the idea that when a memory activates the panic response, then something is "broken" in the brain (in fact, panic shows that the brain is working perfectly), the idea that memories cannot be altered (in fact they cannot NOT be altered), and the idea that after a problematic memory has been reconsolidated by natural means or by guided visualization, it can somehow "go back" to its original state by accident (in fact none of the mice in the research study below had this problem, which is peculiar to human subjects able to imagine themselves into attempted recreations of the original state).

In the rest of this article I will focus on four ways we can more effectively use our memory systems.
- Changing the emotional response we have to particular memories
- Remembering large amounts of new factual information reliably
- Planning for future events more effectively so that we create the results we want in life more fully
- Recovering from physical health issues which are partially recreated by memory

Part B: Changing The Emotional Response To Memories

The Mice Who Conquered Fear With Love and Curiosity

In all the hundreds of research studies refrred to in this article, this is probably my favourite. In 2014, Dr. Susumu Tonegawa and his team at RIKEN-MIT Center for Neural Circuit Genetics conducted an extraordinary experiment which revealed how the "emotional valence" (whether it feels good or bad) on a memory can be changed in a few minutes of "reconsolidation". (Redondo et alia 2014)

"Both the hippocampus and the amygdala are considered critical for memory formation. We wanted to know whether the memory engram [network] was free to associate with positive or negative valences or whether it was fixed with respect to emotion," said Roger Redondo, who along with Joshua Kim is co-first author of this study, in a press release. "We also wanted to know at what point in the circuit the valence is assigned to the engram, in the hippocampus or the amygdala."

Their experiment takes a few sentences to explain, but it is worth it! The first part is a kind of preparation. The experiments were conducted on male mice, who were placed in a room they had never seen before, and divided into two groups. One group received a mild electric shock on their foot while the other group was allowed to socialize with a female mouse. So the two groups of mice both formed memories of the room, but some formed memories of fear and some formed memories of pleasure. Using a biomarker (a chemical called channelrhodopsin-2 or "ChR2", released into the mice brains to mark out the areas of the brain where new connections were growing), the scientists genetically labeled neurons that were active during the formation of either memory. The team then used optogenetics to activate the same set of neurons. This involves shining a light from an LED or laser source outside, through the mouse head - if you hold your hand up in front of a strong light you can see that it shines through the tissue, so this is not surprising. When this light strikes the chemically marked out area in the mouse brain, it triggers the neurons in that area to fire, basically activating the memory network from outside. When the neurons were activated, the mice showed the same response as they did when they originally experienced the event. The mice that had been shocked avoided the room where it had happened, and the mice that had met female mice moved towards the room. the researchers could see the activated circuits inside the mice brains and actually identify the memory of the event, in the hippocampus, and (in mice where this was marked) its connection to the emotional response in the amygdala (to different parts of the amygdala depending on whether the experience was positive or negative).

Next, the researchers gave the mice a new experience, in a new place. The (male) mice who got the mild shock the first time were introduced to some female mice. As they were showing interest in these female mice, the researchers activated the old memory "engram" in the "dorsal dentate gyrus" of the hippocampus. This old memory of being shocked in the room was now connected to the new experience of being interested in the opportunity of meeting the female mice. To the observers' fascination, they could see the memory network changing.

The old connections into the fear area of the amygdala were eliminated, and new connections were made into the curiosity/desire area of the amygdala. Finally the mice were placed back in the room where they had originally been shocked, but this time they immediately showed interest and looked around with positive curiosity. Their memory of the room had changed. Observing the process, the scientists could see that the old memory (or the negative "valence" of the old memory) was simply deleted. The record of being in the room was now associated with positive feelings, essentially creating a new memory.

The effective sequence is to have the mice create a powerful enough positive emotional state, and then, while they are feeling that positive state, to reactivate the place memory of the original event which had been fear-associated. the researchers commented that to transfer this technique to humans, we would only need a way of reactivating the place memory in the hippocampus. In NLP we do this with the process known as anchoring (a precise application of Pavlovian classical conditioning). In a controlled research study published in Germany (Reckert, 1994), Horst Reckert describes how in one session he was able to remove students' test anxiety using the simple technique of anchoring, based on this principle. He had the students recall a powerfully relaxed time, while pressing on a specific point on their hand to "anchor" the event, and then had them use that same pressure on their hand as they thought about the challenging situation. This connected the feeling of relaxation to the experience of sitting in the test room. This is the same principle you experience when you hear a song on the radio that reminds you of the feeling you had years ago when that song first came out.

The most important thing to take away from the research on the mice is that the emotional response connected to memories can be intentionally changed in a very short time, and changed permanently: remember, in the brain there is no "undo" for reconsolidation, there is only more reconsolidation.

Memory Obstruction Versus Memory Reconsolidation

Our growing neurological understanding of the consolidation and reconsolidation of memories is a particularly important issue for PTSD treatments such as the NLP trauma reconsolidation process and NLP eye movement integration. I will comment on each of these, starting with the NLP eye movement integration process. This involves asking the client to re-access a disturbing memory and then try to hold onto that memory while their eyes move from side to side and corner to corner diagonally. For some time, it has been known that moving the eyes causes enormous floods of electrical information across the brain and for this reason, during brain scans, a person is usually instructed to hold their eyes still. We now have research showing that rapid side-to-side eye movements during an event or during active recall of an event prevent the recording of even short term memory traces, and that the result is not a re-ordering of those memories but an interference with the neural circuitry of the memory being formed or reconsolidated (see for example, Engelhard et alia, 2010). This is at least partially the effect of "The NLP Eye Movement process" taught by NP trainers Steve Andreas and John Grinder, and of NLP trainer Andy Austin's "Integral Eye Movement Therapy". Separately from NLP, this kind of method is promoted as EMDR. By calling it "Editing" Grinder refers to it as a type of reconsolidation similar to that experienced by the mice in the experiment above, although instead of connecting the hippocampal memory to a positive place in the amygdala, it would then be connecting it to what Grinder calls a "Know Nothing State' (Grinder 2002)

This is an entirely different process to altering the perceptual position of consolidated long term memories towards what memory researchers refer to as observer memory (i.e. what NLP, with obstinacy, refers to as dissociation - Searching for Memory, Schachter, D.L., 1996, p 21-22). Observer memory is a type of reconsolidation that is done naturally in the brain over long periods of time, especially to distressing memories, and it also seems to require frontal cortex maturation (i.e. it cannot easily be done by a child of say 5 years old). Clinically, we would be better doing eye movement processes with younger children, and with people very close in time to the events they are coping with. The possible loss of memory clarity would be a small price to pay for an effective protection from long term traumatisation. With longer term issues, the NLP Trauma recovery process (the movie theatre technique) may give us better meaning elaboration and subsequent learning about the events being processed.

Training the brain to dissociate from disturbing events is a key to emotional health, as demonstrated in research by Brad Bushman and Dominik Mischkowski (2013). They subjected research students to a situation designed to evoke anger and anxiety. They then asked the students to review the events. Some students were told to adopt a self-immersed perspective ("see the situation unfold through your eyes as if it were happening to you all over again") and then analyze their feelings surrounding the event. Others were told to use the self-distancing perspective ("move away from the situation to a point where you can now watch the event unfold from a distance…watch the situation unfold as if it were happening to the distant you all over again") and then analyze their feelings. The third control group was not told how to view the scene or analyze their feelings. Each group was told the replay the scene in their minds for 45 seconds. The researchers then tested the participants for aggressive thoughts and angry feelings. The difference was dramatic; those students who had dissociated themselves were substantially less distressed and less angry.

This distancing is the basis of the famous NLP phobia-trauma process, which rehearses the brain to reconsolidate a memory as an observer experience by having the client visualise the event happening on a movie screen.. In his book "The Trauma Trap", Dr David Muss MD documents his extensive use of this NLP Trauma Process with victims of PTSD: A policeman involved in the Hillsborough soccer disaster describes how his flashbacks (sudden horrific memories of the trauma), insomnia and alcohol abuse disappeared after two sessions. A patient (Barbara Drake) tells how one session with Dr Muss completely resolved flashbacks and other symptoms resulting from a sexual abuse experience. These and the other stories documented by Muss parallel our own experiences as trainers and Master Practitioners of NLP. Muss says "I know that it has worked for every patient I have dealt with so far, without exception." (Muss, "The Trauma Trap", 1991, p 10). Muss did a pilot study with 70 members of the West Midlands Police Force, who had witnessed major disasters such as the Lockerbie air crash. Of these, 19 qualified as having PTSD. The time between trauma and treatment varied from six weeks to ten years. All participants reported that after an average of three sessions they were completely free of intrusive memories and other PTSD symptoms. Follow-up ranged from 3 months to 2 years, and all gains were sustained over that time.

In 2001, after the 9/11 attacks, New York NLP organisations offered free dissociation trauma cure treatments for New York citizens. their results, over hundreds of people, were so promising that they gained the attention of authorities. In 2014, NLP Trainers, Dr Frank Bourke, Dr Richard Gray and colleagues received a $300,000 grant from New York state and over 5o War Veterans Organisations referred clients to begin a pilot study on the method. 58 veterans were interviewed and evaluated for treatment (52 diagnosed with PTSD). Nearly all of them were combat vets, and they ranged from Vietnam veterans suffering for almost 50 years to vets from Iraq and Afghanistan. Of 33 clients who entered treatment, 26 (using the national PTSD norm of 45 points as cutoff) no longer test as having PTSD; their symptoms were fully alleviated in under five sessions. There were six others who either dropped out or had missing diagnostic scores; one more did not respond to the treatment. As the protocol was tested under strict scientific standards for the first time, it produced results that matched previous success levels. In this study 75% of the treatment pool and 96% of program completers terminated treatment with complete and permanent elimination of the symptoms of PTSD in less than 5 hours of treatment as verified at the two- and six-week follow-ups. The researchers say "According to combined behavioral and instrumental measures, this pilot *completely removed* the PTSD diagnosis in 96% of those who completed treatment. Current VA and Army treatments "statistically improve" PTSD scores 35% of the time (Steenkamp & Litz (2013, 2014). No currently approved treatments for PTSD remove the diagnosis; at best, they only improve the symptom scores." (See Gray and Liotta, 2012)

Part C: Remembering Factual Information Reliably

Memory Pegs and The Journey Method (Method of Loci)

Since memory is so constantly being reorganized, how do people ever recall information accurately? The answer lies not in developing a new ability so much as in utilizing the most stable memory networks you already have, and utilizing the central role of the hippocampus (which is after all essentially a GPS system). Eight time world memory champion Dominic O'Brien had an entry in the Guinness Book of Records for his May 2002 feat of committing to memory a random sequence of 2808 playing cards (54 packs) after looking at each card only once. He was able to correctly recite their order, making only eight errors, four of which he immediately corrected when told he was wrong. In his books he explains that there is nothing genetically different that makes his memory so good. He simply knows how to use the memories and the memory system his brain already uses.

O'Brien simplifies his memory tasks by adding new information to memory "pegs" (things already permanently in place in his memories, that he can hang new information on, just as you could hang clothes on a clothesline using the pegs that are already there). For example, you have probably recalled the Arabic numerals in order, and your memory of them is likely to be perfect, and resilient over time, so they can be used as pegs to hang new images on. If we add images to that list of numbers, you will be able to easily recall those images in sequence too. So if I point out that the number 1 looks like a pen, the number 2 looks like a swan, and the number 3 looks like Mickey Mouse's ears, you will find it easy to remember those three images in that order. Now you can add more detailed images to those so as to remember even random concepts.

Numerical memory pegs:
1. Pen
2. Swan
3. Mickey Mouse's Ears
4. Sailboat
5. Hook
6. Golf Club
7. Cliff
8. Hour glass
9. Pipe
10. Bat and ball

Dominic O'Brien uses the Journey method primarily to recall things such as the list of cards. The journey method is a memory utilization technique in which you use another set of "pegs", taking advantage of your ability to remember a series of specific landmarks chosen from a journey that is already familiar to you such as walking round your house/apartment. In this method, the memory peg idea is used in combination with the place marking system of the hippocampus. The development of the Journey method is attributed to Simonodes of Ceos, an Ancient Greek poet, and it was used extensively by the Ancient Romans, who called it the method of Loci. During the excavation of the rubble of a collapsed dining hall, Simonides was called upon to identify each guest killed. Their bodies had been crushed beyond recognition but he completed the gruesome task by correlating their identities to their positions (loci in Latin) at the table before his departure. He later drew on this experience to develop the 'memory theatre' or 'memory palace', a system for mnemonics (memory) widely used in European societies until the Renaissance.

You use the Journey Method by associating information with landmarks on a journey that you know well. This could, for example, be your journey to work in the morning; the route you use to get to the front door when you get up; the route to visit your parents; or a familiar tour around a holiday destination. John O'Keefe and Lynn Nadel explain that this method directly uses the centrality of the hippocampus in memory, using its location system to record imaginary journeys just as it normally records real journeys. They say: " 'the method of loci', is an imaginal technique known to the ancient Greeks and Romans and described by Yates (1966) in her book The Art of Memory as well as by Luria [the Russian memory expert A. R. Luria] (1969). In this technique the subject memorizes the layout of some building, or the arrangement of shops on a street, or any geographical entity which is composed of a number of discrete loci. When desiring to remember a set of items the subject 'walks' through these loci in their imagination and commits an item to each one by forming an image between the item and any distinguishing feature of that locus. Retrieval of items is achieved by 'walking' through the loci, allowing the latter to activate the desired items. The efficacy of this technique has been well established (Ross and Lawrence 1968, Crovitz 1969, 1971, Briggs, Hawkins and Crovitz 1970, Lea 1975), as is the minimal interference seen with its use." (O'Keefe and Nadel 1978)

Once you are practiced with the technique you will be able to create imaginary journeys that have as many landmark places as you need. To use this technique most effectively, it is often best to prepare the journey beforehand. In this way the landmarks are clear in your mind before you try to commit information to them. One of the ways of doing this is to write down all the landmarks that you plan to use in order on a piece of paper. To remember a list of items, whether these are people, events, concepts or objects, all you need do is associate images of these things with the landmarks on your journey.

This is an extremely effective method of remembering long lists of information. With a sufficiently long journey you could, for example, remember elements on the periodic table, lists of Kings and Presidents, geographical information, or the order of cards in a shuffled pack. One advantage of this technique is that you can use it to work both backwards and forwards, and start anywhere within the route to retrieve information. You could also start other journeys at each landmark.

Part D: Planning For Future Events

Creating Future Memories

Expectations of future events are also created and stored in the brain of course, and here we see a similar pattern to the creation and storage of memory, with the Hippocampus again being central. Construction of a future imagined event looks much the same as reconsolidation of a memory in the brain. That is to say, for the brain, the construction of a future event is much the same as the remembering of an earlier event. Interestingly, the less likely the future "memory" is, the more activity we see in the hippocampus. This suggests that the work the hippocampus does involves connecting or "re-membering" patterns from across the brain – images, sounds, sensations and plans etc. into one memory or event, and the less likely the connection of these parts is, the more complex the job being done by the hippocampus. (Gaesser et alia 2013).

When people complain of memory problems, they are usually complaining of one of two things. The first is difficulty remembering events and facts, which is dealt with using the Journey technique described above. The second is not about memory of the past at all. The person complains that they meant to pick up some bread at the shop on the way home, but they forgot. This is a problem with the effective construction of future events, not with the recollection of pas events. Most people do not solve this by having a "super-memory". They solve it beforehand, by setting up a future cue that will remind them, when they are passing the shop, to go in and get the bread. This skill, called "futurepacing" in NLP, can be learned.

My friend Annette and I shared an office. Each time Annette came to work and saw my cookies, she remembered that it was nice to have a snack available for morning tea. She was committed to buying some to share, but in the meantime she shared mine. After some weeks, we realised that this was a problem of futurepacing. Annette's good intentions (of buying cookies) were anchored to the office (where they were utterly useless - our office did not have a cookie vending machine). I got Annette to imagine herself coming into her local store. I told her to see the things that she would see as she came in the door, and to look over to the shelf where the cookies were. I told her to imagine herself walking over to the shelf and picking up a packet. In this way, her good intention would be likely to be triggered by the naturally occurring sights and feelings of Annette's real life, the exact moment before they were needed. Sure enough, the next time Annette came into the office, she reported success. She had walked into the dairy to buy milk, seen the biscuit shelf, walked over to it ... and realized she had no money in her pocket to buy biscuits! You get the idea though – it takes planning to be able to remember! This is the "preparatory memory" work done by the hippocampus in Gaesser's research (Gaesser et alia 2013). It is the precise sensory-specific goal-setting process which researchers have also discovered is a fundamental of all successful achievement.

Goal-setting

Goal-setting is just a more detailed example of the same process, involving setting up future cues for action leading to a desired result. Richard Wiseman (2009, p 88-93) did a very large study of goal-setting. He tracked 5000 people who had some significant goal they wanted to achieve (everything from starting a new relationship to beginning a new career, from stopping smoking to gaining a qualification). He followed people up over the next year, and found firstly that only 10% ever achieved their goal. It wasn't just bad luck. Dramatic and consistent differences in the psychological techniques they used made those 10% stand out from the rest, as they used their hippocampus in a much more precise way.

Sensory Specific: Firstly, the most successful people did imagine achieving their goal, and were able to list concrete, specific benefits they would get from it, rather than just say that they would "feel happy". They had what Wiseman calls "an objective checklist of benefits" and made these "as concrete as possible", often by writing them down. He notes "… although many people said they aimed to enjoy life more, it was the successful people who explained how they intended to spend two evenings each week with friends and visit one new country each year." At this time, this "future memory" is being created in the brain. (Wiseman, 2009, p 91- 93)

Positive: Secondly, they described their goal positively. Wiseman says "For example, when asked to list the benefits of getting a new job, successful participants might reflect on finding more fulfilling and well-paid employment, whereas their unsuccessful counterparts might focus on a failure leaving them trapped and unhappy." Again, whatever the person imagines happening becomes a "future memory". (Wiseman, 2009, p 92)

Ecological: One surprising result of the research by both Gabrielle Oettingen and Richard Wiseman is that it pays to think about challenges you may face in achieving your goal (even though that may feel unpleasant at the time). After thinking about the positive benefits of achieving their goal, the most successful participants would "spend another few moments reflecting on the type of barriers and problems they are likely to encounter if they attempt to fulfil their ambition…. focusing on what they would do if they encountered the difficulty." (Wiseman, 2009, p 101) Oettingen trained people to do this process, which she calls "doublethink" and NLP would call checking "ecology". She was able to increase their success dramatically just with this step. This is "futurepacing" the challenges and their solution.

Choice Increasing and Celebrated: Related to this NLP concept of ecology is the fact that successful goal-setters made sure that they felt as if their progress was bringing them rewards rather than limiting their choices and creating work. They did this most of all because "As part of their planning, successful participants ensured that each of their sub-goals had a reward attached to it" so that it "gave them something to look forward to and provided a sense of achievement." (Wiseman, 2009, p 93)

Initiated by Self: Successful goal-setters have a plan. They do not leave their goal up to "the law of attraction" or to someone else who will save them. Wiseman notes "Whereas successful and unsuccessful participants might have stated that their aim was to find a new job, it was the successful people who quickly went on to describe how they intended to rewrite their CV in week one, and then apply for one new job every two weeks for the next six months." (Wiseman, 2009, p 91)

First Step Identified: Wiseman found that it was particularly important to break the goal down into small steps and manage one step at a time. "Successful participants broke their overall goal into a series of sub-goals, and thereby created a step-by-step process that helped remove the fear and hesitation often associated with trying to achieve a major life change." (Wiseman, 2009, p 90-91)

Your Resources Identified: In NLP we encourage people to identify both internal and external resources. Wiseman's research studied only external resources, most especially friends, colleagues and family. "Successful participants were far more likely than others to tell their friends, family and colleagues about their goals…. Telling others about your aims helps you achieve them, in part, because friends and family often provide much needed support when the going gets tough." (Wiseman, 2009, p 91) In all these ways, the successful individuals create clear future memories of their goals, and ensure these memories will be constantly reconsolidated.

Taking Care of The Future You

The same thing is true in a larger, life-long, way - it takes planning to enjoy a satisfying future. There have also been studies on people's future perception of themselves, as seen in the brain. Hal Hershfield (Hershfield, 2011) hypothesised that " The more continuity a person shares with his future self—that is, the more that future self feels like a direct extension of who he is now—the more motivated he will be to act in ways that will benefit himself in the future. Conversely, the more the future self feels like a stranger—that is, the more disconnected a person is from his future self—the less motivated he will be to plan for the future." He found that this factor (similarity between the imagined future self and current self) was one of three factors correlated with adequate economic and physical health planning for retirement. The other two were the vividness of the images made of the future self and the positivity of those images (did the person like their future self).

Hershfield summarises studies where brain scans show that when a future or past self is perceived as being similar to the current self, thinking about that self activates the same or close brain areas. In particular, he reports on studies that "scanned subjects with event-related functional magnetic resonance imaging (fMRI) as they judged whether trait words applied to themselves or another person. The investigators found that judgments of self-relevance selectively maintained activation in the medial prefrontal cortex (MPFC) at a baseline rate, while judgments of other-relevance decreased MPFC activation below baseline." Researchers were then able to identify whether the future self seemed similar to the present self by observing the memory structure activated when the person thought of that self.

Remembering to complete daily tasks such as pick up the bread on the way home, reaching specific goals such as creating a new career, and long term life planning such as retirement savings all depend on the activation of convincing future memories. Once again, this is a skill that can be practiced.

Part E: Healing The Body Using Memory

Brain Plasticity

In this final section, we will consider the impact of memories on healing in the body. Firstly, once again, we need to clarify how the brain "remembers" its previous experiences of using the body. In the early twentieth century it was common for people to imagine that the brains memory recall was analogous to a simple phone system where you dialled a number and got a set recorded message. Describing the nervous system as a landline phone system does not do it justice however. In the last fifty years, scientists have discovered that the brain in the head is remarkably flexible and is constantly adjusting to meet the current needs of your system. Some fairly ethically suspect animal research studies in the 1970s began a revolution in the way we think about the brain and healing. The studies by Ashley and Merzenich (Doidge, 2007, p 55-59) showed clearly that a specific area of the brain which ran, for example, the outside of a monkeys hand on one day might not run it the next day. If nerve connections to that part of the hand were severed, then within 24 hours the monkey's brain would have reassigned those brain cells to give it a more exact ability to move a nearby area of the hand which still had connections, or to give better movement in the other hand. Edward Taub also showed (Doidge, 2007, p 136-143) that a monkey's brain rebuilt any severed connections to the hand soon after surgery. These studies revealed that the brain is constantly changing, a skill for which the term "plasticity" was coined. Our brain is constantly, on a day to day basis, reassessing which areas of brain tissue are needed for which tasks, much as a computer reassigns areas of its RAM memory for the programs that we happen to open on it. The "healing" that we see after a stroke is just business as usual, as far as the brain is concerned, as the brain re-evaluates which memories of the body are useful.

The question Taub then sought to answer in his human studies was: why do human brains not simple reconnect after a stroke has produced paralysis? He eventually demonstrated that the only reason this didn't happen was that the brain began to assume that the damage was permanent. If an arm was unable to be moved for a few days, the damaged brain would reassign those brain cells which used to run that arm, and have them run another part of the body more fully. Unless the person with a stroke actually tried very concertedly to move their paralysed arm again, it would simply remain "turned off" as part of the brain attempting to get the best use out of its cranial real estate. In learning terms, the "permanent paralysis" was actually a learned response.

In 2005 and 2006, Taub and his colleagues published studies on his method of actually constraining a person's functional arm in order to "force" their brain to re-grow the neurological map of their "paralyzed" arm. Even people whose paralysis had lasted many years were able to benefit from this process. Since the 1980s, more and more precise ways have been developed to study neurological plasticity (the ability of nerve tissue to adjust like a plastic material) in the functioning human brain. In the 1990s Alvaro Pascual-Leone at Harvard Medical School used transcranial magnetic stimulation (TMS) to scan the brain of blind people as they learned to "read" Braille with their fingertips (Doidge, 2007, p 197-204). His studies showed that the more the person attempted to read Braille, the larger the area of brain devoted to their Braille-reading fingertips became. The changes happened overnight as the brain made continuous re-decisions about how much area to assign to each task. Like the mobile immune system, the brain is continuously re-balancing to create the optimal system over-all. Like any memories, memories of using the body can be enhanced by practice.

Multiple Personality, Memory and Physical Health Changes

One of the most dramatic places to learn about the relationship of the memory system and the body is in studying people who suffer from what is known as multiple personality dissociative disorders. In multiple personality, the person has times when they cannot remember their previous life history because they are using another personality system which has its own "memory system" in the brain. Psychiatrist Don Condie and neurobiologist Guochuan Tsai used a fMRI scanner to study the brain patterns of a woman with "multiple personality disorder". In this disorder, the woman switched regularly between her normal personality and an alter ego called "Guardian". The two personalities had separate memory systems and quite different strategies. The fMRI brain scan showed that each of these two personalities used different regions in the hippocampus to store memories. If the woman only pretended to be a separate person, her brain continued to use her usual areas of the hippocampus to remember events, but as soon as the "Guardian" actually took over her consciousness, it activated precise, different areas of the hippocampus and surrounding temporal cortex (brain areas associated with memory and emotion).(Adler, 1999, p 29-30)

People with multiple personality can exhibit a disease state in one personality which does not turn up in other personalities. Researcher Candace Pert, who pioneeered the whole field of neurotransmitting chemicals, gives a couple of examples of the phenomenon in an interview with Bill Moyers:

"[Candace Pert, Ph.D]: Emotions are in two realms. They can be in the physical realm, where we're talking about molecules whose molecular weight I can tell you, and whose sequences I can write as formulas. And there's another realm that we experience that's not under the purview of science. There are aspects of mind that have qualities that seem to be outside of matter. Let me give you an example. People with multiple personalities sometimes have extremely clear physical symptoms that vary with each personality. One personality can be allergic to cats while another is not. One personality can be diabetic and another not.

[Bill] Moyers: But the multiple personality exists in the same body. The physical matter has not changed from personality to personality.

Pert: But it does. You can measure it. You can show that one personality is making as much insulin as it needs, and the next one, who shows up half an hour later, can't make insulin.

Moyers: So in the person with multiple personalities, the brain is releasing different messengers." (Pert and Moyers, 1993)

Michael Talbot and Greg Hitter collect several other examples of this in their respective books. Talbot says "Frequently a medical condition possessed by one personality will mysteriously vanish when another personality takes over. Dr. Bennet Braun of the International Society for the Study of Multiple Personality, in Chicago, has documented a case in which all of a patient's subpersonalities were allergic to orange juice, except one. If the man drank orange juice when one of his allergic personalities was in control, he would break out in a terrible rash. But if he switched to his nonallergic personality, the rash would instantly start to fade and he could drink orange juice freely.... There are cases of women who have two or three menstrual periods each month because each of their subpersonalities has its own cycle. Speech pathologist Christy Ludlow has found that the voice pattern for each of a multiple's personalities is different, a feat that requires such a deep physiological change that even the most accomplished actor cannot alter his voice enough to disguise his voice pattern. One multiple, admitted to a hospital for diabetes, baffled her doctors by showing no symptoms when one of her nondiabetic personalities was in control. There are accounts of epilepsy coming and going with changes in personality." (Talbot, 1991, p.99)

Greg Hitter confirms "Within a given individual, multiple disease states can exhibit themselves exclusively of each other, depending on the state of consciousness ('personality') currently activated in the conscious mind. Thus, with one personality expressing itself in the conscious mind/body system, the individual can show all the clinical symptoms of diabetes, for example, and require insulin -- while a shift into another personality may result in no presence of any disease state or perhaps the clinically-confirmed appearance of a cardiovascular condition requiring entirely another type of medication and treatment. Thus, clinical measurements show changes not only in immunoreactivity when the individual switches from one personality to another but in bodily functions and metabolism as well, as the subject becomes hypertensive in one personality, diabetic in another, and neither of these in yet other states of consciousness (Hall, N.R.S. et al., 1994; Cosh J., 1996; Hirshberg C. & Barasch M., 1995)." (Hitter, 1997, Introduction)

There is evidence that people with multiple personality activate quite separate areas of the hippocampus as well as quite separate areas in the cortex, as they access each personality. "Having a sense of self is an explicit and high-level functional specialization of the human brain. The anatomical localization of self-awareness and the brain mechanisms involved in consciousness were investigated by functional neuroimaging different emotional mental states of core consciousness in patients with Multiple Personality Disorder (i.e., Dissociative Identity Disorder (DID)). We demonstrate specific changes in localized brain activity consistent with their ability to generate at least two distinct mental states of self-awareness, each with its own access to autobiographical trauma-related memory. Our findings reveal the existence of different regional cerebral blood flow patterns for different senses of self. We present evidence for the medial prefrontal cortex (MPFC) and the posterior associative cortices to have an integral role in conscious experience." (Reinders et alia 2003 p 2119)

This tells us that, to a much larger extent than most people realise, it is our memories that determine, which physical health conditions we experience each day, rather than the actual physical capacities and limits of our body. the memories in the hippocampus do not merely reactivate the specific memory structures in the sensory cortex; they reactivate specific memory structures throughout the body. Our body is to a large extent a memory encoding device itself. Taking charge of our memory could take charge of our body.

Time Lines

The brain remembers the sequence of life events in the hippocampus (just as it remembers the spacial coordinates of events there), using what NLP has termed a "time line". A time line is a spacial metaphor in which events are thought of as occurring along a line which stretches out in one direction to the past, and in another direction to the future. Examples of this way of mentally organising events are referred to in everyday speech; for example when we say "I'm going to put that whole experience *behind* me now." Or "I'm looking *forward* to seeing you again." Boroditsky (2000) tested the relationship between time and space by posing questionnaires to Standford University undergraduates and it was found that there was an obvious relationship between spatial schemas and perception of time. A reaction time method was then adopted by Santiago and his colleagues (2007), who tested the spatial relation of left/right in the person's cognitive conception of time. They found that reaction times were faster when past words were mapped onto the left key and similarly, future words with the right key. Abdul Rahman (2011) confirmed the relationship in another cultural setting in 2011.

This use of spacial distinctions for time was first described in NLP by Connirae and Steve Andreas (1987, p 1-24). Since then, a number of other NLP Practitioners have developed ways to work with the brain's coding of memory. These include "Re-imprinting" and "Change Personal History" (Dilts, Hallbom and Smith, 1990) and "Time Line Therapy™" (James and Woodsmall, 1988). These techniques seem to have a significant effect on physical health conditions. They tend to involve eliciting the time line spacial coordinates and then viewing the original traumatic events from a new time perspective on that line, while connecting to emotional resources from other areas of the person's life.

For example, a one year research study (May 1993-May 1994) into the treatment of asthmatics, using Time Line Therapy™, was done in Denmark. Results were presented at a number of European conferences, including the Danish Society of Allergology Conference (August 1994), and the European Respiratory Society Conference (Nice, France, October 1994). The study was run by General Medical Practitioner Jorgen Lund and NLP Master Practitioner Hanne Lund, from Herning, Denmark. Patients were selected from 8 general practices. 30 were included in the NLP Intervention group, and 16 in the control group. All received basic medical care including being supplied with medication. Most had never heard of NLP before, and many were completely unbelieving in it, or terrified of it. Their motivation to do NLP was generally low. The intervention group had an initial day introduction to NLP and Time Line Therapy™, and then 3-36 hours (average 13) of NLP intervention. The NLP focus was not mainly on the asthma; it was on how the people lived their daily lives. The results affected both the peoples general lives, and their asthma. Patients tended to describe their change subjectively as enabling them to be "more open", get "colossal strength and self confidence" "a new life" etc.

The lung capacity of adult asthmatics tends to decrease by 50ml a year average. This occurred in the control group. Meanwhile the NLP group increased their lung capacity by an average of 200ml (like reversing four years of damage in a year!). Daily variations in peak flow (an indicator of unstable lung function) began at 30%-40%. In the control group they reduced to 25% but in the NLP group they fell to below 10% . Sleep disorders in the control group began at 70% and dropped to 30%. In the NLP group they began at 50% and dropped to ZERO. Use of asthma inhalers and acute medication in the NLP group fell to near ZERO.

Hanne Lund points out that the implications of this project reach far beyond asthma management. The patients who used NLP did not consciously do something different in order to cure their asthma. They had the unconscious areas of the brain respond differently to solve their problems. Lund says "We consider the principles of this integrated work valuable in treatment of patients with any disease, and the next step will be to train medical staff in this model." (Lund, 1995).

Summary

In this essay I extensively reviewed the evidence and consequences of the claim that memories are constantly being reconsolidated. I looked at four specific ways to use this understanding in daily life.

What is Memory: Firstly, I described how the flow of experience is parceled by the brain into discrete events, and memory results from a series of changes in the brain after such an event. These changes occur centrally in the hippocampus, which keeps track of time and space coordinates, in the amygdala, which assesses the emotional impact of each event, and in the sensory cortex where the sensory details of the experience will be registered. In the first days, memories are mainly stored in a buffer area of the hippocampus, and during sleep and re-accessing experiences, they are "reconsolidated" to other brain areas. In this reconsolidation process, procedures are stored separately, and disturbing memories are re-organized as "observer" memories. Several research studies demonstrate that the repeated reconsolidation of memories results in them becoming increasingly less accurate to the original event, even in the case of emotionally significant "flashbulb" memories of major events. For the brain, the aim of storing memories is not to get recording accuracy but to create learned sequences of behaviour (strategies) which are triggered whenever a sensory experience similar to the original one reoccurs.

There are four ways to more effectively utilize this memory system:
Changing Emotional responses to Memories: There are at least three different ways to effectively change the emotional response to a memory, during a window of memory reconsolidation. 1) Anchoring is an NLP technique which involves connecting the spatial memory to a new emotional response. 2) Using rapid side to side and diagonal eye movement while reconsolidating the memory prevents it being laid down in the same brain areas. 3) Rehearsing the person through the NLP movie theatre and rewind process reconsolidates it as an observer memory.
Enhancing Memory of Facts: To enhance memory of facts that you want to protect from reconsolidative changes, you can use memory pegs (which connect the new memories to resilient sequences already stored such as the sequence of numerals) and the journey method (which utilizes the natural spatial sorting of the hippocampus to store specific new memories at each of a number of locations in a pre-established journey.
Planning for Future Events: In the brain constructed future experiences are built in the same memory system as reconsolidated memories. Futurepacing means connecting desired future actions to identified pegs or locations which will trigger their use at appropriate times in the future. Goalsetting is an advanced method of doing this, and involves creating sensory specific future outcome points and plans which take into account the various side-effects of these plans. The image of

your own future self can also be made more vivid, more attractive, and more similar to the current self, to enhance motivation for action supportive of it.

Healing the Body: Memories of body functions such as precise muscle movement skills and immune responses are stored in similar fashion, and can be altered, with effects on the results that the body delivers. In NLP processes such as Time Line Therapy™, the temporal coding of memories in a "time line" is utilized to guide the person to reconsolidate memories and restore body functions.

Author: Richard Bolstad

Fellow Member Trainer (IANLP), Master Trainer (ICI, IN), Doctor of Clinical Hypnotherapy, Time Line Therapy™ Master Trainer, Chi Kung Instructor, Teacher (DipTchTert), Registered Nurse (RCpN)

Richard runs the training organisation 'Transformations International Consulting & Training Ltd', within which he trains with his wife Julia Kurusheva in New Zealand and internationally. He is widely recognised in the NLP community for his promotion of research-based NLP and is a contributing author in the new books *The Clinical Effectiveness of Neurolinguistic Programming: A Critical Appraisal (Advances in Mental Health Research),* and *Innovations in NLP: Innovations for Challenging Times* (where his **RESOLVE** model for NLP coaching is explained).

Richard is the author of many NLP books, published in 8 languages, including *Transforming Communication* and *RESOLVE: A New Model of Therapy*. His Transforming Communication course is taught in Europe, Asia, North America, and Australasia, and is available in more than 12 languages. He is also an expert on the application of NLP to major disaster events and has run training for Trauma Response in Samoa, New Zealand, Japan, Russia, and Bosnia-Herzegovina,

Bibliography:

Abdul Rahman, N. Conceptualisation of Past and Future as Moving from Left to Right
http://ainirahman.wordpress.com/2011/01/20/conceptualisation-of-past-and-future-as-moving-from-right-to-left/
Adler, R. "Crowded Minds" in New Scientist, Vol. 164, No. 2217, p 26-31, December 18, 1999
Andreas, S. and Andreas, C. "Neuro-Linguistic Programming" p 14-35

in Budman, S.H., Hoyt, M.F. and Friedman, S. The First Session In Brief Therapy Guildford Press, New York, 1992

Andreas, S. Virginia Satir: The Patterns Of Her Magic Science and Behaviour, Palo Alto, California, 1991

Andrillon, T., Nir, Y., Cirelli, C., Tononi, G., and Fried, I. "Single-neuron activity and eye movements during human REM sleep and awake vision", Nature Communications, Volume: 6, Article number: 7884, doi:10.1038/ncomms8884, 11 August 2015

Bandler, R. and Grinder, J. Frogs Into Princes Real People Press, Moab, Utah, 1979

Bandler, R. Using Your Brain For A Change Real People Press, Moab, Utah, 1985

Barasch, M. and Hirshberg, C. Remarkable Recovery Headline Books, London, 1995

Barnes, M. Producer, "Hypnosis On Trial" (TV Program) BBC, London, 1982

Bartlett, F.C. Remembering Cambridge University, Cambridge, England, 1932

Bernheim, H. translated by Sandor, R.S. New Studies In Hypnotism International Universities Press, New York, 1980

Bisiach, E. and Luzzatti, C. "Unilateral Neglect of Representational Space" p 129-133 in Cortex, 14 (4), 1978

Boriditsky, L. (2000). Metaphoric structuring: understanding time through spatial metaphors. *Cognition*, 75 (1), 1-28.

Bostic St. Clair, C. and Grinder, J. "The Sins Of The Fathers" p 3-10 in Anchor Point, Vol 16, No. 11, November 2002

Bourke, F. and Gray, R. Research and Recognition Project Completes First Phase of Pre Pilot, 5 December 2014

Brynie, F.H. Brain Sense American Management Association, New York, 2009

Bushman, G. Kross, E. and Mischkowski, D. Journal of Experimental Social Psychology, 2013

Casile, A., & Giese, M. A. "Nonvisual motor training influences biological motion perception", Current Biology 16, 69-74, 2006

Charles B. Brenner and Jeffrey M. Zacks "Why Walking through a Doorway Makes You Forget" December 13, 2011 Scientific American

Charney, E. J. "Postural configurations in psychotherapy", Psychosomatic Medicine, 28, 305-315, 1966

Creswell, J. D., Bursley, D.K., and Satpute, A. B.. Neural Reactivation Links Unconscious Thought to Decision Making Performance. Social Cognitive and Affective Neuroscience, 2013

Dilts, R., Grinder, J., Bandler, R. and DeLozier, J. Neuro-Linguistic Programming: Volume 1 The Study of the Structure of Subjective Experience, Meta Publications, Cupertino, California, 1980

Dilts, R., Hallbom, T. and Smith, S. Beliefs: Pathways To Health And Wellbeing Metamorphous, Portland, Oregon, 1990

Doidge, N., M.D. <u>The Brain That Changes Itself</u>, Penguin Books, London, 2007

Engelhard, I.M., van den Hout, M.A., Janssen, W.C. and van der Beek, J., "Eye movements reduce vividness and emotionality of ''flashforwards''" Behaviour Research and Therapy, 2010

Erickson, M.H. and Rossi, E.L. <u>The February Man</u> Brunner/Mazel, New York, 1989

Freud, S. and Breuer, J. <u>Studies On Hysteria</u> Penguin, Harmondsworth, England, 1974

Freud, S., "Screen Memories". Collected Works of Sigmund Freud, Standard Edition, 3, 1899, p301-322. London: The Hogarth Press

Gaesser,B, Spreng,R.N., McLelland, V.C., Addis, D.R. and Schacter, D.L. "Imagining the Future: Evidence for a Hippocampal Contribution to Constructive Processing", Hippocampus 23:1150–1161 (2013)

Gottman, J.M. <u>The Marriage Clinic</u> W.W. Norton and Co., New York, 1999

Gray, R. and Liotta, R. "PTSD: Extinction, Reconsolidation and the Visual-Kinesthetic Dissociation Protocol" 2012 http://home.comcast.net/~richardmgray/PTSDnVKDprepub.pdf

Greenough, W.T., Withers, G. and Anderson, B. "Experience-Dependent Synaptogenesis as a Plausible Memory Mechanism" p 209-229 in Gormezano, I. And Wasserman, E. ed <u>Learning and Memory: The Behavioural and Biological Substrates</u> Erlbaum & Associates, Hillsdale, New Jersey, 1992

Grinder, John; St. Clair, Carmen, Bostic. (2002). Whispering in the Wind. Scotts Valley,
CA: J & C. Enterprises.

Hall, L.M.., "It's the Frames Stupid: How Meta-States Leave NLP in the Dust" http://www.neurosemantics.com/frames-games/its-the-frames-stupid

Hall, N.R.S. Advances, Issue 10, p.7-15, 1994

Hershfield, H. "Future self-continuity: how conceptions of the future self transform intertemporal choice" Ann N Y Acad Sci. 2011 October ; 1235: 30–43. doi:10.1111/j.1749-6632.2011.06201.x.

Hitter, G.T. <u>Freud's Innuendo and Jamshid's Cup</u>, PsyQuest Books, Los Vegas, 1997

Iyer, S. "Emotional Memory Manipulated: Studying Hippocampus And Amygdala, Scientists Switch Emotions Linked To Memory" Aug 27, 2014

James, T. and Woodsmall, W. Time Line Therapy And The Basis Of Personality, Meta Publications, Cupertino, California, 1988

Kalat, J.W. <u>Biological Psychology</u> Wadsworth Publishing, Belmont, California, 1988

Liu, X. et al. Optogenetic stimulation of a hippocampal engram activates fear memory recall. *Nature* 484, 381–385 (2012)

Loftus, E. "Creating False Memories" p 70-75 in Scientific American, Volume 277, #3, September 1997

Lund, H. "Asthma Management" p 4-6 in The Time Line Therapy Association Journal, Vol 5, Summer 1995

Luria, A.R. <u>Higher Cortical Functions In Man</u>, Basic Books, New York, 1966

Miller, G., Galanter, E. and Pribram, K. <u>Plans And The Structure Of Behaviour</u>, Henry Holt & Co., 1960

Miller, J. "Going Unconscious" in Silvers, R. ed <u>Hidden Histories of Science</u> Granta, London, 1995

Muss, D. "A New Technique For Treating Post-Traumatic Stress Disorder" in British Journal of Clinical Psychology, 30, p 91-92, 1991

Muss, Dr D. The Trauma Trap. Doubleday, London, 1991

O'Brien, D. The Amazing Memory Kit (13 October 2005, Thunder Bay Press, San Diego)

O'Keefe, John; Nadel, Lynn (December 7, 1978). The Hippocampus as a Cognitive Map'. Oxford: Oxford University Press.

Pappas, S., 2011 " Do You Really Remember Where You Were on 9/11?" http://www.livescience.com/15914-flashbulb-memory-september-11.html

Pavlov, I. P. Conditioned Reflexes: An Investigation of the Physiological Activity of the Cerebral Cortex (Oxford Univ. Press, 1927)

Pert, C. and Moyers, B. "The Chemical Communicators" in Moyers, B. ed <u>Healing and the Mind</u>, Doubleday, New York, 1993

Ramirez, S. et al. Creating a false memory in the hippocampus. *Science* 341, 387–391 (2013)

Rasch, B. and Born, J. "About Sleep's Role in Memory" Physiol Rev. 2013 Apr; 93(2): 681–766.doi: 10.1152/physrev.00032.2012

Redondo, R.L., Kim, J., Arons, A.L., Ramirez, S. Liu, X. & Tonegawa, S. "Bidirectional switch of the valence associated with a hippocampal contextual memory engram", Nature Volume: 513, Pages: 426–430, 18 September 2014, doi:10.1038/nature13725

Reinders A.A., Nijenhuis E.R., Paans A.M., Korf J., Willemsen A.T.and den Boer J.A. "One Brain, Two Selves", in Neuroimage. December 2003, Issue 20(4) p. 2119-2125.

Santiago, J., Lupiañez, J., Pérez, E., & Funes, M. (2007). Time (also) flies from left to right. *Psychonomic Bulletin and Review*, 14 (3), 512-516.

Schacter, D.L. <u>Searching For Memory</u> Basic Books, New York, 1996

Simons, D.J. and Levin, D.T. "Failure to detect changes to people during real-world interaction" p 644 in Psychonomic Bulletin And Review, Vol. 4, 1998

Spiegel, H. "Hypnosis and Evidence: Help of Hindrance?" p 73-85 in Annals of the New York Academy of Sciences, 347, 1980

Squire, L. R., and Paller, K. A. "The Biology of Memory", Chapter 3.4 in Williams & Wilkins, Harold I. Kaplan, M.D, Benjamin J. Sadock, M.D and Virginia A. Sadock, M.D.Kaplan & Sadock's Comprehensive Textbook of Psychiatry, 2000 Lippincott

Talbot, M. Holographic Universe, Harper Collins, New York, 1991

Time Line Therapy Association "How False Memories Are Formed" p 1-2 in Time Line Therapy Association Journal, Volume 4, Fall 1994

Wake, L., Gray, R.M. and Bourke, F.S. eds The Clinical Effectiveness of Neurolinguistic Programming Routledge, London, 2013

Wilcox, J., The Transmission and Influence of Qusta ibn Luqa's "On the Difference between Spirit and the Soul", PhD thesis, City University of New York, 1985

Wiseman, R. (2009) 59 Seconds: Think A Little, Change A Lot. London: Macmillan,

Wolpe, J. Psychotherapy by Reciprocal Inhibition (Stanford Univ. Press, 1958)

Yapko, M.D. "Memories of the Future: Regression and Suggestions of Abuse" p 482-494 in Zeig, J.K. ed Ericksonian Methods: The Essence Of The Story Brunner/Mazel, New York, 1994

About The Authors

Principal Author: Richard Bolstad

Fellow Member Trainer (IANLP), Master Trainer (ICI, IN), Doctor of Clinical Hypnotherapy, Time Line Therapy™ Trainer, Chi Kung Instructor, Teacher (DipTchTert), Registered Nurse (RCpN)

Richard runs the training organisation 'Transformations International Consulting & Training Ltd', within which he trains with his life partner Julia Kurusheva in New Zealand and internationally. He is widely recognised in the NLP community for his promotion of research-based NLP and is a contributing author in the new books *The Clinical Effectiveness of Neurolinguistic Programming: A Critical Appraisal (Advances in Mental Health Research),* and *Innovations in NLP: Innovations for Challenging Times* (where his **RESOLVE** model for NLP coaching is explained).

Richard is the author of many NLP books, published in 8 languages, including *Transforming Communication* and *RESOLVE: A New Model of Therapy.* His Transforming Communication course is taught in Europe, Asia, North America, and Australasia, and is available in more than 12 languages. He is also an expert on the application of NLP to major disaster events and has run training for Trauma Response in Samoa, New Zealand, Japan, Russia, and Bosnia-Herzegovina,

Richard's recent work has explored how to vary your therapeutic / coaching styles in relation to the unique personality responses that each client uses, creating a model called **The Wheel Of Change**.

Contributing Author: Julia Kurusheva

Fellow Member Trainer (IANLP), Master Coach (ICI), NZANLP Approved Supervisor, Core Transformation™ Trainer, Chi Kung Instructor, Huna Practitioner, B.Sc. Medical Electronics

Julia works in her private NLP Coaching practice 'Integrace', providing consulting and training services in the area of wellbeing and personal development. She is also a trainer with 'Transformations International Consulting & Training Ltd' and co-trains with her life partner Dr Richard Bolstad in New Zealand and internationally.

With an engineering degree, Julia has sound scientific sense to combine with the visionary and leading edge methods she uses. A varied background in travel and finance industries, and working in different cultures, enriches Julia's understanding of the pressures of corporate life and challenges of change.

Since 2007 Julia has been using and teaching her **SPRINT** model of brief therapy (a simplified model based on RESOLVE, by Dr R Bolstad). In his 48 page study "Structure de Changement en PNL", New Caledonian NLP Trainer Damien Raczy reports on his research into the success of coaching in more than 100 coaching sessions spread over 50 weeks. He found that "The usage of SPRINT is certainly the factor that that most strongly is correlated to successful performance from the standpoint of the customer and from the standpoint of the practitioner."